2311

D0519301

OTHER WORKS BY DAVID MULFORD

The Northern Rhodesia General Election, 1962
Zambia: The Politics of Independence

RECEIVED NOV 19 2014

Packing *for* India

Packing *for* India

A Life of Action in Global Finance and Diplomacy

DAVID MULFORD

Potomac Books

An imprint of the University of Nebraska Press

© 2014 by David Mulford

All rights reserved. Potomac Books is an imprint of the
University of Nebraska Press.
Manufactured in the United States of America.

Library of Congress Cataloging-in-Publication Data

Mulford, David C.
Packing for India: a life of action in global finance and
diplomacy / David Mulford.
pages   cm
ISBN 978-1-61234-715-8 (cloth: alk. paper) 1. Mulford,
David C. 2. Ambassadors—United States—Biography.
3. United States—Foreign relations—India. 4. India—
Foreign relations—United States. 5. United States.
Department of the Treasury—Officials and employees—
Biography. 6. Investment bankers—United States—
Biography. 7. Credit suisse—Officials and employees—
Biography. 8. International finance—Biography. 9.
Economic history—1971–1990. 10. Economic history—
1990–. Title.
E840.8.M75A3 2014
327.73054—dc23
2014023335

Set in Next LT Pro by Lindsey Auten.

To Jeannie,
my love and inspiration

Contents

Preface

Ronald Reagan said, "There is no limit to what a man can do or where he can go if he doesn't mind who gets the credit." Even before I met President Reagan the substance of his statement was my guiding principle, and it remains so today.

This book is about events and transformations in our world these past seventy years that are far bigger than the accomplishments of any one person. Humanity has been on the march. Tolerance and openness have been the currency of change, and passion the force of rising aspirations. Leadership has been tested and often found to be successful.

For reasons not entirely clear to me, I was blessed with an ability to solve complicated problems and to work with diverse and sometimes difficult people. I do not attempt to praise myself or to seek broader recognition. No single man can take sole credit for transformative events, but some people, through their ability to remain secure in their own sense of gravity and to apply reasonable judgment in a variety of challenging situations, can shape complicated . problems and solutions, sometimes in very different worlds.

I believe I have been such a person at times, and I have been lucky to prove it in the longevity and productiveness of my career, not by earning recognition or a fortune doing one thing, but by doing many different and difficult things well.

This book is for those who follow global developments and challenges and who aspire to understand them with a historical perspective. It focuses on the approach I have applied in dealing with these challenges and my life at the forefront of changes to the global economy.

As I journeyed from the relative isolation of a small midwestern town into this wider international world, from the newly independent countries of Africa to the boardrooms of New York, London, and Zurich, from the offices of the Saudi Arabian Monetary Agency in Jeddah and Riyadh to the White House and Treasury Department, from the halls of Oxford to the developing expanse of India, I witnessed and participated in dramatic changes to the world economic system.

In *Packing for India* I describe the private-sector and government decisions that expanded the free flow of capital between countries and the private-market innovators who drove that change. Through the lens of my career and experiences on the cutting edge of those developments, I was able to observe firsthand and sometimes influence unfolding events as a scholar of change in Africa, as a private investment banker, as head of an advisory team to the world's richest kingdom in the great shift of wealth to the OPEC states, as undersecretary for international affairs of the U.S. Treasury Department under Presidents Reagan and George H. W. Bush, as CEO and later chairman international of Credit Suisse First Boston in London, and as U.S. ambassador to India for five years under President George W. Bush.

Oxford in the early sixties opened a new world to me: Europe's societies and governments emerging from the destruction of the war; the Soviet Union dividing Europe and opening the Cold War with America; and African nations moving to independence, bringing the end of colonialism. My research and study as a Rotary International Fellow in 1960 at Cape Town University and my Oxford doctorate research in Zambia during its constitutional transition to independence from 1962 to 1964 reinforced the lessons of discipline and independence I had learned as the son of a suddenly single parent growing up in Illinois.

I describe my experience in the first class of White House Fellows in Washington, finding my career in international finance and moving as an aspiring investment banker with White Weld and Co. into the birthing in London of the eurobond and eurocurrency markets. These were the early forerunners of today's global financial markets.

In 1974, I was the first westerner involved in the creation of the Saudi Arabian government's massive sovereign investment fund during the largest shift in liquid monetary wealth the world had ever seen. For nine years, I led a small group of western investment bankers in Jeddah and Riyadh responsible for the Saudi Arabian Monetary Agency's wealth fund, which rose from virtually zero in 1974 to over $130 billion by 1983 and which required by that time investing some $500 million every market day.

By this time, private-sector and government decisions were driving the free flow of capital between countries, bringing us closer to the emergence of a truly global capital market and a world economy. I walked into this new reality in 1984 when I joined the U.S. Treasury as its senior international policy official during the Reagan and first Bush administrations, which saw the rise of global finance markets in the eighties and early nineties. These were formative years for our modern global economy and financial markets. I then became CEO of Europe and later chairman international of Credit Suisse in the booming market of the nineties, which saw worldwide privatizations, growth reforms in dozens of countries, and the open and productive direction of capital to points of high return with minimal regulatory restraint. These developments brought about profound changes in our world economy, requiring closer cooperation between leading economic powers and the beginning of a historic transformation of the communist world and the rise of emerging market nations in the developing world.

Those experiences aligned to prepare me for service as U.S. Ambassador to India from 2004 to 2009 under President George W. Bush, during which relations between the United States and India were transformed and the world economy was shaken by the global financial crisis of 2008. The change I saw in India was dramatically illustrated by the rise of India's GDP from 2.5 to 4.5 percent annual growth in the first sixty years of India's independence to 9 to 10 percent annual growth from 2004 to 2009. My service concluded with the U.S.–India Civil Nuclear Agreement of 2008, which restored India to the world of civil nuclear commerce from which it had been isolated for thirty-five years and for the first time brought IAEA nuclear safeguards into India's nuclear industry. Trade and investment with the United States blossomed as never before. There were many personal challenges: how to serve as ambassador in a country encompassing one-sixth of humanity; how to run a mission of twenty-three hundred people spread between the embassy and four consulates, with two-thirds of the employees being Indian nationals; how to manage the challenges of our broad and increasingly diverse interface with India, which engaged our two countries in virtually every area of our private sectors and civic societies; how to respond to the inspiration of His Holiness, the Dali Lama and the Tibetan community in exile in Dharamsala and to the remote Kingdom of Bhutan; and how to address the constant concerns about security in and around the embassy and its associated American school, as well as the personal security of the embassy community (terrorist outrages were increasing throughout my service, peaking finally with the attacks on Mumbai and its leading hotels in late November 2008). By the time I left India in 2009, India's vast rural economy had begun a potentially revolutionary transformation that will increasingly incorporate seven hundred million rural inhabitants into the rising national economy.

The summer of 2008, while I was still serving as U.S. ambassador to India, marked the beginning of the global financial crisis that is still running its destructive course. The destabilizing global events of 2008–9 perfectly reflected the scale and diversity of change that had taken place in the previous thirty years in the global economy and international financial markets. I had seen the birth of modern, high-growth India into a world that would never be the same. The leadership role of the United States during the sixty-five years since the end of World War II was eclipsed by this crisis. Our economic model was found wanting in the broader world. Europe's solidarity in the form of its new single currency was under severe challenge, and the Continent, having seen its global influence weaken, was facing a significant threat of economic decline.

Equally important, however, the global economy that I had seen taking shape and played a role in developing was on the verge of revealing a modern miracle. By the end of 2008, the leading developing countries and the emerging market countries were registering a return to growth and prosperity following the external economic shock administered from the developed world. Amid the anxiety over the U.S. and European economic crisis, one had to remember that well over half the people in the world lived in countries that had not had a banking crisis or a crisis of confidence. Instead they had suffered a sharp external economic shock, which they addressed relatively quickly with orthodox economic policy adjustments. The result was a completely new situation. Growth and prosperity were not only more widespread in the world than at any time in modern history, but despite the shock of the crisis in the developed world this growth was clearly proving to be sustained. At all other times of crisis in my experience, the developing world was at the bottom of the stack of nations on the receiving end of economic pain. Now a whole new phenomenon, a newly established pattern of growth, was firmly establishing itself, and emerging market countries were proving they could grow and access capital while the western banking system was in a state of withdrawal.

Full world recovery and sustained growth will require a return of U.S. leadership in the global economy by restoring 5 percent annual growth in the United States, reforming and strengthening international financial institutions and trade organizations, and providing stronger, more credible management of the world's sole reserve currency. A broader view of leadership will be required from the world's leading emerging market countries. In the United States we are faced with evidence of a weakening will to lead, a failure to fulfil our role to provide security and minimal orderly governance in world economic affairs, and a continuing inability to generate sustained growth at home that lifts the world. Moreover, our current government is intruding into our private economy and showing disrespect for the traditional principles of American governance in promoting discord, division, and intrusions into states' rights and individual liberties, all of which hamper our recovery. More than anything, we in the United States need a return to policies that encourage economic growth: reduce and remove taxes and remove regulatory, tax, and government disincentives to private individuals and business.

The world needs us and we need the world if we are to achieve the benefits of open economies, growing world trade, free cross-border movement of capital, sensible rules for the movement of skilled, aspiring people and the free movement of technology. At this time it is by no means clear that we will successfully advance world prosperity by what until now we have called "globalization."

While tracking the rise of the global economy and the expansion of international financial markets over my career, this book is also deeply personal. Based on my experience in this great transformation, it provides a partial record and explanation of important events, reflections on key world leaders, and unique insights into the way forward in our new world.

Packing *for* India

I

Early Years

The diverse and exciting life I have led for the past fifty years draws my reflections back to beginnings. How and when did the boy from a middle-class family in mid-America move into a life of international adventures? Were the seeds always there in the form of Mother, the Scottish immigrant with a German father and Scottish mother? Or could it be in the long American tradition of my father's roots back to East Hampton, New York, in the 1640s?

In retrospect I see that both my parents projected a history larger than themselves. This was not lost on me as a boy, although its formulation was largely conveyed by romantic stories of courage, adventure, and a willingness to face the unknown. From Mother I was treated to tales of the proud, brave Highlanders, fighting wars for the English in remote regions of the world: pictures of men in tartan kilts and tan kit in the deserts of the Middle East, North Africa, and the wilds of India, my namesake, Sir Colin Campbell, holding the thin red line, or at the relief of Lucknow in the Great Indian Mutiny of 1857. Then there were the Scots in the First World War, the "Ladies from Hell," as recounted by Mother, patiently moving forward under fire in the mud and mayhem of trench warfare to the wailing of pipes and the beating of drums. Three of Mother's young cousins were killed in the trenches when she was a girl; only Cyril Andrew Kerr of Glasgow survived, and later he was the first person I met when I left America for the first time. Later still, I realized Mother had left something out: she had never mentioned the role of Scottish Highlanders in the effort by Britain to suppress the American Revolution.

Despite her German father, Richard Mollenhauer of Braunschweig, Mother thought of herself as Scottish, a Campbell, and so my middle name. She had wanted me named Colin Campbell but Dad put his foot down. "The boy will have to fight every day of his life in an American public school against the taunt that he is a girl." Dad won, but only on my first name. He also claimed he was descended from Mary, Queen of Scots, despite the English West Country name of Mulford.

For Dad, his history was America's. The Mulfords around East Hampton and Rensselaerville, New York, were farmers. There was a Mulford regiment in the Revolutionary War drawn from around East Hampton, commanded by Donald Mulford and including Mulfords as about half its number. The Midwest story was that around 1830 John Mulford of Rensselaervilleswore that if he broke one more plough blade in the rocky soil of New England he would go west. By 1840 he was tramping around southern Wisconsin and northern Illinois, writing home of the black earth country that was "40 bushel corn country," where there was all the rich land a man could possibly plough without breaking a single blade.

John settled near the Rock River where the ford occasioned the name of a small village, Rockford. The Mulfords were homesteaders, and by the time I was old enough to look about me, Mulford land seemed spread about the rural east side of Rockford, equidistant between Rockford and Cherry Valley on the Kishwaukee River. Belknap Mulford, my grandfather, owned the big farm "Blackhawk" on the Kishwaukee River, eight hundred acres of rich bottomland and thick woods. We grew up in these woods, playing war and practicing and playing baseball in the meadow areas using dried cow pies for bases. Grandpa said he was land poor, and that seemed right to me.

It was always said that the Mulfords were the true pioneers of Rockford until the 1880s, when Swedish immigrants flocked to Rockford, founding a thriving furniture and woodworking industry. They came to dominate Rockford's east side, though not out so far as Mulford Road, Mulford Wildwood, Mulford Village, Blackhawk Farm, and the old brick Mulford homestead on Charles Street.

My first five years were in the Log Cabin subdivision on Charles Street, not far from the old homestead (now owned by others). My grandfather's Maple Woods, and the "large" cornfield that borders Charles Street Road, was nearby. He and Grandma (Fanny) lived farther along that road, past the Mulford Road crossing in a house called Homewood, set in thirteen acres of woods.

The Mulfords tended to be reclusive and generated an inordinate number of bachelors, some distinctly eccentric, such as Charley, the Canadian trapper and hunter who in his older age spent summers living in my grandfather's garage at Homewood and winters trapping and hunting in Canada. Charley had his long white beard and his hair cut once a year on June 1 and walked every day at sunrise to Cherry Valley (three miles each way) to collect the morning paper.

The Mulfords' moment of fame came in 1885, when at Sunday dinner the family was held up by robbers called the Prairie Bandits. While one of the bandits held a revolver to the head of Mrs. Mulford, all the family's cash and silver were taken. The only artifact from this terrifying event was a silver pocket watch, much admired by us boys, that was left behind by one of the bandits, who had worked as a hired man for the family for the months leading up to the robbery. Another favorite artifact for my brothers and me was, and still is, the original reward poster offering $100 for the arrest of the Prairie Bandits, which hangs in my brother Bill's house at Homewood.

The Mulfords were outdoor people, farmers, woodcutters, and people of strong application to whatever the task at hand. My brothers and I lived outdoors, even when we moved to 1842 East State Street in town. In my first five years in the country I slept out on a screened porch year around, Mother taking me in only if the temperature fell well below freezing. We rode bikes everywhere around town, out the seven miles to Blackhawk Farm and to the thirteen acres of woods that surrounded my grandparent's house on Charles Street Road. Dad took us walking in the woods of Homewood on spring or fall weekends or had us help with wood cutting, brush clearing, or spring burning of the dry grassland and low brush. We went on picnics almost every night in summer at Blackhawk, and we had many other adventures on the farm. The land was cut through by the Kishwaukee, a river we could ford in summer and which was always good for exploration and countless adventures. There was an old natural spring at the bottom of the hill where the big farmhouse stood, where Frank and Loyal Johnson lived with Mary Ellen, Frank's wife, and all the old Labradors: Smokey Joe, Daisy Mae, and Tarzan. Our dog, Yankee, mixed right in and never failed to come home in the car smelling of the cow pies he loved to roll in. The spring had been part of the old Blackhawk Hotel, when the big farmhouse had served as a stage coach stop and hotel on the coach run from Chicago to Galena, hometown of General Ulysses S. Grant, who in our parts was thought to have won the Civil War for the North.

It is hard to capture and convey the freedom, the open happiness, the energy and togetherness we enjoyed as children of Bob and Theo Mulford, lovers of the great outdoors in winter, spring, summer and fall, with activities suited to each season. The only somber and frightening aspect of our early lives was war. We grew up in the shadow of war in Europe, war in the Pacific, the Iron Curtain, the Cold War, the Berlin Airlift, the war in Korea. I was a senior in high school before these frightening conflicts were behind us, except of course, the Cold War with the atom bomb, a constant source of nightmares for my younger brother.

Rockford had Camp Grant in the Second World War, a staging camp that brought thousands of soldiers to town. Mom and Dad made us give up our seats on buses and trains to ladies and soldiers. Our house on State Street was on U.S. Highway 20, before there were Interstates, expressways, and bypasses, so we often observed the endless convoys of army trucks pulling tanks, artillery, and all manner of field equipment. We counted the Army trucks and housed individual soldiers in our spare room, who would stay a few weeks and then suddenly disappear forever. Dad took us to the Illinois Central railroad station several nights a week to see the troop trains come through, some going east for Europe, some going west for California and the Pacific. We took cookies and handed them up to the soldiers crowded in the olive-brown cars, and we watched the big steam locomotives disconnected from the train to ease their way to the water tower two hundred yards down the track and then chuff back to be hooked up again and have their air brakes connected, all prepared for departure. Then, in a great cloud of steam, belching smoke and clanging its bell, the troop train would pull out. We knew from Gabriel Heater on Chicago's wbbm and from the Pathé and Movietone newsreels at the cinema where the boys were going and what they would have to do there.

Rockford was by then a thriving town, home to a large machine tool industry, number ten, we were told, on Germany's bombing list for America. On summer nights we would stop at one of the big factories, the "Black Factory" we called it, where in the gloom everything glowed red under the large drop forges. Down they would strike with a shattering crash and a shower of red sparks. The sides of the Black Factory were open, summer and winter, covered only by large screens like a baseball backstop, and in the summer the men were stripped to the waist with blackened arms and faces.

Dad said that they were making pieces for tanks and guns and half-tracks to fight the Germans and the Japanese. The Black Factory made thundering noises and emitted a heat you could feel from across the street. And although we lived more than a mile away we could hear its pounding working day and night, especially on summer nights when we slept out on the screen porch.

Dad worked at the jl Clark Manufacturing Company, a specialty metals and metal lithography company. They made Johnson & Johnson baby powder cans, Scotch tape holders, Gillette razor blade dispensers, and the black metal paint boxes we used for watercolors at school. But one day Dad brought home one of the new carbine rifles, with its black metal clip snugly fitted under the stock, manufactured by jl Clark. He said this project was secret, but he wanted us to see the weapon American soldiers would use to kill Germans in Europe and Japanese in the Pacific.

In 1944 Grandfather had to admit woodcutters from the federal government into the large tract of woods called Maple Wood to cut down walnut trees for gunstocks for the Pacific. We went out and watched, full of pride that it was Grandpa's walnut trees that would be used for the stocks of rifles needed against the Japanese.

I had seen the first photographs of dead American Marines in the shallow water of a sand beach in the Pacific. The photo was in *Life* magazine, and I stared at it for days, the sand half covering their legs, helmets still on, lifeless in the water, killed by Japanese—the same Japanese we saw in the movies and newsreels. I thought of the big howitzers under the palm trees and camouflage nettings, manned by Americans in helmets, stripped to the waist, handing over shells to go in to the big guns made right here in Rockford at the Black Factory. We knew what the war was about, and we understood it was a life and death struggle for America. We saw gold stars in many neighborhood windows. We knew the names of battles across North Africa, Italy, Europe, and across the vast Pacific: Solomon Islands, Guadalcanal, Iwo Jima, Okinawa. Our neighbor, Major Ben Ryan, was ordered to go to Burma. Before he left he permitted us to handle his rifle, .45 pistol, bayonet, and canteen and to put onto our heads his light helmet and his heavy steel net-covered helmet. From Burma Major Ryan wrote home to his wife Emmy about fighting the Japanese in the jungles. Emmy would read his letters to us. What I remembered most was that Major Ryan had discovered a cobra wrapped around a toilet bowl in the his quarters, an image I often thought of later in India.

When America had won the war we celebrated, madly clanging Mother's pots and pans together until we were virtually deaf. In the burst of excitement that followed victory, Dad brought a new bright blue '46 Plymouth, rationing and shortages died away, and army surplus stores popped up with all the gear a boy could want. We could feel the new America rising from Depression and the war.

But it turned out we hadn't won for good. As I was now about ten, the Berlin Crisis was an exercise in high drama. Who could imagine a plane a minute, in all weather, bringing coal, food, and blankets, with chocolate bars raining from their open doors as they came into land at Tempelhof Airport.

Then Korea. Why were we there, and how could it be that American soldiers did not have the right winter clothes and gear to fight in Korea's frigid winter? It was all new and different because we were not fighting to win. I was now closer to twelve, but I could not conceive of fighting not to win, not to annihilate the enemy. We grew up in a time of total war, total American commitment, and total and comprehensive personal sacrifice by all Americans to win, not to partly win—all these dead soldiers for no territory, no victory. It was a new world of confused values for a young person raised on a diet of war for survival.

While the country was at war abroad, life went on back home. In 1947 brother Bill went to summer camp at Camp Manitowish, then I followed two years later to this most exciting canoe country outpost in the woods and lakes of northern Wisconsin. Camp Manitowish challenged young men to embrace adventure in the wilderness and build character in the tradition of American frontier values by embracing the harsh rigors of adventure in the North woods. Its combination of in-camp activities and six-man canoe trips (including only one counselor) for gradually extended periods, depending on the age and strength of campers, fulfilled for me the perfect mix of adventure, challenge, and self-awareness packed into three and a half short weeks. I loved the big Norway pines, the clear lakes, and the streams, some fast, some meandering through fields of brilliant green reeds and moss covered logs. I reveled in the all-day paddles, the challenge of portaging a canoe single-handed on rough terrain or through muddy swamps, and all the duties of setting up camp, building fires, and cooking the evening meal and breakfast before packing up again for another day on the trail. I could feel myself growing and toughening up, and I could look close up into the wonders of nature.

In the summer of 1950 our world of comfortable family harmony was ripped apart by the death of my father. When I returned from camp in July, Dad was suffering from immensely intense back aches. That same summer Eddie, my young brother, came down with polio and was hospitalized in Rockford. In mid-August Mother took Dad into Chicago for further exploration of his condition.

I had a job that summer mowing the vast front lawn of Keith School, the day school Mom and Dad had put Bill and me into the previous year. I worked with a small hard-to-push hand mower, crossing back and forth across the face of the hill at the school. There was enough grass to mow there to keep a boy busy for a good week, by which time it was nearly ready, in the humid August heat of Rockford, to start over.

One night Mother called Grandma and Grandpa's house from Chicago to tell them that their son, our father, was suffering from an incurable lymphatic cancer that had spread throughout his body. He would live only a short time.

Grandma broke down into hysterical sobbing, and Grandpa was, as usual, stoic and silent. Bill and I did not to speak to Mother until about ten days later when, we were called upon to travel to Chicago with Grandpa to pay a visit to my father. In the meantime, utterly bewildered by how to respond and what to do or say to my crushed grandparents, I did what I had been raised to do—keep going. I went back to mowing the grass at Keith School. It was all I could think to do, and there on the hillside in the hot August sun I mowed and grieved in a confusion of emotions. Looking back now some sixty years later I remember vividly those days of mowing. The steady whir of the blades, the sweat pouring into my tearing eyes, the feeling of utter aloneness. More than any others, those days just after my thirteenth birthday stand in my memory as my transition to manhood. All that followed, for years and years, as I now clearly see, was touched by that shock, those lonely days of hard but steadying work.

A week later we went to Chicago, driving the three hours with Grandpa in a silent car, looking out the windows at the late-August farmland and then at Chicago, with its cramped streets and the hundreds of stops and starts required to get to Billings Hospital. Mother met us and prepared us for our last visit with our father. He would be heavily sedated, she said. He would not be feeling pain. His thoughts would wander. He had not been told that he would not be returning home, and Mother was clear that she had decided that he would not be told that he would die. She said we were to pretend that he would come home and that on no account were we to cry.

And so the last visit to my Dad was made. I remember only the barest essentials of those moments with him. I believe I entered the darkened room alone. Dad greeted me, called me "old top" as he always had when saying good night to me in bed. Then to my surprise he apologized to me for the pain he had caused me the previous year following my undescended testicle operation, when at the dinner table he would make funny comments that got me laughing til the pain in my lower abdomen made me cry. "I never knew it could hurt so much" he said. I was unable to speak. Then he made the observation that at night in his dark room he had a very kind black night nurse who he said he could not see except for her bright white smile in the darkness. I made the necessary statement that he would see me at home in no time. I did not cry, then or afterward, or for a very long time afterward. But I cry now, as I write, as I have many times over the years for those last moments, for the end of his happy life at age forty, for the end of our unique family life of love and adventure, and for Mother, who in her love and her wisdom made what was undoubtedly the right decision for the two of them and therefore for us—sad as it was and still seems in these days. Would Dad have had something to say to me if he had known he was dying? Maybe, or is that is the stuff of movies? I never knew, but I am sure I know what he would have said—"Take care of your mother, and make something of yourself"—not commanded, but straight and loving. How I loved that man who so loved life.

Some days later Mother came back to our house in Rockford. I was in the backyard when she drove the car into the garage. She came around behind the car and said simply, "Your father has gone to Heaven." She did not embrace me but turned and walked inside the house and up to her room. Nothing more was said, perhaps because I shut everything out.

Dad's memorial service was held a few days later. There was no casket. Dad was cremated, so I never saw him again. My parents' view on funerals was that there was no point in open caskets—better to remember people as they were in life. We had no meeting or preparation session for the memorial service—at least not that I was ever aware of. Life with Dad just ended. Mother never cried in public, and she did not talk about Dad. School began. I played football, as it turned out with passionate violence. Brother Bill went away to Wayland Academy in Beaver Dam, Wisconsin, as Mom and Dad had planned, and I became the man in the family. Brother Ed came out of the hospital and began his physical therapy. Life did not return to normal, but Mother did everything in her power to make our life as stable and "normal" as possible. Grandpa drove us to school each day, and Mom came to my football games, which I so desperately wanted Dad to see, and felt deep inside that I was sure he could.

That fall we changed the screens for the storm windows without Dad. I shoveled snow and got a newspaper route to save to go to Camp Manitowish the next summer. This was the beginning of my learning about the world outside our home: delivering the morning paper right in front of every door, every day, meeting the customers to collect each month's bill, seeing inside strange homes, smelling different smells, seeing people in all manner of dress, and hoping for a tip as I handed out Christmas calendars. There was something about the work that I needed, carrying the heavy bundle of papers in the early-morning dark, folding every paper and putting it into my bag, biking around the neighborhood in the early morning stillness or walking through the snow, tossing the papers with perfect accuracy onto each front porch. It was the same need as the need to cut the grass at Keith School while my Dad lay dying in Chicago, though I didn't know it then or for many years after.

Camp Manitowish cost $125 per session in those days. By the following May I had $109 from my paper route and from shoveling snow around the neighborhood. I was worried that I would not make the goal with winter over and with only one month's collections remaining. Mother told me not to worry, I would go to Camp Manitowish anyway, and in mid-June 1951 I did. Years later Mother showed me a letter from Elmer Ott, the camp director, in which he had written that David would come to camp despite his savings shortfall. He had known the whole story, and only Mother could have told him. Why she did not tell me until much afterward I credit to her particular brand of character building, as she would have called it. I am sure she did not wish to take away from the purity of my accomplishment, which to this day remains a proud memory of my early life in an adult world.

I saw much more of the adult world in the next few years. Mother never cried in front of us, and she rarely spoke of Dad except to refer to him when it was a necessary part of conversation. But I heard her cry in her room some nights. I dared not open her door. I knew she intended to be strong, for all of us to be strong, and so we were, and we were free of self-pity. Grandpa never discussed Dad, nor did Grandma, except to say on rare occasions what my Dad would think of something.

He stayed alive to me, though. I did all the things he used to do: wash and wax the car, shovel the snow, cut the grass, rake and burn the leaves, change the screens and storm windows, wash the walls in springtime, paint different rooms each year, wash the dishes for Mom, take out the papers for burning in the back alley, and play sports with a passion no one else in school could match.

My passion for sports and hard work were easy to understand. Although Dad would have been called a salesman, or even perhaps a sales executive, he did hard physical work and made it fun. We had worked in the Victory garden out in the woods of Homewood during the war. I was assigned weeding, and collecting potato bugs and putting them in a can I carried with a bit of kerosene in the bottom. I dug up potatoes and picked beans and peas and sweet corn. Summer evenings were always busy: shucking corn, shelling peas, picking off the tips of beans—all for the purpose of canning or freezing vegetables and fruit for winter.

In winter we had gone as a family out to Homewood, often with family friends, built a fire in the snow, and cut wood to take home for our fireplaces. I learned to work my end of the big two-handed band saw and how to handle an axe for splitting wood. These were days of real accomplishment, with a stock of neatly split wood to load into the cars. In the evening we all sat together by the fire or in the kitchen, listening to Randy Blake and the *Suppertime Frolic* from wLS, Chicago, brought to us by "your friendly Keystone Fence people" in Peoria.

Other nights after the war, Dad would drive us the thirty miles down to Rochelle, a small farming town on the flattening prairie. From Rockford, we went by Camp Grant, where in the war years we could look across at barracks, soldiers, tanks, guns, and above all at the German prisoners who stood along the fence, two hundred yards away, looking at us, standing with their hands raised, holding onto the barbed wire fence.

In Rochelle we would stand on the platform of the red brick railroad station at the edge of town and look several miles up the straight track rising slightly to the distant horizon in the east. The big event of that journey was the high-speed passage thirty minutes apart of two of the four Union Pacific streamliners: the City of Denver, the City of Los Angeles, the City of Portland, and the City of Seattle. These came through every night out of Chicago on their way to the distant west with a force and romance practically too grand for us to stand.

All of a sudden, we could see a bright speck miles away in the early-evening haze of a midwestern summer night. It seemed to sway slightly but not to get closer. When it did start getting closer, Dad would say, "Okay, back against the wall," or "Hang on to one of those iron pillars on the station platform. Otherwise, you'll be sucked under the train."

Eventually, the light was on us from just outside of town, and it swayed back and forth as the engineer began the ear-splitting non-stop whistle he applied through the whole forty seconds it took this yellow and grey monster to roar through Rochelle. Beyond the drama of the whistle, the thunder, and wind of a train going ninety miles an hour, there was a slight curve in the track just on the edge of Rochelle. The engineer applied the brakes in town as the curve approached, and sparks flew from the wheels, some skipping across the platform at our feet. Everything shook and my heart pounded in time with the snapping sound of each passing coach, just as it did when the military drums passed by with the big base drum in parades, and just as it did when the last flash bombs exploded in fireworks displays on the Fourth of July.

Afterward there was an awed silence and the smell of hot steel and cinders. Who, I wondered, was on those trains? They would see things I had never seen, mountains and giant redwoods, the Pacific Ocean, salt water and palm trees. What, I wondered, did a real mountain look like? I knew about open water because you could not see across Lake Michigan or Lake Superior, but our highest mountain was Rib Mountain at Wausau, Wisconsin, 250 miles north and 600 feet high, which we waited each summer for hours to see as we drove north to the lake country of northern Wisconsin.

Then came the second Union Pacific streamliner, and Dad always seemed to know which it was, because he traveled often for JL Clark throughout the Midwest and the South by car or train.

I have remembered these soft summer nights all my life. They spoke of adventure and distant places, of traveling people, of us in our own town on the prairie on the edge of the Great Plains, of a world stretching far beyond us, full of adventure, soldiers, war, and exotic sights. They also spoke of the solidity of our home, our base of happiness. All around Rochelle were endless cornfields where Grandpa said you could hear the corn growing on humid nights. These were my links to the world, along with movies and newsreels for twelve cents on Saturday afternoon showing endless battles and multiple acts of courage and destruction.

When Bill and I turned twelve, Dad took each of us on one of his long business trips. Mine was to Indiana and across to Cincinnati, Ohio, where I saw my first major-league baseball game at Crosley Field. From there we went to Nashville, and Dad showed me Andrew Jackson's Hermitage. Then we drove to Paris, Tennessee, and went fishing with one of Dad's customers. We stayed in the old Greyson Hotel, where on the front porch you could sit in a big wide chair and could watch a steam switch engine go back and forth in the middle of Main Street. After Paris we drove to Memphis and across the Mississippi to Jonesboro, Arkansas, then Cape Girardeau, Missouri, and back to Rockford. I met some of Dad's customers and went to a business lunch with Mr. Ernie Spears, where I embarrassed Dad by responding positively to an offer from Mr. Spears that I have a second hot roast beef sandwich plate. At night we went to Western movies and walked around town, and during his daytime meetings I stayed in the car reading or thinking about the things I was seeing.

These things stopped when Dad died, and sports took over. I knew why I was driven, why I was so violently competitive. In the spring of the year Dad died, he and Mother had portraits taken of all the boys together and each of us separately. When the proofs arrived at the house Dad looked at me in a suit and tie with my hair smashed down and parted up one side and said to Mom, "Get David's done again. Crew cut his hair, put him in an open-collar white shirt and a V-neck sweater. The boy's going to be an athlete!"

And so it was done: a new crew cut, white shirt, and a maroon V-neck sweater. I still have the portrait today. But in all the years that followed I took those words to be my mission and never told a soul, except dear Jeannie many decades later. For whatever athletic ability I inherently had—and it was not insignificant—I had the motivating desire that burned deep inside which never, ever failed me in football, track, basketball, wrestling—all sports of extreme effort—where desire, commitment, training, and fearless competition was required. When I gained a first down or scored a touchdown, broke the tape or set a track record, or simply bloodied an opponent, I thought of Dad, not himself a violent person or an athlete, but of his words "This boy's going to be a great athlete."

Greatness, of course, is relative, as I soon found out. And there is so much more to life than being a good or great athlete. Sports teach many of the principles of success and the better lessons of failure, especially if they come with a measure of humility as the competition improves. I knew it was really about striving for excellence in all things, the ability to turn your hand and mind to many different things. When I began looking past Rockford, beyond my world of passionate involvement in sports to something beyond, it was a long time before I could clearly define my future direction. But I knew these principles were there and that they bore an uncanny resemblance to my early life of work, sports, love, and confidence.

The other change was in my relationship with Mom. Within a

year of my dad's death I felt I was becoming a man, that I had to become a man and take some responsibility. Some of this came out in my willing and enthusiastic embrace of all the work and duties around the house. But there was a new side. I went places with Mom, escorted her if you will, to church, to the store and elsewhere.

One evening when I was fourteen I took her out to dinner at the Wagon Wheel Lodge dining room in Rockton, eighteen miles north of Rockford. Afterward, I had arranged to take her to a Shakespeare play at Beloit College's theater in the round. On that summer evening, she drove, all dressed up, but I had booked the table and bought the tickets because I knew she loved Shakespeare.

We arrived at the Wagon Wheel, which in those days was a beautiful log building of several rooms with giant oak or elm trees growing through its dining rooms, rising up through its vaulted wooden ceiling. The maître d' escorted us to a table just next to the swinging kitchen doors. When we were seated, Mom kindly leaned forward and said, "You *need* to know, for when you are taking ladies out to dine, that he has not given you a good table."

"What do I do?" I asked.

"You would talk to him about a better table, not just beside the kitchen. He has done this because you are young."

So I got up, very uncertain about what to say, and walked back through the rooms to the front desk, where he stood greeting some customers. I waited. When he turned to me I said, "I am with my Mom tonight. It is a special evening, we are going to the play at the college. We think the table you gave us is not so good by the kitchen. Could we have another better table?"

The maître d' looked at me in a different way. He seemed slightly stunned by my request, but I waited for him to speak. "Of course, Mr. Mulford, come back with me and we will look for something better." We were reseated, I had learned a very important lesson. Without the slightest humiliation, and as Jeannie will attest, I have followed this approach to this day when it comes to tables. In fact, when I am seated beside kitchen doors in restaurants, memories of my Mom speaking to me on this subject come back so strongly that I have to get up and ask to be moved even if it turns out not to be possible.

We went out some other evenings, but then she began to build a new life. The most surprising thing she did was to trade in our car for a new fire-engine-red Buick convertible. We boys loved it, and she explained simply that Dad had always said if things go wrong, don't stop living. For us that was enough for the new car and enough for the fact that she began to date again.

She began to see the father of my schoolmate Terry Johnson, whose mother, a Christian Scientist, had died from not being treated by a doctor. Terry and I were inseparable companions, he a year or two younger. We painted the outside of his dad's house one summer and worked at passing and running the football interminably. Frank, Terry's Dad, and Mom started coming to my football games together, whether in Rockford or away.

In all the years I played football in grade school, high school, and college, Mom seldom missed a game, unless it was a college game three or four hundred miles away. In high school we played on Friday nights, and she and Frank were always there, even at games eighty or a hundred miles away and in the cold of approaching winter. She washed my uniform every week and listened to my endless recounting of the particulars of individual plays, which, with my lack of perspective and detachment, I had expected her to understand in every detail. She always listened with a smile.

In fall of 1952 I went from Keith School, the small private day school Bill, Ed, and I attended, to East Rockford High School, a three-year public school of some three thousand students that drew from the entire east side of Rockford.

Two hundred and fifty boys came out for football, whereas at Keith we could barely assemble two full teams of eleven. The boys were from every economic class and ethnic background, including Swedish, Italian, Irish, Scottish, Polish, and African Americans. Many were a year or two older than me, some with heavy beards and well-developed muscles. The sophomore team was separate from the varsity and played the early game on Friday nights, before the varsity took to the field. We all practiced together, at least part of the time. I loved the new level of roughness and the hard contact. I also liked the boys of warmer blood than was usual with the Swedes, many of whom were large and somewhat passive in their approach to the game. They could be very good, but didn't seem to get fired up in the same way.

I had to overcome the fact that I had come from a private school and not from the big junior high school where many of the boys had played. At first, in summer practice, the coaches made snide remarks from time to time, but when they saw the intensity and violence with which I carried out the drills, things soon changed. I made first-team quarterback and played defense as well. The games were major events for me, with endless mental and physical preparation.

I made new friends from new homes and backgrounds. Mom and I went to Sunday lunch at Joe Choppi's house, where Italian was spoken and where lunch had a pasta course and a main course, served by his large mother to a full family table. Other times I went to the homes of Serge Appoloni, Tom Seger, George Biavati, Bobby Gambino, Kenny Zagnoni, and Ryle Schadewalt. Our fullback was Al Walker, who was in my homeroom. He was an African American, a great football player and Golden Gloves boxing champ of Rockford. We were all bound together by the sports we played throughout the year.

My classwork, with the exception of a few subjects with outstanding teachers, was not especially stimulating, unlike the small classes at Keith School. But I got good marks (not straight A's) and, most important, got my eligibility card signed by all my teachers every Friday. Girls came into the picture, but they had to be devotedly interested in sports and be able to put up with my detailed preoccupations with plays, moves, races, and moments of "heroic" accomplishments. In those days, athletes wore Levis and boots; they didn't wear tan cotton trousers, go out for school plays, smoke, or drink, and we weren't particularly social. I did have girlfriends and for a while dated a girl who was a senior when I was a sophomore. She was Italian and smoked and was strikingly attractive, very different from the girls in my class.

In my high-school years I got a job working Saturdays during the school year in Kelly's Meat Market on Broadway, in a neighborhood of Rockford where many customers still spoke Swedish. I drove the truck at age fifteen, delivered Saturday morning orders to private residences, carried a green bag with $3,000 for cashing Friday night paychecks as a service to the customers, picked up sides of beef and boxes of chickens, made sausage, and cleaned the whole shop on Saturday nights, often after returning from an away football or basketball game late Friday night.

I loved the job. It gave me a look into dozens of homes on Saturday mornings, a chance to learn about different foods, such as Swedish lutefisk, which it was my job to shift from one smelly barrel of brine to another as the Swedish Christmas season approached. I worked an eight-hour day, eight to noon and then four to eight Saturday night. In spring I would change into my track outfit in the back room and go close by to Beyer Stadium to run my quarter- and half-mile track races, finishing just around four with the anchor leg of the mile relay. Back at the shop they all wanted to know how I had run that day, though none of them ever came to watch.

Life moved on toward graduation and college. I got more interested in my studies and made better grades. I began the process of choosing the university I would attend. My father was present in my reflections about schools. In the years following his death, I met several counselors at Camp Manitowish who attended Lawrence College in Appleton, Wisconsin. Several of them played football at Lawrence, and my dad had graduated from Lawrence in 1932. He met Mother there when she lived close by in Green Bay, and they married two years later.

I was invited to attend football games at Lawrence, and with grandparents in Green Bay it was natural to go up to Appleton with Mother to see a game and visit Green Bay. I was pulled toward Lawrence because of my history there. Lawrence was an outstanding liberal arts college, I knew Dad had loved it there, and Lawrence had a long history of good football teams.

In my senior year of high school I was selected for Rockford all-star team honors. I had several approaches from large universities to play football, but I found I wanted to follow Dad to Lawrence, a decision I have always valued and thought was right for me. I got a great education at Lawrence, played four years of varsity sports, and in 2000 was inducted into the Lawrence University Intercollegiate Athletics Hall of Fame.

Although I had no father to talk with about my ideas and ambitions, I did have two older men I greatly admired and could talk to freely. One was Keith Dalrymple, who lived across the back alley and took an interest in me during my high-school years. He was an ex-basketball star, and we played many games of horse at the basketball backboard set up in the alley. He had three young sons and sold insurance. I wore Keith down on summer evenings on his front porch with visions and questions about football, basketball, and many other areas of life.

One summer afternoon Mom received a call from a nearby town to say that Keith had been killed by a lightning strike while playing golf. She had to cross the alley to inform Virginia, Keith's wife, and his children of the brutal tragedy. I stayed home, shocked by the loss of my friend and older advisor. Keith's funeral was in central Illinois, but even if it had been in Rockford I doubt if I could have faced seeing him again.

Then there was Ken Pennypacker, truly a major influence on my life. Ken was headmaster at Keith School in my eighth and ninth grades. He was a thin, bespectacled man, a complete non-athlete. He taught English and introduced me to books of substance and excitement: *A Tale of Two Cities*, *Moby Dick*, *Return of the Native*, and a variety of other works. This remarkably gifted teacher befriended me in the years after my father's death. I would often stop and visit him at his home in the years that followed, talking about ideas, asking for advice, and just plain having enjoyable conversations. Ken opened a new world to me. He encouraged a remarkable English woman who taught at Keith to teach us her special, very lively versions of Shakespeare's works. She often read aloud, and she brought to life in her perfect English elocution those dramas so often left for dead by teachers in public schools.

Her name was Miss Harvey. She described England, and more important, Scotland. She drew a picture for me of marching kilted men playing pipes in a crisp and misty early-morning in the highlands—a vision I never forgot and one I came eventually to see. For I remained a proud Scot of the Black Watch tradition, fighting the just wars of England, including the one so recently behind us, though excluding again the Scots' unhelpful role against us in the Revolutionary War, where all good Scots were tough Americans, bred in the eastern mountains and backwoods, crack shots and not so stupid as to march in ranks in the open field.

Miss Harvey talked of how utterly beautiful an English summer day could be, just as Mom described, and she bristled at the stereotyped statements of rainy old England. She and Ken Pennypacker taught us well and opened my eyes to a world beyond Rockford, a world of the mind and spirit and the relevance of history. This retreated somewhat into the shadows during my time in high school, but later in college, there it was, waiting patiently for me to reach out for it.

Ken and I remained close friends. He left Rockford my senior year of high school to become headmaster of the Foot School in New Haven, Connecticut. We corresponded regularly in typewritten letters (I had taken a summer instruction course to learn to type). The letters were thoughtful, full of ideas and information, and for me, some inner thoughts. After my sophomore year, Ken invited me to come to visit his family in New Haven: my first trip out of the Midwest, my first airline trip (United to Hartford), my first view of the sea, my first glimpse of Yale University, and my first visit to New York City.

Ken, coming from Philadelphia, knew all about how New York worked. He took me to a Broadway show and a Dixieland jazz bar on 52nd Street, and we talked and talked about college at Lawrence, how it was going, about girls, sports, and ideas. He never stopped being a teacher, and I knew he believed that I was a natural for teaching. But he also saw that I was a man of action, looking for challenge and adventure.

After I finished college and had gone to South Africa on a Rotary

International fellowship, we continued writing. Ken went on to become the headmaster of the Rockland County Day School at Upper Nyack, New York. He loved it there and I visited him and his family several times. Ken was ultimately diagnosed with multiple sclerosis. He was forced to retire, his letters now more painfully typed with a single finger, short but always great to receive. I saw him a couple of times in their small house in Nyack. The children were now grown, but Ruth, his strong and lovely wife, remained with him until he died, much too young and on the brink of greatness as a headmaster.

For me, it was the old story. Ken was gone, not ever again to be seen or to have a warm and absorbing conversation with. As with my father, there were no last words, no lingering contacts with his family. Sometimes I feel ashamed because I am sure they viewed me as insensitive in the face of this tragedy. But I had been raised in a hard school when it came to sudden tragedy and the disappearance of a part of life. For me it had always been necessary to turn away, turn forward, just as one does for the first down marker as a running back in football. You take the blows, look for the marker, and get up quickly no matter how hard you've been hit, get up with a bounce of defiance, because there is no one there except you, your will and your hope and strength. God rest the soul of my friend and mentor, Ken Pennypacker, whom I have more to thank for than almost any other man I met anywhere over the years. And, Ken, forgive me for my failings with your family.

Two other experiences in my young life left a lasting imprint on the kind of person I would become. One was a single trip I took with my father when I was eleven years old. The other was a series of summer vacations at Echo Lodge on Lake Namakagon in the Wisconsin north woods that Dad always insisted we take, regardless of whatever difficulties or distractions might be facing our family.

The business trip was to Kansas City in the summer of 1947 or 1948. I saw Kansas City as a city in the Old West, which was one of my enduring preoccupations, so the excitement level was palpable.

Traveling to Kansas City from Rockford by train required driving south from town some thirty miles to where two main line railroads crossed at a place called Davis Junction, which comprised only a small brick railroad station near the rail crossing and a water tank for the big steam locomotives that came through. To be standing on the brick platform in the late afternoon in the shadow of the grand water tower, with unbroken views across the open land in every direction, waiting for the express from Chicago to Kansas City, was truly right at the heart of small boy romance.

This steam-driven express did not stop at small towns as it pounded its way to Kansas from the "city of broad shoulders." It had to be notified by telegraph to make the stop at Davis Junction, and as our shadows lengthened that early evening I realized that this great express was stopping just for Dad and me! I wasn't standing, as I did in Rochelle, just to see it roar through the station. We soon saw its light far in the distance, and we could tell that it was slowing for Davis Junction, right in the middle of what must have seemed like nowhere to its passengers.

The giant locomotive hissed slowly into a station hardly as large as the locomotive itself. I didn't even come up to the axle level of the big driving wheels as the breath of that great machine blew hot on me from the big cylinders. It stopped with a jerk. The door on the sleek, dark Pullman car swung open, the steel platform above the steps clanked up against the interior wall of the vestibule, and a small black man, smiling and elegantly uniformed, stepped down on to the brick platform and placed a small, flat-topped iron stool at the bottom step. "Yes sir!" he said to me. "Climb aboard, young man, onto the Kansas City Limited."

I swelled with excitement and did as he directed. The inside of the Pullman car smelled just like a train should. Despite being the only passengers to board, we waited several minutes while the engine was fed from the water tower.

Then I heard the call "All aboard" and the clank of the steel platform in the vestibule falling into place and the door slamming shut. We moved. I could feel the deep individual chuffs of the engine, well-spaced, decisive, then a couple of soft jerks. I knew exactly what was happening outside from watching so many troop trains leave the station down on South Main Street. First the great chuff, then a second, a third, and then perhaps a series of rapid chuffs and some slippage of the big driving wheels on the steel rails. Perhaps the engineer had dropped some sand? In any case we were soon moving faster, and I could hear the muffled sound of the whistle.

I was going to Kansas City. Dad said we would go out to the stockyards, which of course I imagined would be like Abilene or Dodge City, with cowboys packing six-guns in holsters and sitting or lounging along the railings of giant old corrals filled with restless cattle. Shortly after boarding Dad took me back to the observation car on the back of the train, from which you could see the receding rails sliding away as we went west. Then he took me to the bar car for a drink and a sandwich. There men in shirtsleeves smoked cigars and played poker.

By dark we were back in our Pullman car, which by now had been completely made over so that dark green velvet curtains hung continuously along both sides of the aisle, concealing an upper and lower birth. Our porter, as I now knew him, set the ladder for me to climb up into my bunk with a friendly smile and an encouraging series of "sirs" and "young man." Such excitement! The Kansas City Limited swayed and pulsed through the night at what seemed to me the highest of high speeds. I imagined us bursting through one small station after another in the middle of the night, leaving behind those sharp smells of hot steel, smoke, and cinders as the flashing rear lamps disappeared into the prairie. We were going west, west to Kansas, where I knew that the Dalton Brothers, Jessie James, the Prairie Schooners, Wyatt Earp, and all the other frontier heroes had ridden and fought for good or ill.

But Kansas City was not a dusty cow town with cowboys lounging along covered boardwalks. The steaks at the Stockyards Grill were large and tasty, but there were no cowboys and not a single six-gun strapped low on a cowboy's hip. Nevertheless, the excitement of going to Kansas City with Dad stayed with me, just as did the long business trip I took with him the next year through Indiana, Ohio, Kentucky, Tennessee, and Missouri. I saw how he made our living, why he was so successful with people as a salesman, and how he lived when he was away working.

Summer vacations in the north woods were an entirely different thing. For many years we went to Echo Lodge on Lake Namakagon, which was run by Bill and Helen Amos. Echo Lodge was a primitive resort, bereft of both electricity and running water. We stayed in small cabins built of white cedar logs with the gray, stringy bark still on them. Meals were served by Helen, a large-boned Norwegian woman, at the large family table in the lodge, which was covered with a dark yellow oilcloth. Bill and I fetched water every morning from the hand pump behind the lodge, each carrying two heavy pails hung from wood yokes on our bony shoulders down the lane to our cabin. We also helped Bill at the ice house down beside the lake. This was where he and the men buried the large blocks of ice cut from the lake in winter and covered them with layers of sawdust to preserve them through the summer. When ice was required we would help dig a big block out of the sawdust and wait while the hired man lifted it onto a sawhorse with a large pair of tongs. Then we would help saw the block into pieces with a two-man band saw like the one we used in winter to saw logs. Once cut into smaller blocks we would load the blocks into small wagons and deliver them to all the cabins.

We also dug for worms for the fishermen and helped seine minnows in the shallow water along the shore. Dad didn't fish much, so we spent most of the day together on various adventures. Dad made everything fun, from long walks with big sticks to playing kick the stone on the dirt roads around Echo Lodge. He often walked several miles to a crossroads, gas station, or general store. Grandview, the nearest small town, was eighteen miles from Echo Lodge, too far to walk, but exciting to visit because of its large general store with every conceivable thing under the sun to interest everyone from old men to small boys: boats, bear grease, knives, guns, fishing plugs, wool shirts, jackets, jeans, leather belts, canteens, camping equipment, groceries, games, kitchenware, shovels, axes, and on and on, to all kinds of candy, gum and jawbreakers.

In the summer of 1945 Rockford suffered a deadly polio epidemic. Like any parents, mine lived in fear of the dread disease striking their children with the resulting death or paralysis. When we went to Echo Lodge that summer the decision was taken that Bill and I would remain "up north" until the first killing frosts of November and December. I have never known exactly how or even when my parents came to their decision, but the resulting experience for me had an important impact on my ability to deal with sudden change and a wholly transformed environment. At the time and as I look back, remaining at Echo Lodge was an adventure of the first order, and I have no doubt that, along with other sudden changes and challenges over the years, it helped prepare me for the demands of the kind of life I was to lead. The essence of this experience was to require that I deal with whatever situation came to hand entirely on my own. There were no clearers of the way, sponsors, or advisors, just as later there were none of major significance as I made my way through college, South Africa, Boston, Oxford, Wall Street, London, New York, Saudi Arabia, Washington, and India.

Mom and Dad left Echo Lodge in mid-August, and Bill and I were moved into a spare room with one double bed upstairs in the lodge. We continued to work around the lodge and the ice house and in the late-summer vegetable garden. Bill and Helen ran a strict regime, especially Helen. One did not leave food unfinished on one's plate, one ate whatever was served, small cuts and bruises were to be ignored, and one's help was to be forthcoming without complaint or prevarication.

I was eight years old, and Bill was ten. We were bathed once a week on Saturday night in the kitchen, where water was heated on the cookstove and poured into the kind of large shallow tin tub used to collect cinders from coal furnaces to be put out for collection. We were put in the tub together by Helen, who gave a most vigorous and unflinching rubdown with a thick, rough towel when she took us out.

After Labor Day in early September the temperature in northern

Wisconsin drops sharply. Frost and cold morning fog rise above the lakes and swamps, and wood-burning fireplaces and stoves burn all day. Trips to the outhouse, some fifty yards from the house, grew increasingly challenging, especially after dark, now coming early, and in the middle of the night. Looking back, I sometimes wonder I did not simply freeze up and disappear in the outhouse as I used it alone at night, flashlight in hand, surrounded by the dark woods, friendly by day but frightening by night.

We were enrolled in school after Labor Day in Grandview, Wisconsin, a town of some one hundred souls, eighteen miles distant. This necessitated walking approximately one mile out to the main road, which was also not paved, and waiting for a small enclosed van of the type a plumber or house painter might use, which was fixed with two facing benches down the sides and only two small windows in the rear doors by which passengers entered and left. For a boy given to carsickness, the ride to school was a significant challenge. There was no prospect of slowing or stopping the van, no one to change places with, and no place to move that would be better. There was also no way to turn and look ahead out the windshield onto the road (the prescribed tactic in our family for avoiding car sickness) because a partition closed the cab off from our small rear cell.

So the solution was simply not to get carsick. Nothing would be so humiliating in such a small space, with some pretty rough kids of widely differing ages. Bill and I must have seemed like real "city slickers" even though we were well versed in the ways of the woods. Nevertheless, Grandview School was a rough and tumble place. There were several classrooms, but each classroom had more than one age group in it. For lunch we had bear meat stew every day, which tasted slightly sweet but very good after the early-morning departure and a half day at school. Recess, or play period, was among the roughest and most energetic activities I was ever to experience at a school. In my first days at school I vividly recall getting too close to an iron and chain maypole that the girls in particular ran around shouting and laying out feet first to sail around the pole. One of these girls laughingly kicked me in the stomach. She was much older and tougher than me, so after collecting myself from the pain and humiliation of being kicked to the ground by a girl, there was no question of retaliation.

Some of the girls wore lipstick, and a few smoked out behind the outhouses. One such girl of about twelve, to whom I made some smart remark in the school bus, leaned across and scratched my face with her long nails. Again, pain and humiliation. But I got used to school and the rough and tumble playground. And I loved the early-morning walk to the main road and the walk back in the fading day of late afternoon. Of course, what to do about meeting a black bear or a big buck, or a wolf or fox, was a subject of nervous discussion between Bill and me as we walked. Bill Amos's recommendation to just stand still, or alternatively to take off your cap, put it between your teeth and rush shouting at the bear, seemed to be tactics requiring an impossible act of courage—and still do today.

By mid-October the leaves were all down and there was frost in the mornings. Bill and I had lots of work around the lodge, but evenings closed in early and the big kitchen with its warm cookstove always burning was the coziest room in the house.

One Saturday morning in November my parents drove into Echo Lodge to take us home to Rockford. Bill and I were sawing wood with a crossbuck saw that morning and it was snowing large, wet flakes. The adventure was over, but the experience of being away in a strange place stayed with me as a reference point for the future.

2

Oxford and Cape Town

In the summer of 1954, between my junior and senior years at Lawrence, I made a plan to travel through Europe with one of my football teammates. Charlie Scruggs was from South Chicago. He was very smart, a good student majoring in English, and he was very tough. He had cleaned boilers in South Chicago for a summer job and played a deadly safety in football, cutting down runners far bigger than he was. He was fast and could strike with that sharp and violent "crack" that I so admired.

At that time it was unusual for midwestern college students to travel to Europe. We seemed to be the only ones going that summer at Lawrence. Our plan was to bike through Europe on $5 per day, stay in youth hostels, and carry only the bare essentials, which included a football to use for our workouts.

We started by flying from New York to Glasgow, Scotland, where after a very long night in a KLM Super Constellation, which stopped for fuel at Gander, we arrived at Prestwick, Scotland, to be greeted by "uncle" Cyril Andrew Kerr, Mother's friend and correspondent of many years. Andrew, to Charley and me, was a real Scot: checked jacket, mustard waistcoat, tweed cap, small beard, and a civilized Scottish accent. Andrew took us first to a pub and stood us each a pint glass of Guinness, then home to meet his wife, Dickie, who was much younger than Andrew, and from Dundee, north of the Tay, and God's own country in eastern Scotland.

Andrew took us for my first breathtaking view of the Highlands, the naked green hills above Loch Lohman. We bought our bikes and set out for Edinburgh, biking the hilly miles in one day. In Edinburgh, we visited the castle that towers above Princess Street, explored the Rolls of Honour for the names of Mother's long-lost cousins in the trenches of France, and met two charming lassies at one of Edinburgh's old-fashioned dance halls.

Scotland was just the beginning of a glorious adventure that changed my life. Feeling perfectly at home in Britain, I drank in every detail of the buildings, the lanes, the stone walls, the lush greens, the towers and courtyards of Oxford, the sights of London, the theaters, the age and genuine aspect of everything around us. In London, around St Paul's and elsewhere, I was awed by bomb damage left from the war, shells of buildings, partial walls with grass, bushes and trees coming up through the ruins. People dressed as I had seen them in the newsreels of the 1940s. Construction workers wore aged tweed jackets with leather elbow patches and cloth caps, and they smoked pipes while they worked or sat about the street works. Houses, hostels, and bed and breakfast places were cold inside; baths were rare and were always down the hall at the toilets, with the waxlike toilet paper left over from the war, sometimes printed on each sheet with "HMS Government."

The trains were driven by steam engines, the height of romance, and in train restrooms a small plaque invariably appeared stating, "Gentlemen lift the seat," which I was at pains to interpret. Was it a command or an observation? Tea was delicious, teddy boys with duck tails were just appearing, and hitchhiking was easy (we had stored the bikes by then), even on big trucks. We slept in our sleeping bags in fields, parks, and under bridges out of the rain, and every fourth night we took a room and a bath.

By the time we crossed the Channel I knew I would be coming back. I felt an irresistible affinity for Oxford, as if it were just the place for me , and I imagined being a student there, among those beautiful and peaceful colleges, set in the hum and congestion of downtown Oxford.

The rest of the summer was equally intoxicating—Belgium and the World Exposition, where we met and debated with real Russians in the Soviet Pavilion; Germany, where the bomb damage was fearful in its comprehensive presence; Switzerland, Austria, Italy, and France. I returned home hardly able to contain my passion for adventure, to see this extraordinary world, to be a part of it, not a visitor to it. I understood that my life would never be the same, that I would leave home, leave Lawrence, leave America, and find my challenge overseas.

I adopted radically different attitudes my senior year at Lawrence. I tried to drop my major in economics and move to a double major in history and anthropology. The college would not agree, but to their credit they came up with an alternative that marked the high point of my academic experience at Lawrence. By that time I had been awarded a Rotary International Fellowship to Oxford University. These fellowships, awarded by the Rotary International Foundation in Evanston, Illinois, after a national competitive process, provided a one-year fellowship to study at a foreign university selected by the applicant. A fellow was expected to study for one academic year and to act throughout the year as an ambassador to the host country by visiting and speaking at Rotary clubs within the districts surrounding the university.

The Lawrence solution was that I could complete enough economics courses to satisfy my major, choose a course in anthropology, and most remarkably be set up with Lawrence's most talented teacher of history, Professor William Cheney, an Englishman who would give me an individual Oxford-style tutorial course in the history of ideas. Under Professor Cheney I was to read, write a paper, read the paper to him, and discuss it once each week. This arrangement, and the privilege of working with William Cheney, whose knowledge, method of teaching, and pure capacity to entertain with the human realities of history gave me a unique and since-unmatched experience. In our first interview I had artlessly told him that I was intent on changing the world, and many years later he was kind enough to say in public comments that he knew I had meant what I had said and had actually done it.

I graduated that June cum laude with one of the best assets a young person can have: a liberal arts education and a passion for adventure. In my last months at Lawrence I had two other transformative experiences. The first was that I developed a fascination with the movement in Africa toward independence. Ghana had become independent in 1957, Nigeria was on the brink, and other African countries, including white-ruled countries, were moving toward freedom from colonial domination.

The second great change was that I fell in love with a very pretty young Latvian woman, Astrida Akmentins. Astrida and her family had fled from Russia's invasion of Latvia in 1944 and had lived in a refugee camp in southern Bavaria for a number of years before coming to Wisconsin. The spring and summer of 1959 was a fast-moving, highly charged period that culminated in two big decisions: one was to marry Astrida so we could go overseas together, and the other was to petition the Rotary Foundation to grant me my second university preference, Cape Town University in South Africa, instead of Oxford. In addition, I asked, in a personal interview at Rotary International in Evanston, whether they would permit me to use my travel grant to go to Oxford that fall, where I had already been accepted, and then on to Cape Town the following March for the beginning of the school year in the southern hemisphere. To my delight, Rotary agreed, so long as I paid my fees and costs at Oxford myself.

Astrida and I were married in August and two days later set off for England. That summer in England was the warmest and driest for many decades. It was stifling. In London several deaths were attributed to the heat and, unusual in London, it was announced that in view of the heat the Metropolitan Police would be permitted to remove their jackets and neckties. The beautiful green England of the previous summer was dry and brown. None of this diminished the charm of Oxford. We found rooms in Summertown, North Oxford, and I began the academic year as a recognized student studying law.

Oxford in term was exactly what I had wanted it to be. In the pure northern light of early autumn the college buildings of Cotswold stone reflected a soft golden color. Roses continued to bloom in the peaceful courtyards with the bright green lawns and in the gardens that flourished along stone walls. The streets were full of cyclists in short and long black gowns, tearing along between lectures. The alleys and walkways seemed to invite exploration, and behind their many doors and gates one knew there were "secret gardens" with bushes, benches, trees, and flowers. Even the frequent rain seemed right. No one seemed to take much notice of it unless it poured with no break in sight.

My first meeting with my tutor at Exeter College was a startling revelation. I enquired at the porter's lodge just inside the college gate and was directed to the senior fellows' garden, across the courtyard, through a passage and garden to a door that gave into the Senior Fellows' garden. It was a sunny, warm afternoon, and Mr. G. D. G. Hall, subrector of Exeter College, was seated behind a small table big enough only for his book and a tray with teapot and cup. There was a chair across the table for me but no tea cup or offer of tea.

Mr. Hall was a short, compact man who looked healthy and fit. He seemed friendly but reserved.

"I understand you will be here for just one term and that you want to read law," he began.

"Yes, sir."

"I should think the law of torts is where you should begin," he went on.

I wasn't sure what torts were, but it was law and that was what I wanted to learn, so I said yes, the law of torts will be fine.

He asked where I was from in America, and whether I had digs arranged in Oxford. Then he suddenly said, "I am the best lecturer in the faculty of law, but you shouldn't bother coming to my lectures, or anyone else's in the law faculty."

Before I could express my surprise at this statement or ask a question, he went on.

"Here is what I want you to do. Go to Blackwell's Bookshop—do you know where that is—good—and buy [he named the book] and read as much as you can."

"Yes, sir."

"As you read the text, mark the cases referred to in the text or footnotes that you think are most relevant to the subject."

I nodded.

"Then go to the library and read each case you have marked and write a brief precis of the case and why you think it is relevant. Then you will write a brief paper each week on the subject matter as suggested by the cases and come to my rooms to read the paper aloud to me and to then discuss it. Is that clear?"

It was clear, but the reasons and the value of this procedure were fully understood by me only later. Meanwhile, he continued.

"As to lectures, you should by all means go to lectures, but you needn't bother about going to law lectures. Instead, buy the *Oxford Gazette*. Do you know what this is?"

I did not know and said so.

"It is a broadsheet you can buy for a few pence at the bookshop, which will list all the university lectures for Michaelmas term, who is giving them, where they are being given, and the time."

I agreed to buy the *Gazette* right away.

"Then," he said, "go through the *Gazette* and just pick the lectures that interest you in whatever field and go to listen. This will be more useful to you than going to law lectures."

The meeting was over. He took up his book and I left for the bookshop with no further conversation. I was amazed by what he had said and all the things he had not said. His clarity of speech and economy with words impressed me. Instead of feeling at sea with the lean supply of information and direction, I felt exhilarated. I was going to do this by myself. I would have to figure out how to proceed, which cases to mark, and what to write.

I could hardly wait to get started. I went directly to Blackwell's on Broad Street, bought the book and the *Gazette*, stopped at a café for tea, and began reading. The book was dry but written with the same lean clarity of expression as Mr. Hall had used. I found it easy to mark what I thought to be the most relevant cases and understood that I would know whether my judgment was correct only when I had read and written a summary on each case. Meanwhile, I perused the *Gazette*, which was a veritable gold mine of opportunity. I marked lectures in different periods of history, politics, and philosophy, and even chose a lecture in the law of torts. That term I listened to the famous and eccentric Isaiah Berlin, who would lecture on philosophy without interruption and with many amusing side references, while holding his head at what seemed an uncomfortable angle, staring fixedly into the far upper corner of the crowded hall. I also attended the lectures on politics of Professor Max Beloff of All Souls College, not realizing that in two years he would be my supervisor for my doctorate, though not my regular weekly Oxford tutor.

The lectures on law of torts were held at Worcester College, a most beautiful college whose ancient buildings fronted on Walton Street and which had its own secluded lake within its grounds. This lecture room was always particularly cold, but the lecturer, a very entertaining Australian, brought the field of torts vividly to life. He was obviously as much a historian as he was a law professor. Dressed in light brown twill trousers, a mustard waistcoat with brass buttons, and a snappy checked or tweed jacket with his long black gown draped over his shoulders, he would thread his way through the most graphic and amusing cases, some deeply obscure, some with the most pathetic or prosaic circumstances, and some utterly hilarious. He paced while he lectured, smiled, moved his arms and hands to convey the drama or the intricacy of these revelations. I still remember many of these cases: *Rylands v. Fletcher*; the case of the damp firework squib; and the case of the tile on the roof of a pub, dislodged by a bomb in the First World War, which years later slid off the roof, striking an innocent pedestrian in the head. On some days the lecturer would propose his own case situation involving damage to extract from us how we would view such a series of unfolding events that resulted in actionable damages.

That autumn I subjected myself to an intense work program, reading and writing up cases and preparing my weekly paper. The weather soon turned cold and damp, often frosty in the mornings and evenings and frequently with mist or fog. The library at Exeter College was more like a medieval church inside than a library, including the cold rising from the stone floor. As autumn deepened toward winter the cold inside intensified. I took to wearing my long johns, fuzzy-lined ski boots, heavy sweater, and overcoat, and even then I seldom lasted more than two hours before going outside to get warm. Sometimes this meant rushing off to a lecture to get my blood and brain stimulated, and sometimes it meant just going round to the Kemp Café, one floor up over Broad Street and the Corn Market, where for two shillings and six pence I would get a hot meal, complete with pie or crumble for dessert submerged in hot vanilla custard sauce.

The cases were fun to read, sometimes difficult to summarize in two legal-sized pages, and then there was the essay paper to write—and to read. This latter exercise proved challenging because although Mr. Hall assigned a topic for the paper each week, he gave no guidance as to what particulars of the subject should be the focus of my efforts.

On the appointed day for our weekly sessions, I would cross Exeter's front courtyard, enter the far right corner staircase, and climb three flights of stairs to his rooms. There was always a cheery coal fire going, and we sat facing one another, he on a low sofa and me in an easy chair. As I read my paper, Mr. Hall would gradually slide off the sofa onto the floor and stretch his legs out to begin fiddling with a small waste paper basket nearby, always smoking his pipe. Occasionally he would interrupt me to make a point or to ask a question. I handed over my precis papers for the week—handwritten, like my essay—and that was the last I ever saw of them. Mr. Hall never commented on my work, graded it in any fashion, or returned it. What I was pretty certain about is that he was impressed by the sheer volume of cases I chose and prepared, but he never let on what he thought. Later, when I came to see how Oxford really worked—that is, that it was not fashionable to convey the impression that you worked hard, in fact quite the reverse—I could guess at his true response: here is one of these extraordinarily energetic Americans who take everything literally but don't write particularly well!

But I did more than study, and at least conformed to the Oxford tradition of playing a sport after lunch before the early-afternoon darkness descended over the playing fields. Immediately after my lectures I went to what for me, as a middle-distance runner, was the sacred running track on Iffley Road. This was where in 1954 Roger Bannister for the first time ever broke the four-minute barrier for the mile run, and this on a cold and rainy afternoon. I trained at Iffley Road with a small group of dedicated runners, fellows with very impressive track credentials and a fierce dedication to interval training. One afternoon I ran in an inter-college half-mile race and won in close to my best time.

My victory was reported in the *Oxford Times* sports page the next day under the headline "American wins half mile for Exeter College." A few days later I received a handwritten note from Mr. G. D. G. Hall requesting that I come to his rooms the next afternoon. I climbed the three flights of stairs to find him in his usual spot. He got directly to the point. "We are delighted, Mr. Mulford, that you are an outstanding athlete, as seen the other day in your running."

I began to be pleased by the notice of my accomplishment.

"However," he continued, "you must not purport to represent Exeter College again. As you will recall you are a 'recognized student' at Oxford. You are not therefore matriculated as a full member of the University or of Exeter College and cannot represent us in sports."

It was the same clear, lean rhetoric of the law, and this *was* the law, which of course had never occurred to me. I apologized and left his rooms, suitably chastised for my indiscretion, but bemused by the absence of any good-natured tolerance for what had been a rather small sporting event, which, after all I had won.

On two afternoons a week I played rugby with a pickup team called the Oxford Mongrels. This was my first experience of rugby, and because I was an American football running back I was seen as most suitably employed out on the wing, where players ran the ball, pitched it to other backs, and punted. I soon loved the game and discovered that playing a contact game like rugby without additional padding was not as threatening for injury as it would be in American football. Tackling was largely a matter of dragging a runner down from the side as he ran by with the ball, and contact in the scrum was mainly a case of leaning, pushing, and grunting.

What I really found novel was the atmosphere surrounding our matches. They took place in the afternoons against college second teams in what were termed "friendlies." We began in late afternoon, often in the fog or rain, and played on the extremely soft field until dark. We would then have a beer in the clubhouse with the other team—a whole new experience for me compared with American football, where friendly contact with your opponents just didn't happen. Rugby was not nearly as violent as American football, but it was nevertheless physically demanding and rough in a continually fast-moving fashion. The fellows I played with were skilled in many of the game's techniques, especially punting the ball on the run with either foot and drop-kicking the ball on the run for scores.

I was not in Oxford long enough to become well acquainted with my teammates, but I did see some of them around town from time to time. Considering the language sometimes used in the heat of our matches, I was surprised to see many of them in the stiff white collars of aspiring priests or ministers, studying at various religious colleges. By December it was getting dark earlier and earlier, and the season came to an end. From a rugby standpoint I was now ready to go on to Cape Town, where according to my teammates they played real rugby, no holds barred as in gentlemen "friendlies." I would miss those soft, wet afternoons and the luxuriously soft green turf that made falling like landing on a feather bed.

Life for married students at Oxford was fairly isolating, since young people at university in Britain married later. Our friends were mainly Australians, who, like us, married young and often married to come to Oxford. Living quarters in Oxford were plain and very cold. Summertown was a mile and a half from the university in the center of Oxford, a long bike ride in the rain and cold of autumn and winter. Astrida and I lived in two rooms with the bath in the hallway and shared the kitchen with our landlord downstairs. He was Rabbi Lehman, an Orthodox Jew and a classics scholar at the Bodleian Library in Central Oxford. The rabbi also lived in two rooms, one of which was lined floor to ceiling with shelves of books that also came out from the walls in free-standing shelves like a library. There was just enough room for his desk and for a person to walk from the door to the desk, which sat in the front-window alcove. Our contract with Rabbi Lehman specified that we would share the kitchen attached to the back of the house, but the rear garden was not available for our use, unless we needed a five-minute break from studies to gain a few minutes of fresh air.

As far as we were concerned there was plenty of fresh air inside the house. In fact as the weather grew colder ice formed on the inside of our windows There was one small fireplace in each room that had a white filament that would glow red when the gas was ignited to heat the room. Operating the gas fire required inserting a shilling for what seemed a rather short period. In front of the gas fires was the only place laundry could be dried, and this was a long, steamy process. Rabbi Lehman was a deeply shy man who only rarely spoke. We paid him £6 per week. Cooking in the kitchen was akin to cooking in a dripping, steamy cave, to be done as quickly as possible. Rabbi Lehman boiled large pieces of meat for hours on the gas stove, which we did not understand as we were entirely unacquainted with the food practices of Orthodox Jews. This was proven in dramatic fashion one evening when Astrida and I were bundled up in the kitchen preparing dinner. Astrida had innocently borrowed the Rabbi's frying pan to cook bacon, which, as the smells drifted back into the house provoked Rabbi Lehman to storm out of his room shouting, "what is going on here?"

When he saw more exactly what was going on he was further provoked into a frightening display of temper, shouting "I can never use this pan again." We were shocked by this anger and deeply embarrassed by our lack of knowledge and sensitivity to Orthodox requirements and practices. We sheepishly retired to our rooms with tails very much between our legs, cowed by the complexity of matters we knew nothing about at that time and the passion they could provoke when violated.

Relations were soon restored with Rabbi Lehman, who remained reclusive but friendly when some matter needed discussion. He studied all day every day in his library-like sitting room. I knocked on his door one frigid morning in December when water in the kitchen had frozen over in a pan. He answered the door in an overcoat and gloves with the fingertips cut off so he could write freely. He had a terrible cold that had left him with a red, weeping nose. I expressed my concern about his being unwell and obviously very cold, to which he responded by saying that he never turned on any heat until the first of January. Later I learned that he was regarded at Bodleian as a true eccentric, having been lost in the preparation of his dissertation for nearly fifteen years. When we left in early February he seemed genuinely sorry to see us go.

3

Africa

At last, Africa!

We were set to depart Southampton in early February 1960 on the Union Castle Line's *Carnarvon Castle*—fifteen days to Cape Town. The big steel trunk and the footlocker were packed, the brightly colored cardboard Union Castle tags were laboriously filled out, and all our effects except what we would need on the ship were sent by rail for loading at Southampton. It was a thrill each time I wrote the words "Cape Town, South Africa." This was adventure of the first order. My imagination raced with excitement, visualizing utterly new sights and sounds, different people and landscapes, the unknown challenges of living in a warm climate country, let alone seeing wild animals and native peoples.

I had carefully read the history of South Africa, which had greatly surprised me in certain of its elements, such as the migration of Afrikaners into the unsettled interior to escape the unwelcome presence of the British in the Cape Province and later Durban. Their conflict with African tribes who had moved south from tribal wars farther north also raised similarities with the opening of the American West. I had no previous knowledge of how the four main provincial states (Cape Province, Natal, Orange Free State, and Transvaal) had come together in the union of South Africa. Nor had I any real idea of the violence and suffering of the Boer War and what clearly was a defeat of major proportions for the British. Still less did I know about the Zulus, the Basutos, and the tribes of the Eastern Cape, except for the vision left from boyhood adventure movies that portrayed Africans in general as dangerous, primitive, and violent—characteristics I was to learn that had no basis whatsoever in reality.

We cast off from Southampton for Africa on a cold, wet, and thoroughly gloomy early-February day. We had the lowest-cost inside cabin. The *Carnarvon Castle* had been built in the early 1930s and was not air conditioned. Salt water baths were available, and the interior décor of the ship appeared not to have been refurbished since the time of its building. It was even more English in appearance than the rather worn and stifling appearance of public places in Britain at the end of the 1950s. We were assigned a table with two English spinsters traveling to South Africa and another South African couple who said they had left their full staff in place in Cape Town to look after their cat while they spent several months visiting England. Our waiter was a pleasant man who regularly made voyages to Cape Town and on around Africa to Durban, Lourenço Marques, Dar es Salaam, Zanzibar, Mombassa, and the Red Sea to the Suez Canal. Such delightful and exciting names and places I knew I would have to see. He was also quick to remind us of the temperatures ranging up to 140 degrees in the galley in the Red Sea. The fact that our ship was not air conditioned as we toiled across the swells in the Bay of Biscay didn't at that point seem to matter.

After three days you didn't need an overcoat to go on deck. In five days we were in shirtsleeves and summer frocks. Then we entered the tropics off the coast of Africa, which despite peering to the east everyday we never could see. By day nine or ten we were churning through the calm between the trade winds of the two hemispheres, the surface as calm and mirrorlike in the mornings as a windless Wisconsin lake. We and other young people slept on deck to avoid the stuffy heat of our small interior cabin, and there were celebrations and shenanigans as we crossed the equator.

Now we were nearing Africa, and the talk among the passengers was of Africa. Some were going "up country" into the hinterland. I heard words referring to the Veld, the bush, the Karoo, the Transvaal, the Drakensberg, the Interior. Bush outfits began to appear, distinguishing the Africa hands from the rest of us. One also heard countless remarks, some insensitive and disturbing, about the natives, about the new regime of apartheid and about Bantustans in the Transkei and elsewhere. Clearly there was tension here, a sort of undercurrent of racial hostility that was hard to square with how I had grown up, accepting as friends and teammates boys of many different backgrounds, including African Americans. I was uncomfortable with these loose and offensive generalizations but engaged in no debate with people older and apparently more set in their views.

After fourteen days, in which the *Carnarvon Castle* had become in a sense our home, an announcement was made that we would arrive in Cape Town the next morning. Long before dawn a bell like those that toll for Evensong in Oxford chapels began to toll in steady strokes. I rushed up onto the deck, where I was greeted by the softest breeze I can remember, wafting off shore and bearing the smell of land. Then I could make out lights far across a broad bay and the shape of land and hills against the lightening sky. Now Cape Town itself was unmistakably visible, nestled beneath Table Mountain, its outline stark against the morning sky with a small white cloud sitting over part of its utterly flat surface. This was its "table cloth," and beneath the rim rising from the city were countless sparkling lights that had yet to be extinguished for the day.

It was the most perfect arrival anyone could wish for, especially any adventurer thirsting to see a new and exotic continent. There we were, at the very place where the English sailing ships had berthed to take on provisions and fresh water on their voyages to India and the Far East. This was the Cape of Good Hope, not just any cape, the southernmost tip of Africa, which all captains, sailors, soldiers, explorers, and settlers east of Suez knew. This was where the South Atlantic and yes, let me say it, the Indian Ocean met, the turbulent sea Conrad had written about, the place David Livingstone had come to enter Africa to begin his great mission.

Africa was becoming free. I was here, at Africa's door, ready to be a visiting Rotary Scholar, ready to attend Cape Town University, and ready above all to travel to the interior, forgetting perhaps as I was later to learn that the heart of Africa was yet as far away as crossing the United States of America.

Could there be a more breathtaking place than the University of Cape Town, set high against the rising base of Table Mountain and looking out across the Cape Flats to the mountain ridges of the interior and across Table Bay, Cape Town's natural harbor? I could hardly contain myself over the multitude of flowers, exotic trees, and plants, birds, colors, smells, and the quality of light that filtered through trees in the mornings of those first days. The most delicious grapes were for sale on the street, as it was March, harvest time and the end of summer. We had to get used to being served morning tea in our hotel room as soon as we awakened by an African or Cape Coloured member of the hotel staff. On our first morning after a knock on the door a man entered with a tray in hand. I thought he was invading our room and leaped out of bed before noticing he was just bringing tea and morning salutations, which included a completely new word for me: "Where you want the tray, boss?" Boss? It brought new visions of command and domination that made me feel uneasy.

The Rotarians of Rondebosch, my host club and the town where the university was situated, gave us a gracious welcome. We could tell they were surprised by how young we were to be married, and once again we soon discovered that at Cape Town there were no other married students. We found housing in Newlands and registered at the university and at our home Rotary Club. We were then directed to Pietermaritzburg, a thousand miles up the coast and inland from Durban, to attend the annual Rotary Conference for South Africa.

Pietermaritzburg was a small, picturesque town, called by everyone "sleepy," situated on the edge of the Valley of a Thousand Hills in Zululand. Huge shade trees and old whitewashed buildings, including the hotel, gave the town the atmosphere of old South Africa.

At the conference I was called upon to give my first speech in South Africa, which I did together with Elvis Mason, a Rotary fellow from Beaumont, Texas. It was soon made clear to us that a Rotary fellow from America, if not unique, was certainly very unusual in South Africa. We were told that we were to be put to work in whatever free time we had from our studies by visiting and speaking at all the Rotary Clubs in the district. We would be hosted by families and assisted by them in our travel from club to club during the long university holiday in midwinter, June to July.

This was no small assignment. There were fifty-two clubs in the district, which covered an area twelve hundred miles long by five hundred miles across, quite unlike a midwestern American district comprising a county or two. The district ran from Cape Town to Eshowe, near the border with Mozambique, then inland to encompass the interior of South Africa, except for Johannesburg and Pretoria in the Transvaal.

To Elvis, who became a lifelong friend, and me this seemed a preposterous assignment, but during the course of the next nine months we both made the effort to live up to the Rotarians' expectations. In the end I visited fifty-one of the fifty-two clubs (the only exception being Upington in the Kalahari Desert) in three of South Africa's four states. I was received with open, friendly hospitality by families all over South Africa. Travel was mainly by road, with one family handing me over to the next host family halfway between the two towns.

I often say that my year in South Africa firmly started me on the road to an international career. Traveling across this great country, meeting people, speaking at luncheons and dinners, absorbing the unique aspects of urban and rural South Africa was a gift for me of inestimable value. Around Cape Town I would drive out for the day to nearby towns in my old 1952 Ford Prefect to attend and speak at luncheons. I had prepared and then started to memorize speeches on three themes of American life: one to explain how America elects its president, which in 1960 was a subject of much interest; the second explained the educational system in America; and the third was my attempt to provide an explanation of race relations in America in the 1950s.

At first I was extremely nervous about giving a speech to a seated crowd following lunch and a brief Rotary singing session. I soon conquered this by thinking, "I am their guest, I am expected to speak, my audience is friendly, and it is a captive audience. I must use this time and these opportunities to teach myself how to relax, to speak with few or perhaps no notes, and finally to be confident in the knowledge that I had been invited by them to speak and that I must therefore engage first their attention and second their sustained interest." I found that eye contact with my audience was essential, that I must continuously think of them and not of myself and how I was doing. During the year I learned to relax, how and when, and when not, to try a humorous remark or story, and perhaps how to begin to read a crowd and the degree of engagement I was achieving as I went along. I learned never to speak down to a group, and I sought to explain my subject clearly, to educate through clarity of expression. I worked at eliminating the "uh, ah" intrusions that are the enemy of clear expression and undermine the momentum of a speaker's theme. Finally, I tried simply to let my personality show through so my listeners would know who I was, even if they did not necessarily agree with certain of my comments or observations. By the end of the year I was sure I had made important progress.

What was surprising to me was the importance given by the Rotarians in the small, often isolated towns, to my visits. This was extremely touching, as was the family hospitality and effort to make sure we were exposed to the best their area had to offer. It was not uncommon that dinner in these towns would be a black tie affair with wives attending, which to a small-town small-college midwestern American, twenty-two years of age, was humbling and seemed to demand of me the best possible performance as an ambassador of my country.

I met and stayed with a wide variety of interesting people all over the country. In Oudtshoorn I stayed on an ostrich farm with a man whose wife had recently left him. I rode an ostrich across a small field, which was apparently as chancy as riding a wild pony. In Cradock I met a war veteran who had been captured in the collapse of Tobruk, put into a German prison camp in Italy, and then escaped from a slow-moving freight train in the Italian Alps as they were being removed to Germany late in the war. He survived by working his way down the mountainous spine of Italy, staying with farm families until he ran into the Americans coming north.

In Mossel Bay I stayed with a family where the father of two young sons had been blown out of a bomber at twelve thousand feet over Italy and fallen with a partially opened parachute into a tree. He had lost both legs at the knee but was able to run about throwing a rugby ball with almost as much agility as anyone else. In Ladysmith I was taken through the town streets where many British solders had fallen to Boer snipers in the surrounding hills before its ultimate relief by British troops, including then-journalist Winston Churchill. I saw small companies, farms, and a lady in Graaff Reinet who occupied an entire block closed in up to thirty feet high with screening; inside were hundreds of birds that had full access to her open house.

These towns were in the high country, well inland from Port Elizabeth, in the rising hills of the Drakensberg Mountains. It was bitter cold in the mornings and at night. I traveled there by overnight train, a milk train that stopped at virtually every ranch to drop off freight and pick up farm products, including milk. I looked out the window or stood on the open platform between the carriages to watch the loading and to see Africans, women and children beside fires, wrapped in colorful Basuto blankets.

Race relations and attitudes to Africans were inevitably a consistent theme on these visits. Conversation with families always got around to the question of how Africans were treated and why they had to continue in their present place in South Africa's white society. Attitudes between English and Afrikaans-speaking South Africans were very different. I found that English-speaking South Africans were often more liberal but sometimes treated their African house and grounds or farm staff with less respect than did Afrikaans families, who were less flexible politically about possible change but seemed more respectful to those who worked closely with them in their homes.

Nevertheless, the attitudes of superiority, the constant denigration of Africans, wore heavily on me. As a visitor and guest I did not feel I could argue these matters with every family and Rotarians hosting me in South Africa. I knew my own mind, and at Cape Town University I was learning a great deal about how the laws and administration of African (Native) affairs actually operated on the ground. The picture was not uplifting, not optimistic, and could, it seemed to me, be justly characterized as inhuman. The Sharpeville massacre, which took place in Cape Town's townships shortly after my arrival, made a deep and disgusting impression on me. At Sharpeville, the police opened fire on a large group of Africans who were unarmed and protesting against the imposition of the new Nationalist government's policy of apartheid. Sixty-eight Africans were killed outright in the shooting. I wrote a passionate descriptive article and sent it back to my hometown newspaper.

Countering these feelings of disgust were the often paternalistic views of many decent, hardworking white South Africans toward the Africans they knew and with whom they often worked. These relations were often friendly and well-meant within the context of race relations in South Africa at the time. Fear of change, of possible violent extremism, colored the view of most people I met, especially white women. As a result, I listened to interminable dissertations, keeping my own counsel and concluding that it would be decades before race relations in South Africa would change. This judgment had an important bearing on the path I chose for my academic career over the next five years.

In the course of my year in South Africa—attending classes, traveling across the country, meeting people in their homes and Rotary Club associations, seeing at close hand the life that Europeans, Africans, Asians, and Cape Coloureds (a group of mixed-race people descended from Europeans, Bushmen and Hottentots) actually lived, the magnitude of South Africa's entrenched tragedy penetrated ever deeper into my mind. In the aftermath of the Sharpeville killings and the ongoing implementation of apartheid, my studies at the university took on a whole new dimension. Anthropology was in itself deeply interesting, despite the the influence of South Africa's political and racial agenda. I took both the opening course and the advanced course in the single year. Some of the subject matter, which I retained for future use in Zambia, centered on Barotseland in the far west of Northern Rhodesia (now Zambia). Barotseland and its unique society occupied the great flood plain of the Zambezi River, which made its way from the Belgian Congo to Victoria Falls and on to the Indian Ocean.

However, the two courses that really opened my mind were in comparative native administration and law. These were taught by Professor Jack Simons, a brilliant and articulate lecturer who had been imprisoned for his views by the Nationalists and continued to work under a restraining order restricting his free movement beyond the immediate area of Cape Town. One course reviewed the different methods of government and the administration used by the various colonial powers in their approach to governing their territories in Africa. This covered the British approach of indirect rule; the Belgian approach of ruthless suppression; the French method of government directly from the metropole of Paris with cultural assimilation of the most educated African class; and the Portuguese policy of assimilation within the territory itself. The rule of the white-dominated territories of the British were also treated, such as Kenya (the Mau Mau uprising was still a very recent experience there), Southern and Northern Rhodesia, and the French experience in Algeria. The sweep of this course was breathtaking and totally absorbing to me, especially as countries in West Africa and the Belgian Congo were in transition to some form of independence.

The second course focused on the respective differences between "customary native law" in Africa, British common law, and the Roman Dutch law of South Africa. The most riveting illustration of the conflict in law between these systems were between customary law and Roman Dutch law in South Africa. These stemmed from radical differences in how such matters as marriage, property rights, family law, inheritance, and freedom of movement were dealt with. The roots of apartheid, extended from the religious philosophy of the Dutch Reformed Church, as well as from the fact that Roman Dutch law applied by the Nationalist politicians in power was used to isolate and remove rights of all kinds from nonwhites in South Africa. Rural Africans in their "homelands" (Bantustans, or reserves) generally shared land in common rather than owning land individually. When they came to town, or simply into white areas, they did not and in fact could not own land where often they lived and worked for generations.

One example of the conflict in law that I particularly remember was the case of an African man run down and killed as he walked along a road at night by a drunken white driver. The man's wife's application for damages to sustain herself and family was denied by the South African court on the grounds that they had been married by customary law, which was not recognized either by the Dutch Reformed Church or by Roman Dutch law in South Africa. This would presumably also apply to the devastated families of those killed at Sharpeville. In fact, the reality in South Africa was that Africans had no rights of substance in the areas where vast numbers of them lived and worked, and the rural multitudes were similarly disenfranchised, except that in traditional African matters customary law continued to be observed.

However imperfect my knowledge may have been when viewed from the technical standpoint, the big picture was depressingly clear. South Africa was a country of comprehensive racial persecution and unfairness based solely on race. The elaborate differentiation between Africans, Coloureds, and Asians were buttressed by both law and social custom. Africans were very poor, often without basic education and health care, especially in the rural areas, but on top of this they were treated, very often without ill will, as people without status or rights apart from those bestowed by customary law and society. It was this constant, omnipresent weight of nonrecognition and essential injustice that weighed one down. Yet the country of South Africa was beautiful beyond imagining, as it remains today, governed by its African majority.

Somehow, despite the sheer magnitude of the diverse and utterly new experiences I was having in South Africa in 1960, I managed to maintain my equilibrium and to enjoy South Africa. The course-work was deeply stimulating and my classmates were friendly. I played rugby, even in Newlands stadium against the very rough boys from Stellenbosch University. I ran the half mile on a grass track at Rondebosch. The Rotary visits continued to be enjoyable and educational as I moved out into the country. However, when it came time to leave, I was ready to go.

One reason that leaving was easy is that I had laid a plan for returning home by traveling the length of Africa via the East Coast. I had written ahead to Rotary clubs in Tanganyika, Zanzibar, Mombassa, and Nairobi. Astrida and I left Cape Town early one morning in the first days of December on South African Airways to Durban. From Durban we had booked space on an East African Airways DC3 aircraft that worked its way up the east coast of Africa. The captain and first officer were father and son, both from Australia and both, as we learned, black belt karate experts. The flight attendant was a blond Dutch-speaking woman from Indonesia. The handful of passengers included a Kenyan farmer who had taken another mans' wife fishing in South Africa. There was also a heavy-set Polish general in a rumpled white linen double-breasted suit who carried an ancient, overstuffed soft leather bag as his briefcase, which he seemed to guard carefully during the whole trip.

The trip consisted of flying most of the rest of the day straddling the coastline of the Indian Ocean at a height of about three thousand feet. The ticket included an overnight stop at a small town in Northern Mozambique, with hotel room and dinner included in the fare. We landed on a dirt airstrip in late afternoon and taxied to a terminal no bigger than a small shed. The earth was red and the vegetation brilliant green. The drive into the town was beautiful. We drove down a red dirt boulevard with freshly painted white curbs and a median filled with bright orange flame trees in full bloom whose trunks were also painted white.

The hotel was on the sea, in effect a large, modest house with a broad front veranda facing the sea. Behind the hotel was a small station for a narrow-gauge railroad, and two hundred yards north of the hotel, a long jetty stuck far out into the sea—which reminded me of the painting on the cover of my copy of Joseph Conrad's *Victory*. In fact, the whole place and its atmosphere reminded me of the setting Conrad depicted in his novel.

After a simple but wonderful dinner of fresh giant lobsters at a large round table that seated the captain, crew, and passengers of our flight, I wandered over to the railway station. A wood-burning locomotive stood panting in the dark, fire visible through cracks in the side of its firebox. It was primarily, though not exclusively, a freight train, and it was being unloaded by scores of porters in little more than loincloths, who carried boxes and machine parts on their heads under the supervision of Portuguese soldiers with rifles and machine guns. Women, children, and a variety of dogs sat around in the dust in the oppressive heat and, the scene was lit by the engine and a few oil lanterns. Here, I thought, was the real Africa, Conrad's heart of darkness. We could be in a novel with the plot set among the passengers and crew of an unusual flight, thrown together by chance, making their way up the coast of Portuguese Africa and Tanganyika.

The next day we returned to the small shed at the airstrip, had ourselves and our luggage weighed, and, after flying most of the day, arrived in Dar es Salaam, still only halfway up Africa's Indian Ocean coast. We stayed with an Indian Rotarian (those were the days when the East Africa Indian community was still an accepted part of local society). The house was a complex of rooms with latticework and sheer white curtains billowing inward by the steady wind from the sea. The man's wife was hardly visible, but he was friendly and enthusiastic to show us Dar es Salaam.

A few days later we went to Zanzibar, an exotic island where the Arab world clearly met Africa. Zanzibar was lovely, its palm groves saturated with the scent of cloves, which settled more heavily in the warm evening. We stayed with a British colonial officer who had been born in Uganda and had been away from East Africa long enough only to be educated at public school and Oxford. Each night we dined with him in his garden, served by tall black men in white gowns and white turbans. It was my first view of mosques, carved doors, graceful minarets, and sleepy dhows drifting in the harbors waiting for the seasonal winds that would take them back to Arabia.

Mombassa and Nairobi were distinctly different from other places we had seen in Africa. The blight of Mau Mau, the violence that overtook rural Kenya in the late 1950s, was still noticeably present.

Three years later, in December 1963, Jomo Kenyatta, Kenya's African leader, released months earlier from prison, would formally accept the Act of Independence from Prince Phillip. I was present at that event, as I was back in Kenya preparing the index for my soon-to-be-published book on the 1962 Northern Rhodesia General Election that brought Kenneth Kaunda to power in the transition from white minority to black majority rule.

From Nairobi it was on to Cairo, where four years after Jamal Nasser's rise to power the streets of Cairo seemed deserted, with soldiers at main intersections warming themselves around open fires built with what looked like broken pieces of furniture. Astrida and I saw the pyramids and became desperately ill from Egyptian food. It seemed a blessing to visit Rotarians in Athens a few days later and then to return to the States to see our families after a year and a half away.

4

Boston, Oxford, Northern Rhodesia

Despite there being a great deal to digest and to reflect upon from my year and a half at Oxford University and Cape Town, my future direction was remarkably clear to me at the end of 1960.

I had dropped the idea of going to law school and instead would pursue a master's degree in political science with a specialization in Africa. When I finished in a year's time at Boston University, I would try to return to Oxford to seek my doctorate. Astrida was pregnant with our first son, Ian, who was due in June. It was, as they say, all work and little play for the whole of the next twelve months.

On the question of where to direct my studies on Africa I had decided that South Africa had no chance of moving to black majority government anytime in the foreseeable future, which I put at twenty-five years. On the other hand I was preoccupied with the process by which white-settled countries in Africa would move toward a transition to African government and independence. The independence movement was well on its way in both British and French West Africa. Transition toward black rule had advanced in East Africa, but Central Africa seemed to me the place where the chances were best for a transition from white minority rule to black majority government without producing a mass exodus of the settled white population. This seemed especially to be the prospect in what was then Northern Rhodesia, the northernmost state in the Federation of Rhodesia and Nyasaland.

However, the developing political situation in Northern Rhodesia and within the broader Federation of Rhodesia and Nyasaland was increasingly threatening in 1960 and 1961 as rising African nationalist political parties agitated for independence and the breakup of the federation. Serious violence was on the increase, some of it directed at the settled white population in the towns, on the farms, and in the rich copper belt in the north.

Northern Rhodesia was differentiated from Southern Rhodesia by the fact that it was by law a protectorate under the British government. This meant that despite being a state within the federation, Britain retained the authority to impose the constitution that would govern Northern Rhodesia, but this was not the case for Southern Rhodesia, Britain's self-governing colony in the south. The ability and willingness of Britain to exercise its constitution-making authority in the north and its inability to exercise its weakened authority over the south led ultimately to the breakup of the federation and Southern Rhodesia's unilateral declaration of independence. This highly unusual state of affairs, which began to unfold in 1961, intrigued me and seemed to offer an ideal laboratory for the study of constitutional engineering for a political transition in Northern Rhodesia from white minority rule to black majority government and independence, hopefully without driving out the territory's settled white population.

In June 1961, British Secretary of State for the Colonies Sir Ian McLeod announced new constitutional proposals for Northern Rhodesia. I studied these proposals, which some members of parliament referred to as a "dogs breakfast," and which among the white population in the Federation of Rhodesia and Nyasaland were seen as nothing short of subversive, with the intent of destroying the Federation, Britain's own creation of an earlier time. To me McLeod's proposals seemed to offer the possibility of a peaceful transition to multiracial government on a democratic format in the north, which was simply out of the question in Southern Rhodesia.

McLeod's complex plan, perhaps rightly derided by opponents as too complex and "too clever by half," would force political parties to appeal to both blacks and whites and to obtain at least a minimum degree of support from both main racial groups. As I studied the plan and its later revisions I thought it was a stroke of genius on a continent where other efforts to promote a transition to multiracial governance had failed.

As a result I wrote my master's degree paper in my last semester at Boston University on the McLeod Constitutional Plan for Northern Rhodesia. Since that semester would conclude at the end of January 1962, and since I had been accepted to return to Oxford University at the conclusion of my master's degree program at Boston, I was in a tearing hurry to return to Oxford, where as a doctoral candidate I could focus my energy on Northern Rhodesia and its new constitution.

Once again, the problem was the discontinuity of academic years and the normal timetable for academic scholarships. The previous spring I had applied for and won a Woodrow Wilson International Fellowship for the academic year September 1961 through June 1962. I wanted to begin at Oxford in Trinity term (spring) 1962, so once again, as I had done with Rotary International in 1959, I approached the Woodrow Wilson Foundation in Princeton to ask whether the balance of my fellowship could be used at Oxford. I was asked to file a written request, which I did, laying out the substance of my study topic and spelling out the need to get to England in time to follow the McLeod Constitution implementation in the form of new electoral laws and a general election in Northern Rhodesia sometime in late 1962. To my delight, and to the credit of the Woodrow Wilson Foundation, they agreed to allow me to use the remaining half of my fellowship to begin at Oxford in April 1962.

Before leaving Boston, I had one other exposure that profoundly influenced my outlook for the future. This was my other master's degree specialization, comparative government, a course requirement together with political philosophy for my master's degree. In the course work I was exposed to the comparative history and functioning of the major forms of government in Europe. They were, chiefly, in the UK, France, Germany, and the Soviet Union. The modern history of these countries, and especially the focus on their respective constitutions and governance, were fascinating to me and have remained useful over my entire career.

A very special dimension of the experience was a course I cross-registered into at Harvard, called "The Theory of International Relations." This was taught by Dr. Henry Kissinger, the most brilliant lecturer I heard in my academic career. He brought this field to life in both historical and contemporary terms, and he linked it with his new and highly influential book on nuclear deterrence, *The Necessity of Choice*. Many years later I was to meet Henry Kissinger and establish a friendship with him that has been one of the great pleasures of my adult life. Henry is an original mind in every sense, as evidenced by the fact that one cannot listen to him without learning of a new dimension or a new perspective on the complex issues of relations between nations.

Meanwhile, Mr. McLeod's final constitutional proposals were announced in March 1962 and set out new electoral arrangements for Northern Rhodesia's presently all-white legislative council, which previously was elected by a small, virtually all-white electorate in a territory whose population was made up of approximately seventy thousand whites and four million unenfranchised Africans, many of whom were illiterate or semiliterate. According to McLeod's proposals, there would be an upper roll of voters and a lower roll of voters. All voters, regardless of the roll on which they were registered, had to possess four general qualifications: literacy in English, aged at least twenty-one years, two years' continuous residence in the Federation of Rhodesia and Nyasaland, and citizenship in the Federation or the United Kingdom. Persons who satisfied these requirements were qualified under one of the two sets of additional qualifications for either the upper or lower roll. Voters in the upper roll would have qualifications governed by income, education, and property and would be mainly but not entirely composed of whites. Voters in the lower roll included all other voters who met the four basic requirements or some additional considerations related to position in the community (chiefs, elders, and ex-servicemen). The lower roll would be mainly but not exclusively composed of Africans.

The country was divided into three sets of fifteen constituencies: upper roll, lower roll, and national. Each set of constituencies covered the entire country, and every voter had two votes to cast in the election: one for his respective upper or lower roll candidate, and one for a national candidate in his respective national constituency.

The objective of the constitution's complex electoral system was to permit the two main racial groups to elect candidates of their own race and party in the upper and lower constituencies respectively but also to require a multiracial approach in the crucial national constituencies. To be successful in a national constituency a candidate would have to attract a minimum of support from each voter roll, or, in effect, under the complex rules regarding the calculation of votes cast, from 10 percent of the voters of each race. For more details on this complex electoral system, see my book *Zambia: The Politics of Independence, 1957–1964* (Oxford University Press, 1967.)

In early March Astrida and I crossed the north Atlantic on the ss *France*, making its second west-to-east voyage. We were three at this point. Ian had been born the previous June in Boston, and here he was, now nine months old and crossing a stormy North Atlantic.

That spring England saw a series of westerly gales coming one after the other through March and most of April. We settled in a stone cottage in Woodstock called Chaucer's Cottage, joined to the larger Chaucer's House that stood just outside the village gate to Blenheim Palace. Like all other accommodations at that time in England, Chaucer's Cottage, though charming, was cold inside year-round.

This time at Oxford I was matriculated initially as a bachelor of letters student and assigned Mr. George Bennett of New College and Queen Elizabeth House, a British Commonwealth historian, as my tutor. My supervisor was to be Professor Max Beloff of All Souls College, a man of prodigious reputation I was to see approximately semiannually and on the occasion of my final oral examination a few years later.

The most significant development of that first term was my decision to attend a seminar course being given by Professor Margery Perham at Nuffield College, another graduate research college at Oxford like my home college of St Antony's. This decision was based solely on my experience at Cape Town, where the study of

British colonial indirect rule in Africa had introduced me to the famous Lord Lugard of West Africa and his trusted assistant, Margery Perham. Professor Perham was now considerably older, and Lord Lugard had long since died, but they had been the early theorists and practitioners of indirect rule in Africa. Indirect rule was the British system of leaving vast tracts of Africa free to govern themselves under native institutions and customs under the overall authority of a small number of British colonial officers assigned to oversee hundreds of thousands of square miles of African territory. Those officers, mostly educated at Oxford and Cambridge in history, politics, economics, and the classics, were robust men for all seasons. They toured their areas of responsibilities and exercised their influence through traditional authorities, backed by a minute military force in the form of police authority. They sought to encourage local administration and courts. They worked with Christian missions and local medical facilities to improve education, agriculture, and health standards. Oxford at this time was in the last years of generating these unique and highly educated adventurers, but clearly their days as rulers of the British bush were numbered.

Margery Perham took an immediate interest in my project, and toward the end of term delivered the exciting news that the British government's Department of Technical Cooperation, under the Colonial Office, soon to be renamed the Commonwealth Relations Office, was planning a grant for that summer and autumn to study the implementation of the McLeod Constitution and the general election to be held later that year in Northern Rhodesia under the new constitution's electoral arrangements.

As the Northern Rhodesia legislative council elections would be modeled on British parliamentary elections, I immediately bought and read the studies produced on British general elections by Butler and Rose. I sought to become virtually overnight a psephologist (student of elections), a particularly British term that has never found its way into the lexicon of American academia.

In the days of advancing spring, Professor Perham contacted the Colonial Office and arranged for me to be interviewed. She felt I was the ideal candidate because I had studied in South Africa and had been working for nearly a year on the unfolding of the McLeod Constitution. I went to London the following week—early June—to visit the Colonial Office, which was located in a small street running behind Westminster Abbey. It had turned into a warm spring day, and I was in a heavy wool suit. I was shown into a large office and introduced to a man who to me seemed the very sort one would expect to find in the Colonial Office. I noticed his bowler hat and umbrella, tightly rolled, hanging on the coat peg next to his desk. He asked me some questions, which I answered with strength and clarity. Northern Rhodesia was by now a topic on which I had considerable knowledge but also on which it was fair to say there were few people competing for recognition.

Yet the man seemed preoccupied, even a little uncomfortable, as I went on. I couldn't think what the problem was. Perhaps I was making exactly the wrong impression with my confident espousal of the progress I had so far achieved on my project. By this time I was perspiring, regretting my decision to wear a wool suit that chilly early morning in Oxford.

Suddenly he cleared his throat and shifted sharply in his seat. "Please excuse me," he said. "I have been preoccupied with a problem ever since you entered the office."

"Oh," I thought and perhaps even said.

"Yes, you see when Margery Perham called us she gave no indication that you are an American."

There was a pause.

"You see, the department is spending British taxpayers funds on the project, and you are not a citizen of the UK."

My hopes were receding fast.

"I've been thinking what to do. You obviously know the subject thoroughly. The election will be set for early November, just after the dry season in Central Africa. Preparations must begin at once, and campaigning will no doubt be underway by September. There is not a moment to be lost."

I waited for his thought process to continue, hardly knowing what to say. Was this positive, or was it negative?

"How long are you in London?" he asked.

"Just today" I responded, "but . . . I can stay over if need be." Hanging on now to the slightest hope.

"Do you know the London School of Oriental and African Studies?"

"I know of it," I said, which was just barely true.

"There is an eminent constitutional law professor there, Professor Kenneth Robinson. I am thinking of contacting him to discuss this matter."

I nodded, waiting.

"Why don't you go across the street where there is a canteen in the basement and come back at two-thirty this afternoon."

And so I went across to a cavernous subterranean room that seemed to go back under Dean's Yard and chose between toad in the hole (sausages in pudding) and bubble and squeak (a fry-up of cooked potatoes and vegetables). At two-thirty I was back across the street. The Colonial Office official seemed brighter. He said I was to see Professor Robinson at four-thirty and run through my project with him, and if Professor Robinson approved, they would send me shortly to Northern Rhodesia to begin work on the ground.

I left at once for the School of Oriental and African Studies in the Bloomsbury district of London, where at four-thirty I met with the eminent and dignified Professor Robinson in his spacious first-floor office. We covered the ground, and after an hour and a half he said he would recommend that the Colonial Office send me to Central Africa.

By early July 1962 I was on my way to Northern Rhodesia. I had all the necessary inoculations and had bought appropriate bush clothes at the shop in Cambridge Circus that had supplied generations of aspiring district commissioners. I boarded a BOAC Comet 4 airliner for Rome, Benghazi, and Nairobi, with a change to an old Dakota (Douglas) DC3 from Nairobi to Ndola and Lusaka.

This was real adventure! The captain circled the DC3 two times around Mount Kilimanjaro so we could see into the crater, which seemed only a few feet beneath us. Then we bumped our way through the updrafts from the heat below until we landed finally at Lusaka, the capital of Northern Rhodesia. That night I stayed in a one-story hotel with covered walkways around a courtyard to the rooms. I could smell the coal fire heating the water for travelers and the wax that Africans applied to the smooth red cement floor with brushes strapped to their bare feet. That night was my first night under mosquito netting with a slow fan moving the air in the dark. Too excited to fall asleep, all I could think of was that I was in the interior of Africa at last, ready for whatever was to come.

Northern Rhodesia (present-day Zambia) was a large country (about 290,000 square miles, slighty larger than Texas, at about 268,000 square miles) that was shaped rather like a large somewhat lopsided butterfly. On a map, the body of the butterfly would be akin to the "line of rail" and the country's one partly hard-surface road that ran virtually north and south the length of the body of the butterfly. The wings spread to either side were vast, thinly populated areas whose dirt roads and tracks all ran back to the central body. This meant that traveling from the far east or west of Northern Rhodesia to areas in the northwest, northeast, southwest, or southeast was impossible without returning hundreds of miles to the central column of rail and road that stretched from Victoria Falls in the south to the copper belt near the Belgian Congo in the north. Even then, to get farther north to Bemba Land required crossing the so-called "pedicle" of Katanga, part of the Belgian Congo, which created a fifty-mile-wide finger puncturing deep into northeastern Northern Rhodesia. At the time of the 1962 election, Katanga, led by Maurice (Moise) Tshombe, had seceded from the Republic of Congo, which led to civil war and made the "pedicle" dangerous to cross.

I met with Mr. North, the very able Chief Secretary of Northern Rhodesia, to be briefed on the plans and progress of the election. The electoral commission was delineating the new constituencies, framing up the two electoral rolls, and designing the ballots to be used in this first-ever attempt to create near-universal suffrage for an election in Northern Rhodesia. There was a massive learning challenge for me, and I realized that most of it would have to be self-taught.

In addition, there were the political parties and candidates to master, the latter, apart from the principal leaders, still to emerge. Although the election itself was still months away, interest in the election and prospects for the various political groupings was running very high. The two leading African political party leaders were Kenneth Kaunda and Harry Nkumbula. Both were fiery advocates of majority government and independence for Northern Rhodesia from both the Federation of Rhodesia and Nyasaland and from the British government. They were seasoned nationalist politicians who had been imprisoned at one or another point by the British government which administered law and order in the territory, assisted by the elected membership and leader of the Legislative Council.

Kenneth Kaunda was a resolute Christian from the north who had formed the United National Independence Party (UNIP) and forged it into a large-scale messianic political party, bound to achieve independence at virtually any price. Harry Nkumbula, from the south, was significantly older than Kaunda and was the leader of the African Nationalist Party (ANC), the oldest African political party in Northern Rhodesia. Nkumbula was the more sedate leader, although his personal conduct regarding ladies and drink left much to be desired as seen from outside his home area in the south. He was often referred to as "Slow Coach" in the more passionate circles of African Nationalism and was not trusted to be as sufficiently hostile to and divorced from the representatives of the British government. One could say that the ANC and Harry Nkumbula were a good deal more mellow than UNIP and its leader, Kenneth Kaunda.

I based myself some six or seven miles out of Lusaka at the Rhodes-Livingston Institute, a very modest research center not far from Chisamba Mission where David Livingstone had reportedly died, and more important, perhaps, where his loyal servants had cut out his heart and buried it at Chisamba Mission. From there those same servants carried his body to the east coast of Africa and then accompanied it by sea to England, where the great but diminutive hero was laid to rest in Westminster Abbey.

At the institute, where living conditions were very basic, I delved into the archives of local newspapers to better understand the politicians and passions leading up to the McLeod Constitution and the impending general election. The African nationalist demonstrations and protests and the self-serving defenses of the white political class were suddenly left behind. Everyone was focused on the new challenge for political power, and how to organize and campaign to achieve a measure of cross-racial support, or at the very least not to alienate members of the other race, whose votes would be needed to achieve power by winning the majority of the fifteen national seats. Complicating the challenge was the fact that there were two African political parties, one of whom, the ANC, was seen as less extremist than UNIP.

Soon I realized that I would need to get out into the country to see the electoral preparations in progress and meet and evaluate the candidates. I had bought a rather heavily used Land Rover, whose front vents and side windows were the only source of air movement in the increasing heat of the dry season. Dust came in from everywhere, covering everything with a fine grit. I drove north to Kitwe and Ndola on the copper belt to begin my interviews and later to attend political party rallies and election meetings. At about this time, Astrida came from Oxford with Ian, now over a year old. We lived in a unit at the Rhodes Livingstone Institute and hired "Jacques the Cook," an aged African man who doubled as the snake killer in the African compound behind the institute.

In Lusaka I had met a number of British government officials and many of the leading politicians. At first I met mainly whites, but as word spread of my purpose in being in Northern Rhodesia I began to meet African politicians. Eventually I met Kenneth Kaunda in his two-room house in one of Lusaka's black townships. These were makeshift communities with dirt streets, little in the way of plumbing, and overrun by children and stray dogs. The houses (and usually the people) smelled of wood smoke and of the earth. At night, most neighborhoods were lit only by the odd electric light and by firelight from lanterns or cooking fires.

Between my research in the newspaper section of the institute's library and my visits with officials and political leaders I soon commanded an in-depth knowledge of the political scene. The next step was to meet people more widely throughout the country, ordinary citizens, political operators, and local officials outside the capital city. This was the purpose of my trips up to the towns on the copper belt and a long drive to the small towns along the "line of rail" to Livingstone on the border with Southern Rhodesia. This driving was mainly on dusty dirt or gravel roads, which spread a thick red dust over everything inside the Land Rover.

Guest houses and hotels followed the same routine for travelers. When you arrived in late afternoon (one never drove after dark), there was a strong smell of wood or coal smoke from the fires built in late afternoon to heat water for bathing. Dinner was a simple affair; most travelers seemed to have a Scotch or brandy and water out on the always-present veranda, with ceiling fans stirring the air and smell of the African evening in the high plateau country. Everyone made an early start in the morning after a cold wash up or shower and a hearty breakfast of bacon and eggs. The reward on the southern border was the gentle, old-fashioned tin roofed town of Livingston and the mighty Victoria Falls, which spreads itself grandly across the Zambezi River.

The village of Victoria Falls on the Southern Rhodesia side of the river offered the most spectacular distant views of the falls and the National Railway bridge that spanned the exit gorge just below them. A cloud of mist rose above the falls, and one could easily imagine David Livingstone walking toward his great discovery and seeing what first appeared as smoke in the distance as he approached.

Up close the falls were frightening and beautiful. There were no guardrails along the numerous paths that meandered through the exotic rain forests or along the wet and misty rim. Wherever one looked there were dramatic sights, whether at the massive volumes of water, the thick green vegetation, the rocks, the brilliant tropical flowers and grasses, or the dry-colored bush beyond the banks of the river. What struck me the most, however, was the vast span of whitewater that plunged smoothly over the rim and seemed to draw you down with it as you stared at the wall of water plunging directly at you a few feet away across a narrow gap, down some 350 feet into the narrow cauldron below. A narrow suspension walkway could be taken to a heavily foliaged island on the top of a column of rock in the middle of the falls. As one edged out across its slippery surface, gripping tightly to the cable handrails, the speed and violence of the falling water and the soaking mist in the air all caused a frightening sense of disorientation. It seemed that the island should have been swept away thousands of years ago.

My trip plan changed when I was offered a ride in an airplane up the Zambezi River to a small administrative outpost at Sesheke. Sesheke was some 150 miles upriver, about halfway to Barotseland in the far west of Northern Rhodesia. I had met the British district officer at Sesheke, Philip Bowcock, at Oxford some months before his posting. He was married with two small children and had served previously in the southern part of Anglo-Egyptian Sudan and loved his work. It was arranged that I should stay at the his residence.

The airplane was a single engine Beaver that flew upriver every week or so, with mail, fresh vegetables, and meat for the posts along the river, eventually to Mongu, the British administrative center for Barotseland. The pilot was a typical bush pilot, friendly and adventurous. When we took off early in the morning from the Livingstone airstrip his first maneuver was to circle three times very low over Victoria Falls so I could "get a good look at it." He shouted back to me (it was a two-seater) that because it was late in the dry season with only a month until the rains, the river and falls were at low volume. I tried to imagine the roar of the falls close up in the flood season.

We flew steadily up the great brown river, seeing hippos from time to time and other animals watering along its shores. At Sesheke airstrip the pilot made a sudden steep decline, which he explained was necessary for him to examine the condition of the dirt runway and to scare off any lions or other animals that might interfere with our landing. We flew the length of the runway at a height of what seemed to be about thirty feet while he leaned out his windows to check for ruts or potholes. We flew one direction, then zoomed up sharply and around to fly down the strip in the opposite direction. He was obviously enjoying himself, but I felt a little queasy. I was glad to be on the ground with the mail, the meat, and the vegetables. In a few minutes he had unloaded, wished me well, and taken off for the next outpost. I was taken by Land Rover to the district commissioner's house.

I spent two days and two nights at Sesheke, and the memory I have of the post remains clear to this day, nearly fifty years on. The house was a low, one-floor cement structure, cream in color and framed by a long roof-covered veranda. There was a red dirt circular drive in front of the house and a backyard of grass that ran some fifty yards back to the top of a high bank overlooking the river. The grass stopped at a low fence at the top of the hill, where the land dropped sharply through small trees to the river. I was advised that no one, and especially not the children, was to go down the hill to the river because of the large population of crocodiles living along the shore.

There was no electricity at the post for any extensive lighting. If there were a small generator for low-demand essential services I never heard it running. The district commissioner's office was a short distance away at the end of a drive lined with white-painted stones. Before the office, a flagpole flew the Union Jack in a small circular bed of bushes surrounded by white-painted stones.

We had dinner together that night and talked about how the district was run, what was happening among Africans in the vast bush area surrounding Sesheke, what state the electoral preparation process was in, and how in Phillip's opinion the election would go in his area. Sesheke district would, he thought, largely support the ANC and Harry Nkumula. There were few, if any, white voters in the district beyond those employed by the government. As soon as it began to get dark the gas lanterns in the hall and on the tables in the dining room and living room were lit. After dinner, when we had finished our talk, we sat around for a time reading to the soft hiss of the lanterns, which from time to time grew dim and had to be pumped up by hand.

Just after dawn the next morning Phillip and I were outside for the raising of the flag and his inspection of the African police. These men were lined up at attention in a semicircle around the flagpole, dressed as smartly and as crisp in movement as any military group I have ever seen. Every man was dressed in light tan shorts that ended just above the knees. These were starched and pressed with the sharpest of creases. Each man wore a light gray flannel-looking shirt with a brown leather belt up over one shoulder and through one of the shoulder straps next to the collar. Dark blue, thick wool socks reached just below the knee, neatly folded over with a small ribbon showing from the fold and shiny black hobnailed boots. On their heads were white pith helmets, which contrasted strikingly with their dark faces.

Phillip Bowcock commanded the police, administered the entire district of hundreds of square miles, and was the chief justice of the district, hearing and settling all manner of cases in Sesheke and on tour around the district. He was the manager and symbol of British authority in that large section of Northern Rhodesia, along the Zambezi and far inland into the bush. He himself was dressed in tan, well-pressed shorts and shirt, a helmet, and he carried a leather swagger stick in his hand or under his arm. He ran Sesheke district alone with one other white British officer.

I have remembered this visit as my view of the last of British indirect rule in Africa. It would be many months before power would pass in Northern Rhodesia, but in Sesheke I witnessed a system and a person who embodied the best aspects of the modest British presence in rural Africa. Phillip Bowcock was an energetic, well-educated Englishman, an outdoorsman, a man of broad experience in all the elements of life in an African community, and more important, a man of steady, quiet commitment to his work and way of life. He knew about Africa, its people, and their tribal affairs and practices and customs. He kept order, dispensed justice, coordinated activities with mission schools, and worked every single day. I admired the man and the decent, well-intentioned system and culture he represented.

On the second day Phillip advised me that two men were expected to come through in a Land Rover traveling on to Mongu. He arranged for me to join them the next day for the drive to Barotseland over the many miles of dirt tracks along the river.

We set off early in the morning on the longest continuously rough ride I have ever endured. I was seated in the middle of the front and only "soft" seat in an aging Land Rover, with nothing to hold on to except from time to time the tall floor-based gear shift that stuck up between my legs. The road was little more than an uneven and exceedingly rough track. Its roughness was enhanced for long distances by a washboarding of the road accomplished by Africans cutting the tall dry grasses and laying them in bundles across the road. The grass bundles were then covered with the soft sand running along beside the road, which if entered by a Land Rover, would have been exceedingly difficult to exit without becoming stuck.

On a number of occasions we had to cross and recross the great river. This involved running the Land Rover up two sturdy boards onto a wooden raft only slightly larger than the vehicle. The raft was hooked to a steel cable strung across the river to prevent it from being swept downstream. A second cable was hooked to the prow of the raft to pull it across the river by means of a small gasoline-powered motor on the far shore. Placed in a prominent position on the approach to the landing was a roughly made sign board that read "Beware crocodiles and hippos." While crossing, we three occupants of the Land Rover stood on the narrow space along the side of the vehicle, enjoying a good stretch and keeping our eyes carefully focused on the moving river water a few inches below us. Every crossing was the same, and all were accomplished with a great deal of shouting back and forth across the river.

As we moved west the surrounding vegetation changed from trees and bushes on fairly high ground above the river to mainly grasses eight to ten fee tall, with gnarled trees on small mounds occasionally protruding above the grass. This was clearly the fringe of the great Zambezi floodplain, which, beginning each November with the rains, formed a vast lake. The rough track we were negotiating would clearly be well under water in a few weeks.

This floodplain was called Barotseland after the large but isolated Barotse tribe, whose cycle of life and form of government were directly and profoundly influenced by their physical surroundings. In the post-flood period each year and the ensuing dry season, the Barotse people lived in small villages on the hundreds of mounds that rose up from the floor of the plain. From these mounds they would descend to the floor of the plain to farm the rich bottom-land soil until harvest time just before the rains set in. As the water levels rose across the floodplain, reducing the size of the mounds and covering many of them altogether, the Barotse people made an annual migration to the higher ground around the capital of Mongu. The annual move was carried out in large barges pad-dled by dozens of men, and their occupants reflected Barotseland's elaborate system of governance. The king and royal family would travel in the royal barge; members of their equivalent of a parlia-ment would be paddled in another; a third would be reserved for high court judges; and many others were used to move the multi-tude of commoners.

This spectacle was still many weeks away, but the approaching general election provided plenty of interest in the meantime. After two days of meeting local politicians and officials I was offered a ride on an incoming government aircraft from Lusaka that was trans-porting election ballots to various far-flung administrative centers. The aircraft was a small two-engine plane with four seats. I was the only passenger the following morning when we took off for Mwinilungu in the farthest northwest corner of Northern Rhode-sia. Mwinilungu was surrounded by the beginning of the tall rain forest that stretched northward into the nearby Congo. We spent the day around the post and then set off for Lusaka on what proved to be a very entertaining ride. The young solo pilot flying at about three thousand feet would spot gatherings or herds of wild game, which he would circle and drop down near the ground to survey. This sent the animals, mostly zebras, deer, water buffaloes and ante-lopes, charging off in all directions. I was grateful for the quick ride back to the line of rail, despite the numerous plunging detours.

By now the campaign had begun. I made two other extensive trips in my Land Rover, one to the far eastern border with Nyas-aland and the other up into the Northern Province referred to as Bemba Land and the home base for Dr. Kaunda's United National Independence Party. In each case my objectives were to observe local campaigning, meet candidates and officials, and in particular to see how the multitudes of newly enfranchised voters were being instructed on how to mark the two types of ballots that would be provided at polling stations to each voter.

The visit to the Northern Province was especially informative and exciting. The drive north from the copper belt involved crossing an approximately forty-mile stretch of road through Katanga, a province of the newly independent Republic of the Congo. Katanga was in revolt against the new central government and in effect in a state of violent civil war. Guerilla groups reportedly roamed Katanga and had harassed travelers moving across the "pedicle" territory.

The procedure for the crossing was to present one's documents at the border post between Northern Rhodesia and Katanga. A pink copy of the form, which was required to be completed by each driver of a vehicle crossing the pedicle, was to be submitted at the border post on the other side. As I climbed into my vehicle to begin the drive north my assistant and Bemba translator from the Rhodes-Livingstone Institute asked if I could give a ride to a Bemba man whose mother he said had died. Since I knew little about my assistant and nothing of the man asking for the ride, I was in a difficult spot. Was this man a guerilla? Was he going to his mother's funeral, or was his plan to rob or perhaps kill me? Did my assistant know this man, were they in league? If I declined assistance, what would my assistant who I needed in the coming days think of me? Would he think me unfeeling or unreasonably cautious regarding Africans?

In less than a minute I decided I could not say no to the man without losing the confidence, sympathy, and respect of my African assistant. I would need his support, cooperation, and accurate translation services in the coming days in a strange area with rural tribal people who in a few weeks would vote in a historic and transformative election.

The man climbed into the back of the Land Rover and to my further discomfort seated himself on the bench on the driver's side immediately behind me. I could see him only partially in my rearview mirror as I drove north through the dusty bush of Katanga. An hour later we crossed the northern border, and after a further hour we arrived in the provincial center, Fort Roseberry.

My quick decision to give a lift across Katanga to a man I did not know seemed to be rewarded the next day. My Bemba assistant went all-out to help me meet local campaigners, including an expedition to meet villagers and village organizers deep in the bush. We left Fort Roseberry the next morning and drove on a track through a highly varied landscape. I wondered whether this was the country in which it was said that Kenneth Kaunda had come face-to-face with a lion and escaped. We crossed open country, bush, and a well-forested area, arriving around noon in a larger village of huts with one cement house and a school. I was offered tea and a snack by the owner of the cement house before being taken to a sizeable structure built of wooden poles and thatch.

Waiting for me there was a large group of organizers seated in rows on the ground with a blackboard on a tripod facing the groups. There were few windows in the structure, so it had little air movement in the heat and very limited light. A single straight-backed chair had been set for me on the uneven dirt floor. The atmosphere in the room was heavy with the smell of sweat and woodsmoke, which was ever-present in rural and township Africa.

My assistant and the organizer from Fort Roseberry, who spoke English, gave me an elaborate introduction, which was decidedly different from the outline I had provided to them. My version had emphasized that I was an academic studying the general election, that I was a politically neutral observer, and that I had come to visit them to hear their views and comments about the election process and their own approach to campaigning. Instead, it was explained that I had come from the great distance of England, across the sea and across the vast territory of Africa, that I was a very famous professor at Oxford University, and that I was there specifically to help them (UNIP) win the election.

This was of course a violation of the guidelines which under my grant governed my visit to Northern Rhodesia. I felt, however, that under the circumstances it would be harmful not to let the introduction stand, so I proceeded to conduct an instruction class for most of the rest of the afternoon. This covered an explanation of the new constitution, the electoral arrangements for all the voters of Northern Rhodesia, how the voting would take place, how winners would be determined, why each voter had two votes to cast, and how the newly issued ballot samples (specifically designed for semiliterate voters) were to be marked to avoid being spoiled. With translation, this took a great deal of time, but I remember vividly today the rapt attention and wide-eyed interest I commanded among the seated group that day in the fading afternoon light. In fact, from this experience, and others like it, including the big African political rallies I attended, I carried away with me an understanding of how precious, how steeped in optimism, and how powerful is the act of voting in the minds of people who aspire to freedom. In aging and settled democracies this realization is harder to distill, but there in Bemba Land, in the remoteness of the Northern Province, it was written on every face. That night I made the drive on the dirt track through the bush back to Fort Roseberry by the light of a full moon.

The trip back to the copper belt provided my most frightening experience in Africa. At the border on the north side of the pedicle a line of large trucks waited on the dusty road in front of the white gate that marked the border of Katanga. To one side was a small cement shed that served as the border post. It had a single window outside before which stood half a dozen of the drivers of the large tractor trailer trucks parked across the road. It was midday, very hot, and I was alone this time, as my assistant had decided to stay in Fort Roseberry to visit family.

The truck drivers, all Africans, motioned me to the front of the line. On the other side of the open window was a desk or counter-top, behind which sat a disheveled looking African dressed in a white gown. On the counter top before him was the pad of forms to be completed in triplicate for the crossing and a black glistening sub-machine gun. He was drunk on "melee melee" beer, which I could smell from the several feet away as I stood with my passport in hand. I had not needed to show my passport on the crossing coming north, and I did not wish to show it for this crossing, because reports that the United States had supplied bombs used by the central government of the Congo to bomb Maurice Tshombe's breakaway province of Katanga had inflamed anti-American feelings in the area.

The border guard spoke some English and asked me to tell him my particulars so he could fill in the form himself. I noticed as I gave him my name and address that he was only semiliterate, despite the fact that he spoke some English. He completed the form, running all the letters and numbers together in an orderly printed fashion. Then he picked up the machine gun in his left hand and said in a loud voice:

"You are a South African pig!" He waved the machine gun around while he shouted, "We know all about what you do in South Africa."

"No," I responded, "I am from Rhodesia, not South Africa."

Then I was desperately frightened that he would demand to see my passport, discover that I was an American, and who knows what would have happened next. At that moment I remembered the tragic photo of a year earlier of a white man climbing out of a Volkswagen with his hands raised in desperation and the Volkswagen full of holes from bullets that had just killed his wife. That photo had been taken at one of the Congo border posts.

Then I noticed that the truck drivers had begun to laugh. Apparently this was good entertainment. I spoke again.

"Please finish the form so I can go. Here are three shillings," which I then placed on the desk. The machine gun had now come down to his side and was pointed at the floor.

I saw that the man was weeping.

"I'm sorry," he said. "You can see that my government gives me a job I cannot do."

"I'm sorry," I replied.

"It's two and six," he said.

"That's okay," I said, hoping he would hand me the pink slip of paper I needed. "Keep the sixpence."

"What!" he shouted. "Are you bribing me?" The gun came up again and swung about as he waved his arms.

"Wait for change," he said, and he pushed back from the counter and walked unsteadily through a door behind him into the bright sunlight of a rear yard. The floor there was dirt, and women and children sat on it, along with a dog. The laughing among the truck drivers behind me started up again. I turned and tried to laugh with them.

Soon the man came back with the sixpence, which he placed in my hand with the pink form. I thanked him, nodded to the truck drivers and walked across to my Land Rover. I don't know how close I came to disaster that day, but I was relieved to be back in my Land Rover, driving as fast as the dirt road would permit, happy that I had not had to show him my American passport.

Other tests came in the form of large African nationalist rallies that were held outside the mainly white towns. These were often attended by thousands of boisterous Africans, the big rallies usually being held on Saturdays and Sundays. It was late October, very hot, and the end of the dry season south of the equator, often referred to as the suicide month by whites. The rains would come in mid-November after the poll.

The rallies were all-day affairs, with people sitting in rows on the ground under the hot sun. The leaders would stand ten or twelve feet above the crowds on giant anthills that were spread through the bush. They spoke at length, usually in English, because the presence of six or seven regional or tribal languages in Northern Rhodesia made English the lingua franca of politics. No food was provided, and I was invariably the only white person present. People were friendly, asking who I was and what I was doing there. Water was brought around by women carrying white enameled pails with matching dippers. A woman would stand in her long gown at the end of a row of spectators, and the dipper full of water would be passed down the row, each person drinking until the dipper was empty. The lady would then fill the dipper again and it would be passed down the line by those who had drunk to those who were yet to have water. When the dipper came to me, all eyes were on me to see if I would drink out of the common cup. I was thirsty, but I also knew I had to drink. Not knowing where the water was from made this difficult and so did the multitude of mouths that had shared the cup. But I drank, and drank deeply. The water was warm but seemed delicious. When I handed the dipper back up the line there were lots of smiles, the kind of wide, unrestrained smiles one so often finds in rural Africa.

Northern Rhodesia's general election took place on October 30, 1962. Voter turnout exceeded 88 percent. Despite the cross-racial voting requirement and efforts made by political parties of both races, conclusive voting results were not achieved in all of the national constituencies. In this situation the law called for by-elections to be held in those constituencies in six weeks. On December 12, 1962, the national constituencies that had failed to produce definitive results in the general election were successfully decided, as party and racial differences were resolved. Thus, by the end of 1962, Northern Rhodesia had elected and formed a coalition government between the two African political parties in a legislative council composed of eighteen African members, seventeen Europeans, one Asian, and one Euro-African.

The two African political parties, UNIP and ANC, formed the new government, which included three European ministers. As to the McLeod Constitution, it had succeeded in bringing the races into active, peaceful contact, but voting results showed that the "nonracial" political approach explicitly encouraged by its design was not generally achieved. Election results in the national constituencies clearly indicated that while Europeans and Africans voted for each other's candidates, both had refused to support candidates who genuinely represented the opposite race. Political parties in Northern Rhodesia were firmly based on racial lines, and voters essentially saw parties as organizations representing one or other of the two races, irrespective of the race of the parties' respective candidates in the election. Yet the constitution had brought Northern Rhodesia's races into closer contact. They had shared a common political arena, and the territory's political parties had joined in an electoral contest that gave the stamp of legitimacy to Northern Rhodesia's crucial step from minority white to majority black government.

Kenneth Kaunda became leader of government business under the British Governor General, the Queen's representative in the protectorate of Northern Rhodesia. A peaceful transition from white minority government to African majority rule was accomplished without crisis or upheaval, and Northern Rhodesia went on to become the independent African state of Zambia and a member of the Commonwealth under President Kaunda in October 1964.

During this transition, there was no outbreak of mass violence and there was no exodus of the settled white population. All in all,

I felt I had participated in and witnessed a remarkable achievement of political and constitutional engineering.

After the election Astrida, Ian, and I headed home to Oxford, where I planned to write and publish my psephological study of the election in what I hoped would be record time. I had returned to England just in time for the bitterly cold winter of 1962–63. In Woodstock, where we lived, the town's water supply froze in the ground for six weeks, during which we had to fill pails from spigots on the back of a water truck that came through the village each day. The snow was deep and everything froze, including steam engines running on the Western Region railways and Blenheim Palace pond, which hosted ice skating for weeks on end. I settled in the upstairs room of Chaucer's Cottage and tried to write a thousand words of finished text every day, including Sundays, in an effort to finish my book while the subject was still topical.

My tutor, George Bennett at Queen Elizabeth House, was of invaluable assistance to me as I struggled to write what I hoped would be my first book. Mr. Bennett patiently showed me how to ruthlessly revise and improve my daily product by marking up a page or two to illustrate what might be accomplished with a sufficiently detached discipline in my approach to my own work. It was not easy but my book began to take shape.

As winter turned to glorious spring I found interest in the possible publication of my book with Pergamon Press of Oxford, a company founded by the famous Mr. Robert Maxwell, later of very mixed reputation and who ultimately died at sea on his yacht under mysterious circumstances. My manuscript was reviewed by a Scandinavian woman who taught at Oxford and apparently acted as a kind of editor for the Press. She told me that my manuscript was accepted for publication as soon as it could be completed. I was ecstatic, standing, I thought, on the edge of a major accomplishment.

Instead, I was standing on the edge of one of my first big decisions, a professional decision involving a principle of fundamental importance. A few weeks after the exciting news that Pergamon

Press would publish my book, I was informed that for publication to go forward I would need to pay a stipend of £1,600. She explained that this was a perfectly normal practice in the publishing industry in order to help defray the initial costs of publication and publicity.

I was dumbfounded by this news, outraged and humiliated. It was out of the question that I should pay someone to publish my work, which I knew to be both timely and reasonably good. A few days later, after some deep soul searching since I had no other option for publication, I demanded the return of my manuscript, indicating that I would not agree to publish it with Pergamon with or without the stipend.

For several critical weeks I was at a complete loss. Time was passing. In Northern Rhodesia the British government had declared that there would be a new election set for 1963 under a new constitution and that this election would be followed by the independence of Northern Rhodesia in early 1964. I needed to see my book published in a timely fashion and return to work on my doctorate.

Mr. Bennett came to the rescue with the suggestion that I should submit the manuscript to Oxford University Press in London, the commercial arm, as he called it, of this famous old publishing company. The manuscript was submitted to a personal friend of Mr. Bennett, who agreed to read it immediately and give us an answer up or down. Some days later I met Mr. Bennett in London to visit the Oxford University Press office in Dover Street.

I have two distinct memories of that day. The first was that Oxford Press had indeed decided to publish the book as *The Northern Rhodesia General Election, 1962*, and that to ensure its rapid publication it would be printed in East Africa as a paperback and released in 1964 by Oxford University Press, Nairobi. The second memory derived from a brief conversation after our meeting with Mr. Bennett on the sidewalk outside the very elegant townhouse that housed the offices of Oxford University Press. The building had tall, elegant windows with a large iron rail fence across the front. From the sidewalk I could look down into a deep well, where the basement windows opened onto a small subterranean court. Mr. Bennett, who was not given to making personal remarks, suddenly said, "My father was a butcher. He worked in a place like that."

He then turned and walked away. Nothing more was ever said by him on this subject. I have, however, wondered over the years about his comment, because it revealed so much about what I already knew about Oxford and what I did not know about him. Oxford was a place of privilege in Britain. I had met a few scholarship boys, as they were called, boys from modest middle- or working-class backgrounds. At that time they were very few, and among the dons they were fewer still, or perhaps harder to identify. Most dons, or tutors, were by American standards very reserved. Certainly this applied to George Bennett, so his comment seemed very revealing and deeply personal. He was a butcher's son but had become a distinguished Commonwealth historian at Oxford. I wondered whether my own modest background and my struggle to put my doctoral studies on hold and see through my book on the election had struck a deeper chord within him. I never knew, of course, because our relationship never became informal or familiar—a fact of life at Oxford that I had come to accept.

My mother came to visit in June. She had come to see Edward, my second son, who had been born in early May. I had to build a fire for Mother everyday in Chaucer's Cottage to counter the chill coming up through the floor. The two of us drove out for a few days to Gloucestershire and on to the Wye River Valley in South Wales.

In conversation with my mother I revealed to her that I knew what I wanted to do. As usual, it was a broad idea that only set a general direction, but it was carefully considered, nevertheless, and it set a course which I stayed on over all the years of my professional life. I told her that I wanted to develop the ability to "learn how a particular country works." I wanted to be able to visit a country and in a relatively short period get to the bottom of how that country functioned—its economy, its politics, and its society. I explained that I thought this could be a practical profession, not academic, but an expertise born of hands-on engagement, which over time and with practice could be developed into a talent that could produce relatively quick results.

By November I was in Kenya, confined to a room in the Nairobi Club, where I composed the index for my book. This is a task which if done by a professional would have cost me over £300. I saved the money but the exercise necessitated the careful reading of my own book and noting down under countless headings on dozens of sheets of paper the relevant page for every name, place, or subject as they presented themselves. At the end of three weeks I had finished. The book was to be published in January 1964. Before leaving Kenya, I attended Kenya's own independence celebration in December 1963. Prince Phillip, representing the queen, handed over power at midnight that night to Jomo Kenyatta, the nationalist leader who had risen in the Mau Mau days of the 1950s. It was the one and only time I witnessed the independence of a new nation in Africa, and the evening was raw with emotion and pride.

A few days later I returned to Northern Rhodesia, this time to do research for my dissertation, which was on the broad topic of the rise of African national political parties and Northern Rhodesia's transition to independence. Dr. Kaunda was the new leader of government business in a legislative council controlled by the United National Independence Party, with an African majority. Dr. Kaunda had moved from his two-room house in the African township to a government minister's house near the governor general's mansion. Others I had met during the campaign of the previous year were now serving as ministers in the government.

I spent approximately six months in Northern Rhodesia, focusing on research in the archives and libraries, some of which were in towns other than the capital, Lusaka. I applied to the office of the governor general seeking access to official papers I had heard were housed in the grounds of Government House. To my great surprise I was given access to these files, which were kept in a newly built brick structure on the grounds of the mansion.

When I understood the magnitude and the importance of the records that had been opened to me I was stunned by the opportunity and rather humbled by the trust that was being placed in me by the soon-to-depart British government in Northern Rhodesia. The files ranged in their markings from confidential to secret and top secret. They produced a comprehensive record of the years leading up to the election of 1962. Some of the materials were Special Branch (intelligence or police) records and were extremely sensitive. As is the practice in the British civil service, notations, some quite lengthy, had been made in the margins, or in some cases individual names had been inserted as a particular file made its way through the administration for consideration or decision. This provided a remarkably clear and orderly picture of the British response to passing events, some of which had been turbulent or extremely politically sensitive as the nationalists engaged with and challenged in many cases the local government.

My hours each day were strictly limited from nine to four, at which point the files were collected and locked away in a large vault. Obviously, these were sensitive records that had been removed from the newly elected African transition government, and it was easy to see why. Classified "secret" and "strictly confidential," the files contained reports by British government Special Branch officials in Northern Rhodesia covering a wide variety of extremely sensitive matters relating to the previous government's handling of the rising African nationalist political movement.

My research technique was to carry a small portable typewriter into the office each day with a spool of tape that was half red ink and half black ink. I would read the files and type in black the directly transcribed material from the file that I felt it was important to preserve. Since there was a vast collection of files this required fast reading and disciplined selectivity. Then, when required, I would enter in red type my own observations or thoughts as I worked through the records. I felt at the time the helpful shadow of my law work at Oxford with Mr. Hall of Exeter College. When I came to writing my dissertation, the technique I had chosen to use proved to be invaluable.

One day, after a few weeks, I realized that I needed to retrieve a certain file I had read earlier to clarify or verify some particular fact or event. I asked the clerk if he would kindly retrieve the file in question. He looked at me with an expression of modest surprise and said, "Did you not know, mate, these files are being burned."

"Burned? Destroyed?" I was shocked, but of course I should not have been. Obviously, at independence there would be a new sovereign government that would be able to access anything it wanted. These files, filled with sensitive, often graphic material about incidents of intimidation and violent acts against the authorities, were accompanied by revealing comments, observations, and evidence of decisions taken by the British which, if not removed, would be seen after independence by very different eyes. One could imagine the political sensitivities these would stir up between the government of Great Britain and the newly independent Zambia, the newest member of the Commonwealth.

Still, why wouldn't the files have been preserved and shipped for safe keeping in archives in Britain? To an academic it seemed inconceivable that such a valuable treasure of records should be destroyed; but Special Branch and security personnel were more concerned about secrecy and eliminating evidence of their thoughts and actions. I realized from then on that I must work fast to see all the records I possibly could and to record the key elements of this documentary history as faithfully and thoroughly as I could. My red notes of observations became more important as a means of giving perspective to the relatively limited raw data I could actually transcribe. I worked feverishly each day and protected my growing composition of data in the realization that I would be the sole custodian of this valuable record.

On one point I knew there would be a complication. As I was given access to the documents, I was required to sign an agreement that I would abide by the Official Secrets Act of the United Kingdom, which would restrict my use of the material I was now researching. I knew that this was a complex legal area and that no one in country could give me sound and trustworthy advice. Thus I decided simply to go ahead with the task at hand and to cross the "official secrets" bridge when eventually I got to it. This proved to be a sound decision, as I discovered two years later.

When after many months I had read all the files that remained available I left Northern Rhodesia for Oxford, with my large and very weighty treasure carefully packed in my personal baggage. Once back at St. Antony's College I began to write what would become my doctoral dissertation and a book entitled *Zambia: the Politics of Independence, 1957–1964.*

As a result, there was one final chapter for me with Zambia. My dissertation was a long and difficult enterprise made more difficult by the graphic sensitively of my material. Nevertheless I wrote the dissertation fully utilizing the restricted material because I believed its preservation was a matter of academic freedom that justified the risk I was taking. In May 1966 I returned to Oxford from Washington DC, to take my doctoral oral examination.

I was examined by Professor Beloff and an outside academic from another British university. It lasted most of the morning in a large lecture room in "the schools," an impressive old building at the lower end of the High Street. I was told immediately afterward that I had passed the examination and set off at once to meet with Mr. Bennett at Linacre House, where he also held an appointment in what was to be a new college.

The moment was memorable in a very Oxford sort of way. When I entered a small reception room I advised Mr. Bennett that I had passed my orals.

"Well done," he replied.

After a few moments of awkward silence Mr. Bennett asked, "Would you like a sherry?" He turned to the sideboard and poured two dry sherries.

"Well, congratulations," he said as he lifted his glass.

A momentary swelling of pride caused me to say suddenly, "Well I suppose I should call you George now?"

To which he immediately replied, "Well, if you think you are up to it!"

And that was the last time I referred to him or addressed him as anything other than Mr. Bennett.

Several years later I learned that he had died of cancer at what was a relatively young age. He was the man who taught me the discipline of writing, how to say clearly what you wanted to say with a minimum of words. He also respected my effort to do original research in the living field of contemporary affairs, where I had begun to understand the geneses of decision and action in public affairs. It had been a formative experience for me to find my way through the confusion and passion of Zambia's transition to independence. As an academic I had been close to the "action," but not in it. Now I knew I wanted to move to a life of action. I didn't know where, but I knew it was not going to be in either Africa or academia.

But first there was the issue of the Official Secrets Act to deal with before my dissertation could be published by Oxford University Press. I sought legal advice regarding the application of UK law to classified documents, which although now destroyed in Zambia, had contained sensitive information that otherwise would have been the property of the new sovereign government of Zambia. The final legal advice on this matter was that the British government's authority over the classified information in my manuscript no longer existed after Zambia's independence. On the other hand, I was advised to clear the manuscript with the new government of Zambia.

I contacted the now-president of Zambia, Kenneth Kaunda, who passed the manuscript to his attorney general and invited me to visit Zambia to discuss its clearance. This I did a few weeks later and was invited to dine with President Kaunda at Government House. Dinner was set for 7 p.m., and upon arrival I found it was to be a one-on-one dinner at a small table in the center of the state ballroom, attended by at least twenty ot twenty-five servers. At 7 p.m., President Kaunda entered the ballroom carrying a large portable radio, which he placed on the table. He asked if I would mind waiting the start of dinner for ten minutes and pushed the "on" button of the radio. The next thing I heard were the sharp pips announcing the BBC World News Service. President Kaunda then listened silently to the ten-minute report, after which he turned the radio off and laughingly said, "This is the only way I can find out what is going on in my country."

At the end of dinner, President Kaunda said there would be no problem clearing the manuscript and that he had invited his attorney general to Government House that evening to execute the necessary documentation with me. I have been ever grateful to this impressive leader for his tolerance and understanding.

5

Oxford, Washington, Investment Banking

I was in my own transition to independence and had been for nearly two years. In early autumn 1964 I took a break from the writing of my dissertation in Oxford to make a visit to the United States. My purpose was very simple. It was not to find a job, but instead simply to meet as many different kinds of people in widely diverse fields to discover what their line of work actually was, how they approached it, what they believed they accomplished, and where it might lead them in the future. I put a great deal of effort into contacting people, either through friends or other contacts, or simply by making a direct approach myself.

In the event I was surprised by how accessible many senior people proved to be. I called on people in major corporations, foundations, universities, and government, as well as visiting with old friends such as Ken Pennypacker in Upper Nyack, outside New York. The other surprise was that when it became clear that I was not seeking a job, but simply trying to explore and think ahead, people were not merely accessible but opened up to me at length in answering my questions. In short, I learned that people responded to someone younger and enjoyed talking about themselves, reflecting sometimes about their own careers. I was especially impressed that some very senior people took a significant period of time to simply visit and explain what they were trying to do.

One of those people was John Gardner, at the time president of the Carnegie Corporation in New York and later the founder of Common Cause. When I explained how I had approached my graduate study in South Africa, Boston, Oxford, and Central Africa over the past five years and that I was looking for a life of action in a field that mattered, John Gardner gave me very good advice and a suggested course of action. He thought I should continue at Oxford to complete my doctorate and then return to America.

I would then have been away for five of the past six years. He felt I should find a way of re-integrating into America, and his suggestion was that I should apply for a new program that Carnegie Corporation had been instrumental in developing with the Kennedy and then the Johnson administrations. The program was to be called the White House Fellowship Program and was due to begin in September 1965 in Washington. Mr. Gardner outlined the program, which was open to all people between the ages of twenty-three and thirty-seven from any and all fields of activity. Fifteen Fellows would be selected to spend one year in Washington, with four assigned to the White House and the other eleven to a cabinet secretary.

The purpose of the program was to expose Fellows at a relatively young age to the very senior levels of U.S. government with the understanding that they would return to their professional fields outside government, serving in future as a pool of talent knowledgeable about opportunities for service at senior levels themselves. Mr. Gardner pointed out that if I entered the competition and succeeded in obtaining a White House Fellowship it might prove to be an ideal way to reintegrate into the United States and help me find my career path. He was right on both counts.

Applications for the program were due in November. The form was lengthy, with many sections addressing local community and public service, about which I had very little to enter. On the other hand, my adventures in Africa were very original at that time, and my academic record was sound. I applied and heard nothing through all the winter months at Oxford, nearly finishing the draft of my dissertation. In April I was interviewed at the U.S. Embassy in London for what I was told was the international area of the White House Fellowship program. In May I received a letter informing me that

I had been selected as one of forty-five finalists invited to appear in Washington for a weekend of interviews at Airlie House in rural northern Virginia.

Until I actually arrived in Washington the possibility of winning a White House Fellowship had seemed very remote. I had not been exposed to any of the excitement of the competition and had virtually no information about how the program would work. When I arrived at Airlie House, however, I met the other finalists and my attitude was instantly transformed. My old competitive instincts immediately asserted themselves. I understood that this was a very big deal, an opportunity, as it were, of a lifetime, and that the competition for the final fifteen Fellows would be fierce. How I had made it this far with so little understanding of the competitive process and the magnitude of opportunity the program would provide I wrote off to having been isolated among the "spires of Oxford."

Before many hours of that weekend had passed, I was taken by the idea that this was basically like a Foreign Office recruitment selection weekend in England, where, as one heard, candidates were asked questions and demonstrated that they could dine with a knife and fork. But Airlie proved to be much more comprehensive. The panel comprised many distinguished Americans: David Rockefeller; John Macy, head of the U.S. Civil Service; several university presidents; and at least one U.S. senator, Margaret Chase Smith of Maine. Multiple interviews with the panel aggressively probed matters of public policy, world affairs, and the role of government. Free time between interviews was spent at the large swimming pool, exchanging views with the other finalists or walking around Airlie's lovely grounds concentrating on the matter at hand.

On Monday following the weekend the final fifteen Fellows would be announced, and we were all invited to attend a White House reception that evening to meet President and Mrs. Lyndon Johnson. The list of Fellows was issued around three in the afternoon, and my name was on the list. It would not be an exaggeration to say I was overwhelmed with emotion and later with sheer excitement about what I knew to be a remarkable opportunity. I called my mother long-distance in Rockford and choking up in tears told her the news. She said she wasn't surprised, as I suppose all mothers do in such circumstances, but to me it all seemed to be some sort of miracle and still does to this day.

At the White House we were each introduced to President and Mrs. Johnson in the East Room and afterward there were drinks, a buffet dinner, and dancing to a live orchestra on the back lawn of the White House. The next morning we were asked to report to Washington in late August to attend two weeks of briefing before our assignment to specific departments. Briefing books on the structure and operation of the federal government were provided by the Brookings Institution for summer reading, with information about a program of continuing education that would be run by Brookings in parallel all year with our departmental assignments.

There was now not a day to lose back at Oxford, finishing all but the final two chapters of my dissertation, making arrangements for moving to Washington, and beginning the search for housing. Finalizing the text of my dissertation and writing the final chapters would be done in the early morning hours of the next six months in Washington. In the meantime, I was discovering a whole new life and career in finance and public affairs.

The first thing to be decided by the first class of White House Fellows was which White House or departmental assignment to designate as your preference. We were asked to list our top three choices in preferential order. This posed a particular problem for me, because although the State Department would be the most prestigious assignment and would offer a major learning experience, I had not been impressed by the State Department people I had seen in Africa and London, including the American ambassador in South Africa. In addition, I no longer wished to be seen as an Africanist, specializing in the State Department in African Affiars, because the newly independent nations of Africa seemed to me to be headed in the wrong direction, with the widespread philosophy of one-party democracy taking hold, even in Zambia. I was afraid I might end up being asked to specialize in African affairs and thereby fail to achieve the broad exposure I was seeking to both U.S. domestic and international affairs.

My decision was based on another of the many rather uncomplicated deliberative processes that have marked my important career decisions. First, I had majored in economics at Lawrence, and although I had not liked economics very much I did know something about it. Second, my exposure to public life and to the deeply entrenched problems of Africa had taught me that successfully seizing the initiative, resolving problems with workable solutions, and in general "getting things done" invariably required finance, that is to say, money, and its effective deployment. I was also learning that tax and budget issues were a lively component of politics and public life. I wanted to learn more about the practical realities of finance and how the American economy really worked. Hence, I put down the U.S. Treasury as my first choice, which no one else as far as I could tell wanted. And Treasury is where I was assigned, to Secretary Henry Fowler. This really was a new beginning.

The White House Fellowship Program has gone through various phases since its launch in 1965. It has been a uniquely successful program, which over the years created a large reservoir of talented people with public policy aspirations and the skills and disposition to deliver benefits to the U.S. government. The fact that Fellows were selected from outside government on the strength of private-sector credentials has helped ensure the availability of "new blood" for successive administrations. The program, when it was functioning most effectively, provided cabinet-level exposure to the public policy process, as well as an organized public policy education program that exposed Fellows to a full range of federal government departments and agencies, also at very senior levels. At the end of one year, Fellows came away with broad-based practical knowledge about the structure and functioning of the federal government, an appreciation of the political process in government, and in light of their experience, a far greater likelihood that they would serve in government at some point in their career. This latter point was especially important because Fellows would understand that the financial and personal privacy sacrifices one makes serving in the U.S. government would be worth it, because they knew from first-hand experience that an individual could make a real difference in our form of government. Certainly, this was my own personal experience when, seventeen years after being a White House Fellow, I served for nine years as assistant and later undersecretary of treasury for international affairs and five years as U.S. ambassador to India.

In the opening phase of the White House Fellows program the idea was that Fellows would work in the office of the secretary of the department, rather than be assigned to some particular job farther down in the bureaucracy. The support necessary to make this high-level arrangement a continuing reality during the full year of the program was provided on a sustained basis by President Johnson and his senior White House staff. The president had written all cabinet secretaries expressing the importance that he attached to the program and the necessity for Fellows to be placed in close proximity to the secretary. We also had four personal evening meals in the White House mess with just President Johnson and sometimes his chief of staff, Jack Valenti. We were included in certain White House events. I remember vividly, for example, being present at a large meeting of members of Congress with President Johnson at which he harangued members, as only he could do, to support a given piece of Great Society legislation. In addition, the fifteen Fellows met, often for a lunch or a dinner, with individual cabinet secretaries or agency heads for a free form discussion. Because we Fellows all held top-secret security clearance, these discussions often touched on extremely sensitive issues. As young, possibly naïve, participants, we Fellows were invariably outspoken, which at times I sensed was appreciated by our respective hosts. At these meetings I met and have vivid recollections of Robert McNamara at the Pentagon; Dean Rusk at the State Department; John Gardner, founder of the White House Fellowship Program and Secretary of Health, Education and Welfare; McGeorge Bundy, National Security Advisor; and Vice President Hubert Humphrey, one of America's great and always constructive liberals. We also met as a small group with large numbers of senators and congressmen, engaging frequently in substantive exchanges of views.

For all of us it was a heady and uplifting experience. It was hard work as well, with long hours, because much of the substance that goes on between cabinet members and their counterparts in other departments takes place after hours. It was not unusual to come home at night at nine o'clock and then to be up at five for two hours' work on my dissertation before going to the Treasury at eight. My reward was that every day was utterly fascinating, absorbing, and usually a new learning experience. I was assigned to be the special assistant to Deputy Secretary of the Treasury Joseph Barr, who sat next door to the office of Secretary Henry Fowler. I was given plenty to do, provided with access to virtually every area in Treasury, and taken along to meetings with other departments, to the White House, or to private meetings on the Hill with members of Congress. I was also sometimes permitted to listen in on telephone calls or conferences.

In order to do my job as Joe Barr's special assistant, I had to read and occasionally comment on virtually all the paper coming forward to the deputy and the secretary. This gave me a comprehensive exposure to Treasury affairs and to the multitude of policy issues Treasury dealt with on a daily basis. At that time, the office of the secretary was responsible for, among other things, domestic and international economic policy, taxation policy, the Internal Revenue Service, Customs, the U.S. Mint, the Bureau of Alcohol, Tobacco and Firearms, and the U.S. Secret Service. I came, during the course of the year, to understand Treasury's unique position in the structure of the U.S. government. Treasury was the government's senior economic policy agency, the keeper of knowledge of taxation, the link agency with the Federal Reserve, the issuer and manager of U.S. currency and debt and the fiscal agent of the U.S. Congress. This latter function, together with Treasury's institutional knowledge of taxation, placed it in a somewhat closer, often more cooperative, position with Congress than other departments and agencies.

As the year progressed I found myself drawn toward the international side of Treasury, partly I suppose by my own background in International Affairs. There had been developments in recent years that posed new policy challenges for the United States in the international field. The miraculous rise of postwar Germany and the general recovery of Western Europe resulted in the restoration of convertibility among a number of European currencies. The American commitment to the Vietnam War was impacting U.S. interest rates, which rose to levels not seen for decades; signs of inflation appeared, and the nation developed its first postwar balance of payments problem. President Johnson's Great Society program was under challenge from the rising costs of war in Vietnam, which was leading us to the years of "guns and butter" economics. Foreign aid and new resource commitments to the World Bank had become contentious issues in Congress as expenditures rose and concerns for the U.S. economy deepened.

Three important developments took place in this period that had a profound influence on my future career, though at the time I could not know how significant their influence would be.

In the mid-1960s, in response to its growing balance of payments problem the. United States closed its capital market by imposing the Interest Equalization Tax (IET). When I started at Treasury in September 1965, I did not fully understand the implications of this measure, other than the fact that it had closed the U.S. market to foreign borrowers. Within eighteen months I would understand and be acting on the unintended consequences of this action.

The second development was the introduction of a program to discourage capital outflows by U.S. corporations designed by Treasury and imposed by the Commerce Department's newly created Office of Foreign Direct Investment (OFDI). This program was aimed at forcing U.S. companies with large overseas investments to raise the capital required for these operations from sources outside the United States instead of transferring funds directly out of the United States. The program was introduced during my time at Treasury, so I understood it more clearly than I did the implications of the IET. Taken together, however, the two measures in effect constituted a form of capital controls in the U.S. markets.

The third development had to do with the international monetary system and the necessity for the United States to take the two unusual measures outlined above. Secretary Fowler had formed an advisory body called the Dillon Committee for International Monetary Reform. The committee was chaired by Mr. C. Douglas Dillon, a Republican and former secretary of Treasury under President John. F. Kennedy, and it was comprised of eight or ten wise and influential Americans including David Rockfeller of Chase Manhattan Bank; McChesney Martin, governor of the Federal Reserve; John Macy, head of the U.S. Civil Service; Edward Bernstein; and Paul Volker. Its purpose was to study, discuss, and make recommendations to the secretary of Treasury concerning the rising balance of payments problem facing the United States resulting from the postwar economic recovery of Europe, especially the so called German miracle; the return of currency convertibility in Europe in the late 1950s; and the evolving challenges posed to the international monetary system that had emerged after the war with the United States at its center, and supported by the Bretton Woods Institutions, namely the World Bank and the International Monetary Fund, established at the end of the Second World War.

Secretary Fowler asked me to attend the meetings of the Dillon Committee as an observer—the only observer, as it happened. Committee meetings were held every few weeks in a large conference room and often went well into the evening. At first, I was somewhat overwhelmed by this entirely new and apparently esoteric field of knowledge and public policy. I mostly listened to the flowing discussion, took a few notes, and read the background papers prepared for the meetings, which presumed a high degree of knowledge and so at first were difficult to follow.

Gradually, the subject began to come to life for me. An organized and coherent international monetary system had been formed after the Second World War and the Great Depression of the 1930s. It was based on a fixed value link between gold and the U.S. dollar, set at $35.00 per ounce of gold. The U.S. held the overwhelming bulk of gold reserves in the devastated postwar world. Most other countries were starved of gold reserves and had run their economies behind elaborate foreign exchange and strict capital controls. Their currencies were not convertible into other currencies, and in Europe the recovery that followed the war was financed by loans and grants under the Marshall Plan and the World Bank. Recovery proceeded, and as trade between the United States and Europe increased, financial tension and imbalances also increased, especially between the United States and Germany, facilitated by the reintroduction of convertibility between currencies. The imbalances were exacerbated by the rising demands on the United States for the war in Vietnam. As the United States was the centerpiece of the system and the dollar's fixed value link with gold was the foundation of the system, changing and building holdings of dollars outside the United States represented a threat to the stability of the system. This was our balance of payments problem. Dollars could be put forward to the United States under the system in exchange for gold at the fixed price of $35.00. As overseas balances of dollars built up, and the prospects for rising inflation in the United States took hold, gold prices away from the official community rose well above the official price of $35.00. As the world economy recovered, and the United States seemed to be losing some control over its stable price levels and interest rates under the duress of heavy spending for both Vietnam and Great Society programs, confidence in the United States as the anchor of the monetary system began to weaken. Later, in the crisis of 1971, the United States would terminate the dollar's fixed rate link to gold. For me, at Treasury in 1965–66, the subject matter and deliberations of the Dillon Committee opened a new world.

What impressed me the most was to discover that there was a functioning world financial system that bound together the leading nations of the world. At that time, this was admittedly a restricted group, because the early postwar world was still deeply fragmented. The only capital available to developing countries and to many recovering countries was drawn from either U.S. foreign aid, Soviet foreign aid, or the World Bank. Cross-border capital flows from one country to another were modest to nonexistent, with the exception of flows from the United States. Our balance of payments problem had, however, caused us to begin to restrict those flows.

I began to see the world differently. The simplistic but very practical idea I had developed in Africa, namely that all projects or policy ideas to improve things centered in the final analysis on money, took on a new clarity. If there were to be a developing and improving world, finance would be requred to support development on a scale well beyond present government capacities, and this finance would have to cross international borders.

The effect on me of this overly simplistic conclusion was as if a light bulb had suddenly gone off inside my head. What I wanted, I realized, after the academic world and my adventures in Europe and Africa, was a career in international finance. Since banking was the one business area I had not explored in my 1964 visit to the United States, I was uncertain about how one would enter the field of international finance, if indeed there were such a discreetly defined field of activity. To me, the field was not to be confused with international relations, which was about diplomacy, treaties, and international organizations. International finance would surely be about doing things, financing real projects and businesses that were accomplishing concrete objectives.

This breakthrough was not solely the result of my attendance at the Dillon Committee meetings. It was also influenced by the whole of my Treasury experience. I learned to pay attention to markets, both stocks and the Treasury market, to learn about gold operations, to see the connection between money and action in government. It seemed I was entering a world peopled by a relatively small number of participants who really understood these concerns. It seemed a special world, mysterious to some extent, but capable of great accomplishments, not of wealth necessarily, but of change and new beginnings.

I had developed a friendly relationship with Assistant Secretary of International Affairs Winthrop Knowlton. He had come to Treasury from the Wall Street firm White, Weld & Co., where he had been the head of research and had written a best-selling financial book entitled *The Growth Stocks*.

As I watched him function in the Treasury, I was fascinated by the range of subjects that he and his people seemed to know. There seemed no end to the flows of discovery and to the various complexities that surrounded economic and financial issues. And I was able to connect the importance or relevance of these issues to the real world around me. Treasury's business, it seemed, reached everywhere: into other departments, the White House, Congress, the banking community, the Federal Reserve, the State Department, and the private economy at large.

When I expressed my interest to Win Knowlton toward the end of the year, he immediately said he would arrange for me to meet people on Wall Street at commercial banks and investment banks. His brother, Hugh Knowlton, was the managing partner of Smith Barney on Wall Street, and Win seemed to know virtually everyone else in the New York financial community.

I made several visits to Wall Street to meet with and interview both investment banks and the large commercial banks, thanks almost entirely to the kind assistance of Win Knowlton. I was amazed by what I found and knew at once that I had found the field I wanted to enter. I had not been to business school, a disadvantage I sensed, but not one in my view that could not be overcome. I had a unique background and a demonstrated track record of self-starting accomplishment that gave me confidence in the interviewing process. I had read a record of court proceedings against Wall Street investment banking firms in the 1930s in which the judge provided a helpful guide to the origins and histories of the major firms. I found the commercial banks strikingly different from the investment banks. Banks like Chase and JP Morgan were multifloor operations with huge open areas filled with row upon row of desks populated by people who looked suspiciously like clerks. There was a "groupness," a buttoned-down sameness about the big banks, though clearly they did very important, large-scale business, including outside the United States, which was an important factor for me.

The investment banks were far smaller. The people had more of an edge and seemed more worldly, livelier in their conversation and demeanor. They also dressed with more style. They were, however, less international and were closely linked in their activities to the Securities and Exchange Commission (SEC). Everything seemed to require a prospectus; several years of hard-slogging technical work had to be accomplished before one got too far into the business. For most of them, international business was limited to nonexistent, and seemed to be reserved to a very few senior people.

White, Weld & Co., was an exception. It had an important foreign business, especially in stock brokerage, but it also had a London office engaged in foreign financings in what was termed the new eurobond market. Several of its partners were Europeans living overseas and clearly making a major impact on the firm. They were obviously respected and had made their first mark by building and then dismantling a successful business in Venezuela in the late 1950s and early 1960s. One of the senior partners in New York was Belgian, another was a White Russian émigré, and the younger partners in Europe were English, Russian, French, and Swiss. Here was a firm doing its international business overseas and conducting it with non-American partners. This seemd to me to be the right way to do international business.

To make my choice, I had to decide between commercial banking and investment banking. Apart from the superficial differences I had noted on my visits, I based my ultimate decision on a set of simple facts, just as I had done with other important decisions. This reasoning went as follows. A commercial banker sits on a stack of money and decides whose application for borrowing from the stack of money qualifies for a loan from the bank. The investment banker has only limited capital, sits on no stack of money within the bank, and effectively considers what people and projects warrant financing with other people's money. Investment banking seemed more creative and more demanding, with new ideas and tailor-made solutions to financing challenges. There was something exciting about the idea of taking risk in the underwriting process. This was the basis on which I chose investment banking. I chose White, Weld because they seemed to be a truly international firm doing their business overseas, and I would be the only American at the working level in the foreign department.

When the interviews were over I met separately with two senior partners. One, Jean Cattier, the Belgian, asked if I liked good food and explained that good food was an important part of international investment banking. The other partner, David Weld, a low key, white-haired Bostonian, said that I had an interesting background and that White, Weld would offer me a job. He went on to say that they would only be able to offer me a salary of $12,000 because at this point I didn't really know anything! He knew I had a PhD, had gone to Cape Town and Oxford universities, worked in Africa, and been a White House Fellow, but he was right: in his world I didn't know anything. I took the job and felt I was on top of the world.

It was a new world with a great deal to learn and much I did not understand. I enrolled in the evening program at the New York Institute of Finance. I sat in the investment banking work pen, closely positioned next to the research department. I learned about companies, stocks, brokerage, accounts, and how to read a balance sheet and income statement, and I studied for the NASD certification examination. Learning wasn't easy, in part because colleagues who responded to my frequent questions seemed to assume that I knew much more than was actually the case, and one couldn't go on indefinitely asking follow-ups.

Gradually I learned in those first six months, and I began to understand the investment banking culture at White,Weld. David Weld had explained in the meeting when he offered me a job that I would be eligible for a year-end bonus on top of my $12,000 salary and that this might run in the neighborhood of $1,200 to $1,400, depending upon my performance and the profitably of the firm. The culture was clearly preoccupied with the bonus possibilities, which I discovered could be many multiples of one's base salary. A good bonus depended on performance, which in turn translated into generating or "bringing in" new business. The bigger the fees associated with new business, the larger the bonus potential. Clearly, the moral of this story was to think big, because winning and executing a large piece of business did not require significantly more time or energy than did a small piece of business.

I came to two conclusions. First, I would prove to Mr. Weld that I was worth many more times the $1,200 to $1,400 bonus he had mentioned at our meeting, and second, that I needed to focus on new business right from the beginning, even if I was still in a learning or training mode. As usual, there was no time to lose. Stock offerings, whether initial public offerings (IPOs) or secondary sales (subsequent offerings of shares of companies already listed on the stock exchange) carried the largest underwriting fees. I soon identified a company in my hometown: JL Clark Manufacturing Company, where my father had worked in the 1940s. Mother had kept the modest stock holding my father left when he died in 1950, and in 1964 the company had gone public with a significant increase in liquid value for my mother's holding. I understood the company might be considering a secondary offering, so I went to see members of senior management, some of whom I had known as a boy, to begin to learn more about the company and to build a relationship with them.

Shortly after beginning my campaign for new business in the Midwest, I was assigned the task of reviewing the presentation of monthly brokerage account statements. I was given great stacks of statements to review and from them learned about various kinds of brokerage transactions and whether their presentation in statements made sense for nonprofessional customers. I was to report my findings to Mr. Emery Katzenbach, the senior managing partner of White, Weld. Later, I learned that I was given the assignment in order to bring a fresh, if inexperienced, view to this problem that would help overcome resistance to change in the back office of the firm. Far more important to me than the outcome with the dark forces of the back office was the fact that as a part of this process I was sent to Europe by Mr. Katzenbach to visit two of our offices, London and Zurich, which gave me my first opportunity to meet the foreign partners of White, Weld. These men were Stani Yassukovich and John Stancliffe in London, and young John Cattier and Bob Genillard in Zurich. Interest in the project at hand was minimal. Instead, at a lunch our discussions were about international developments and projects, a combination destined to stir very deeply my broader interests. These meetings convinced me I was on the right track and had joined the right firm.

This was when I first heard of eurobonds, and suddenly the significance of what I had learned at Treasury and sitting in at the Dillon Committee meetings came to life. The closing of the U.S. capital market to foreign outflows (IET) and the impact of the OFDI program in forcing American companies to look offshore for sources of capital to finance their international operations had had the largely unintended consequence of sparking the still fledgling eurobond market. The young and creative partners of White, Weld were among the leading architects and innovators of this new and exciting market.

It is important to understand what a eurobond was and what it did for markets at the time. Obviously, it was a debt instrument, a note (5 years) or bond (longer maturity) denominated in U.S. dollars. These dollars, however, were euro dollars, that is, dollars owned by non-Americans or nonresident Americans. There were lots of such dollars around because of America's growing balance of payments problem. In any case, the debt instruments issued by American companies' finance subsidiaries, usually situated in Delaware or the Netherlands Antilles, were in a form that was not registered, as all domestic U.S. bond instruments were, with the U.S. Securities and Exchange Commission. These bonds, known as eurobonds, had other special features. They were issued in denominations of $1,000 each in bearer form as opposed to registered form, which meant that the issuing company had no record of the bond's owners, so simple possession of the bond was proof of ownership. Eurobonds paid interest free of all tax encumbrances, including any withholding tax imposed by any authority on payment of interest. Thus, the receipt of both principal and interest payments could remain anonymous. Eurobonds were not saleable into the United States, and arrangements had to be made upon initial sale and subsequent trading of the bonds that would preclude them from migrating to the U.S. market. Hence, they were an offshore instrument bought by non-U.S. buyers and traded for dollars already outside the U.S. Their issue involved no further contribution to America's growing balance of payments deficit, and so no new outflow from the United States.

The euro market was small, still in its infancy, but I knew that the supply of dollars outside the United States was large and would grow. Limitations on the market were that the dollars were spread widely and held mainly by individuals, as opposed to large institutional investors. Most investors demanded anonymity, chiefly for tax reasons, and most required a high degree of liquidity; hence the $1,000 bearer instrument denominations. Investors also required that the credit of issuers be of the very highest quality, so the market was a big-name market, open only to major corporations and top governments. At this stage, the eurobond market was also beginning to finance leading non-U.S. names, provided that the established conditions of issue could be met.

Shortly after my visit to Europe, I was sent to London to work on a new and exciting project: the preparation with two other banks of our proposal for financing the Channel Tunnel. Here was a true cross-border project, estimated at that time to require some £820 million of financing. I was low man on our team, calculating what seemed to be endless columns of numbers running out years into the future, but I could participate in the drafting of the plan. I was struck at the time by how lean and efficient the language was that set out the financing plan for this vast, historic project. The tunnel would not be built for many years, and when it was it cost far more than the figures we had used at the time. White, Weld was not part of the ultimate financing group, but the "Chunnel" project remained a part of me.

I stayed on in London for nearly two years, working on eurobond issues. It was demanding but exciting work. Looking back over these many years, what was most exciting was that the few of us in the office were responsible for all aspects of the work. The office was small—only two of us working under two partners plus the traders and support staff. I was directly engaged in the solicitation of business, preparing financing proposals, writing the prospectus in preparation for an offering, writing the invitation telex that would go out to underwriters and selling group members, staying late into the night actually feeding the telex tapes through the telex machines, keeping the order book while the deal was out on offer in the market, pricing the issue (setting its terms) when the book was closed, and allotting the bonds according to the assessment of the quality of each participant's demand. This was old-fashioned investment banking in its most comprehensive form. The advancing specialization in Wall Street that divided business getters from those who prepared the documents, from those who did the research, from those who constructed the syndicate and priced the transaction, and from the traders in the open market had not yet taken over in eurobond London. We all did everything: solicited the business, prepared documentation, put together the syndicate of banks to sell the issue, allocated the bonds with a view to the after-market performance of the issue—all vital elements that if well performed, generated significant credibility and therefore value for those on the front line trying to win new business. In later years I often saw investment bankers marketing proposals who did not possess a confident and detailed understanding of the market that was to buy their deal. In London in those early years I had a fully integrated experience base, and I learned the first and most important principle, namely that the market determined whether a deal was doable and its price.

Learning who comprised the market was particularly fascinating for me. Making up the list of old established European names, for any given issue, or unfamiliar names from the Middle East, Africa, or the Caribbean, confirmed for me the sense that we were raising funds from across national borders, that we were tapping resources spread widely around Europe and other areas. It was by no means a global market at that time, nor did the euro market reach into the various national markets of Europe, which were still heavily regulated on a national basis and surrounded by capital controls and foreign exchange restrictions that kept them isolated from other nations. One came to think of the euro market as a thin layer of dollar financing actively superimposed over the national markets of Europe. Still, as I sent the telexes out late into the night to the long list of impressive names, I felt a sense of uplifting pride that we were at the cutting edge of a new world of expanding finance, beyond the reach of individual governments where the code of responsibility for control and quality lay with us, the bankers.

The market grew rapidly, and White, Weld (later Credit Suisse

White Weld) usually occupied the top spot in euro market league tables. Issues which in the beginning were only $10 to 15 million grew to $25 to $30 million. Bonds convertible into the common stock of American companies were introduced in 1968. These were popular because they carried a fixed rate of interest but were convertible at the option of the holder after a period of time at a premium price into the underlying common stock of the American parent company. Governments of Mexico, Japan, European countries, and other European institutions also entered the market. By 1970 I was back in New York heading up White, Weld's international corporate finance effort. I was at that point thoroughly grounded in the euro markets and marketing offshore finance proposals to leading companies all over the United States. In 1968 JL Clark Manufacturing Company, later named Clarcor, and Sundstrand Corporation, both of Rockford, had done secondary stock offerings, and my bonus for my second full year at White, Weld was $45,000, well above the $1,200 to $1,400 figure David Weld had suggested might be possible the day I was hired. I loved my work. I felt a distinct calling toward a financing world of expanding scale with what seemed virtually limitless opportunities.

The new international market was not without its shocks and moments of uncertainty and even destabilization. In a market that was relatively free and unregulated, except by the industry itself, unexpected developments or traumatic events could have deeply threatening repercussions. The devaluation of sterling in 1967 by the government of British Prime Minister Harold Wilson was one such event. The dollar crisis in 1971, which resulted in the breaking of the dollar's fixed value link to gold was another. The bankruptcy of Herstatt Bank in Germany in 1974 shook the euro market, and so did the sudden and drastic oil price increase in late 1973. But the euro market not only survived but prospered and continued to innovate.

Issues appeared denominated in other currencies, such as the deutsche mark and Swiss franc, which offered alternatives, often at substantially lower rates, to U.S. dollar issues. Composites of currencies also appeared, such as the European Unit of Account, which through a complicated basket of currencies structure offered a low-risk means of diversification away from the dollar. Participation by European banks also changed dramatically, as they organized to seize the lead manager role in more issues. In the opening phase of the euro market, many of these huge banks participated only as selling group members; but soon they became underwriters, then lead managers as the market expanded and they exercised their very considerable financial power.

Among all the unexpected events and shocks to the financial markets in these years, the most profound was the oil price increase of late 1973. Virtually overnight the oil-producing states engineered a massive shift in wealth, unprecedented then and still now, for its speed and magnitude. Within months the developed nations of the West and Japan were faced with slowing growth and rising balance of payments problems. Massive liquidity was building in the OPEC states, especially in Saudi Arabia and the Gulf States, as recession and financial dislocation faced the world's leading economic powers.

Fear and loathing in the Western countries was palpable as a new, highly inflated price of the commodity we depended on above all others made itself felt across the full breadth of society. Formerly obscure, remote kingdoms, assumed by the public to be primitive relics of the past, suddenly assumed a threatening image of unlimited financial power and influence. The Kingdom of Saudi Arabia had been thought to be a remote desert kingdom of six million primarily fundamentalist Muslim people ruled until 1964 by King Saud, who led an ostentatious and capricious lifestyle, reportedly divorcing wives and marrying new ones every few days. By 1974, it was thought that the kingdom, now ruled by the wise and conservative King Faisal under the ultraconservative Wahabi sect of Islam's strict Sharia law (which called for, among other things, beheading criminals for capital offenses and stoning women for infidelity), would shortly have enough money to buy the entire New York Stock Exchange. Many Westerners at the time thought the barbarians were truly at the gates with the financial power to choke us into poverty.

6

Arabia

I grew a moustache while on vacation at our family's remote Wisconsin lake cabin in the summer of 1974. I don't know why. When I returned to work in New York in August I left the moustache in place. There was general approval around the office so I kept it in place—for over twenty-one years.

Perhaps the moustache was predicting my future? Before three months had passed I was in Jeddah, Saudi Arabia, looking like a slightly lighter version of most other men.

In the spring of 1974 the world was struck with the first evidence of the massive transfer of financial resources that flowed to the OPEC states from the oil price increase of December 1973. The sudden wealth of Saudi Arabia was simply mind blowing to investment bankers, aspiring entrepreneurs, and con artists of every description. The largest commercial banks suddenly enjoyed massive deposit flows as the new Saudi liquidity sought the security of leading world banks, especially those in the United States, the United Kingdom, Germany, and Switzerland. Dreams of $100, $200, $300 million or even $1 billion in private financings or massive syndicated bank credits that ostensibly needed underpinning by the Saudi Arabian Monetary Agency (SAMA) literally obsessed the world banking community. The worlds' media began to speculate and extrapolate numbers that showed the Saudis developing the wherewithal to buy up the NYSE, dominate the financing of governments, and in short, to rapidly develop the ability to control the world.

All of us aspired to "do a Saudi deal"—$100 or $200 million or so overnight. But Saudi Arabia was remote, withdrawn, and mysterious. Obtaining a visa made it a hard place to visit. Communication was virtually impossible, unless through sheer diligence at a telex machine or dialing a telephone one might suddenly break through. But even then, there was no reply; just silence, surrounded by swirling rumors.

The most prominent representative of Saudi Arabia's new wealth that summer and fall was one Anwar Ali, the governor of SAMA, Saudi Arabia's central bank of issue and the repository of the Saudi government's mushrooming wealth. We knew by then that there were two young commercial bankers working at SAMA to assist in managing its deposit function with the banks—one from JP Morgan and the other from UBS in Switzerland. Those lucky enough to obtain a visa and to pin down an airline seat on the twice-a-week flights from several European capitals might actually see these gentlemen from time to time, but only briefly due to the rumored pressure of their work. It was also rumored, and later confirmed directly to me, that they were deeply unhappy, living alone, isolated, and under difficult conditions as, in effect, bonded laborers. But a few private financings began to be done with SAMA, and how exciting, rewarding, and reputation enhancing these private placements were! My firm, White, Weld & Co., did a $100 million medium-term placement for British Columbia Hydro in October 1974. I secured the mandate for the deal in a single afternoon, and the placement was done a few days later for a fee well in excess of $5 million.

Suddenly, in October of 1974 there was a change. My firm, White, Weld & Co., in New York, was approached by the retiring chairman of JP Morgan, John Meyer. SAMA, it seemed, wished to consider hiring a team of advisors to help it begin to dig out from under the vast flow of dollar liquidity, to help set up a more coherent and structured investment program. This news was the equivalent of a high-voltage electric shock.

When the big money began to flow into SAMA in March 1974 (cash arrived approximately 3 months after oil was raised and sold), King Faisal of Saudi Arabia, acting on the recommendation of Anwar Ali, sought advice from "three wise men" of global banking. These men were John Meyer of JP Morgan, Richard Fleming of Robert Flemings in London, and Dr. Alfred Schaefer, former chairman of UBS in Switzerland and an expert in gold markets. Anwar Ali, a Pakistani serving in Saudi Arabia, had been the governor of SAMA for sixteen years, during which he was under the direct supervision of King Faisal.

As of November 1974, King Faisal had authorized only eighteen major international banks around the world to receive SAMA deposits. As I came to know later a new bank could be added only after the most careful scrutiny and the consent of the king and his council of ministers. In the autumn of 1974 this select group of banks was experiencing a surfeit of deposits. I learned later that some banks had begun to express concerns about the magnitude of their Saudi deposits and the undue risk exposure to Saudi Arabia that was building in their banks as a proportion of their total deposit base.

In late October I had the honor of meeting with Anwar Ali at the World Bank Annual Meeting in Washington, with several senior members of White, Weld. Our chairman had been approached by John Meyer, who asked whether in principle White, Weld would be willing to consider assembling a small team of "real international investment bankers," as opposed to research analysts or portfolio/deposit managers, to work for what would have to be an extended period of time at SAMA in Jeddah.

Our selection as a candidate for this possible assignment was typical of the mysterious (to us) ways of the kingdom. When Faisal, before becoming king, had served in New York as Saudi Arabia's representative to the UN he had been treated by a Dr. Freeman, whose son, Robert, was now a stockbroker at White, Weld. This was how our name came forward. John Meyer supported White, Weld because we were a private investment bank, a leading international firm in what was still a relatively young euro market, and we had the people and the expertise to help the Saudis break away from excessive dependence on the big commercial banks.

Tragically, a few days after our meeting with Anwar Ali he died in New York of a massive heart attack. This event proved to be catalytic in Saudi Arabia: SAMA was left leaderless, with only one member of its staff charged with responsibility for international investments.

Within days we were asked to travel to Saudi Arabia to meet SAMA's senior management. We were asked if we would be willing to make a joint presentation to SAMA with Baring Brothers of London, a private merchant bank with outstanding international credentials. And so by the third week of November, a prized visa in hand to the Kingdom of Saudi Arabia, I flew to Jeddah with Paul Hallingby, president of White, Weld; Bob Freeman, Dr. Freeman's son; and Nicholas Baring and Leonard Ingrams of Baring Brothers, London.

We set off from London for a three-day visit on the British Airways nonstop to Jeddah, Saudi Arabia's costal city on the Red Sea and at that time the desert kingdom's window on the world.

Little did I know that here, for me, would begin a most extraordinary nine-year odyssey.

I could smell Jeddah and feel its humidity well before we landed in the middle of the sultry night. The airport was a shambles, yet the atmosphere was intimidating. There was no air conditioning. The sides of the airport were in fact open, but the Saudis looked cool in their white gowns. I had never seen a Saudi in his *thobe* (white robe) and *ghutra* (headdress) before. The sight gave some pause. I really had arrived somewhere different and exotic that clearly recommended the exercise of caution and forethought.

Visas reviewed and stamps administered with some impressive thumping of our landing cards and passports, we moved to the customs hall. This was a most extraordinary sight. There were several long tables attended by Saudis in full dress carefully going through every bag or suitcase open on the table. Milling around was an army of what I soon understood were Yemenis, lifting and shifting cases, each wearing a *futa* (long skirt), cotton tops, and paper-thin sandals. Behind us, as we waited at the tables, was a pile of unclaimed cases, bags, and boxes that rose all the way to the twenty-foot ceiling, completely filling the corner of the hall. Yemenis were hunting through this massive pile for pieces of luggage and shouting back and forth. Meanwhile, I gripped my small, fit-under-the-seat one-suit folding bag in one hand and my briefcase, which looked strangely foreign, in the other. The examination was rigorous, with items taken out and inspected closely.

A few feet away a customs officer shouted "What is this?" holding up a bottle of Scotch whiskey. "There is more here," he pointed to the bottom of the hapless visitor's footlocker.

"It's my medicine," the man pleaded. "My doctor requires that I take it."

"Take him away," shouted the officer—in Arabic, but the meaning was clear as two police officers came forward to escort the man from the hall.

My first night in Jeddah was both memorable and disappointing to my image of the great desert of Arabia. We stayed across from the airport in the Kandara Palace Hotel, supposedly Jeddah's best. It smelled of mold mixed with a mild sewer smell; that night, contrary to all my expectations, there struck a massive thunder and lightning storm with heavy rain. I lay in bed awakened by the storm and the sound of sirens and general running about in the hall outside my room. Why should it rain? And why so hard? I thought I was coming to the desert, and here it was raining and storming like a summer night in Wisconsin.

I needn't have been disappointed. When the puddles disappeared in the steamy sunshine the next day, we did not see rain again for the next two years.

That morning we met the management of SAMA after eating a very carefully selected breakfast in the hotel dining room. We met in a small, exceedingly warm office. The Saudi team consisted of Mr. Ahmed Abdulatif, head of the International Department; Controller General Sheik Abdul Wahab; and Mr. Ahmed Saeed, a Pakistani in a leisure suit. There were the five of us from White, Weld and Barings. The meeting was formal but friendly. Many questions were asked of us but little information was given. A follow-up meeting took place that afternoon, and it was agreed we should meet again the next day.

In the intervening period something mysterious happened. At the meeting the following day, the Saudis came rapidly to the point, with several stunning observations, a list of clear requests, and a plan for moving ahead. Mr. Abdulatif, smiling infectiously and sitting cross-legged in his chair, his attractively stitched red leather sandals on the floor in front of him, explained that SAMA was hopelessly behind. Money was coming in too fast—around $100 million a day—and bookings of deposits and a few treasury purchases were weeks behind.

SAMA needed to diversify away from the banks, he explained. They needed the help of "real investment bankers" who would commit to stay five years and be sworn to secrecy. These investment bankers would help negotiate direct-country loans, then corporate loans to the safest and strongest companies in the world; and finally, they would create some form of equity portfolios that would give SAMA exposure to the West—all without upsetting Western markets and inviting scrutiny and possibly retaliation.

Their proposal was that Mr. Ingrams and I would stay on for one month, until the hajj in late December, to learn and to appraise their needs. We would then be permitted to go home for three weeks and to bring back recommendations for the kind of team and contract arrangements that would be required for SAMA.

They went on to propose that Mr. Ingrams and I begin work the next morning, and in return the Saudis pledged to begin evening discussions of contractual working arrangements jointly with the two firms. Until then, we would work without fees. Our first loyalty would be to SAMA, though we could still be paid by our home firms and retain our benefits.

The atmosphere was warming up. Mr. Saeed, the Pakistani administrator, added helpfully, meaning to be humorous, that while we were in Saudi Arabia we would be their "prisoners" with our passports held by SAMA. This proved to be the case and over the years wasn't always humorous

There was virtually nothing to say—except that Mr. Ingrams and I would indeed remain in Jeddah, working during the day and discussing working arrangements for a team at night.

A month later I was home for Christmas with no contract in hand. Our contract was eventually completed and signed the following April after a long and difficult negotiation. In the meantime, with our passports retained by SAMA, we were virtually prisoners, working six days a week on the basis of a handshake, with no agreed compensation and no contact with the home firm for the next five months. The only way to convey the nature of the odyssey that followed is to tell the tales of this extraordinary challenge.

On the first morning we were shown into a small room with a few soft chairs and a low coffee table with a rough mosaic top. After a while we decided we needed to learn about what resources SAMA now had and how they were presently invested. We found our way to a small office on the third floor of our very dilapidated building. In the room, six desks were pushed closely together and six Saudis sat cross-legged on the desktops drinking sweet tea, their sandals lined up neatly on the floor. Before them lay large, leather-bound, open ledger books in which line after line of entries had been made by hand in beautiful Arabic script. I was reminded of my student days at Oxford, where my savings account book for Barclays Bank was processed by clerks on stools who entered with the greatest care and elegance any deposit of whatever amount I had made that day. How, I wondered, did they manage to scribe such beautiful numbers with that long sweeping symbol for pounds sterling?

These large books, and more like them, were lined up on two shelves. Each book represented one of SAMA's eighteen deposit banks. Every deposit entry was a thing of beauty, but they were unreadable by me or Leonard.

"How do you look at your whole portfolio of deposits say, for example, by their maturity structure?" we asked. They didn't keep a spreadsheet record of maturities, they explained. But they did have, on a single piece of lined paper, a long handwritten list showing the total deposits of SAMA with all eighteen depository banks.

My eye went to the bottom of the column, which was in Arabic numbers. The total at the bottom read something like $20,160. As an investment banker I automatically added three zeros. "Over 20 million dollars," I observed. "No," they corrected me, "here you have to add six zeros."

Pause. So, over 20 billion dollars had been spread among eighteen banks, much of the money, as we learned shortly afterward, on current account, that is, not earning interest. No wonder they wanted to move away from an excessive dependence on commercial banks!

This was a shock but I soon understood some reasons for this state of affairs. In part it was a function of simply being overwhelmed and having hopeless international communication difficulties, not directly because of the casual greed of the banks. On the other hand, the deafening silence from SAMA on some pools of liquidity surely was encouraging banks to let sleeping non-interest-bearing dogs lie.

Our next days settled into a pattern: work in the morning, break for a quick and high-risk Kandara Palace lunch; then rush around town seeing and pricing housing, cars, food, possible schools, and staff; then returning to SAMA to either work late into the evening or meet with the Saudis to discuss how our contract arrangements might work.

These were demanding activities. Good housing was scarce, and rents were rising by the week as landlords watched the influx of foreigners into Jeddah. We needed drivers immediately to avoid the very considerable risks of driving oneself in Jeddah. Houses came with only the walls, no furnishings, air conditioning units, appliances, or even cabinets in kitchens or baths, so our team members would need every conceivable thing required to set up house. The choice of such items was depressingly limited, but they still needed to be priced for the purpose of calculating the needs of our contract.

At work we began writing brief explanatory papers describing, for example, how Federal Reserve Auctions of U.S. Treasuries worked and the various U.S. government agencies that issued high-grade bonds and notes—Fannie Mae, Federal Home Loan Bank (FHLB), Federal Housing Administration (FHA), Farmers Home Administration (FmHA)—and what in each case was the basis of their creditworthiness. We wrote papers on various other subjects, including selected countries. These were very short, usually three pages typed by a Pakistani typist and limited by the number of pages that he could fit into a typewriter with carbon copy papers. No copy machines were made available to us for the first three years. The result was that the papers had black smudges spread throughout and hand-made corrections. We also read piles of financing proposals and materials in boxes full of telexed offerings from around the world, which were spread in disorder several feet deep along the hallways.

Most days Ahmed Abdulatif invited us in the late morning to sit in his office to meet bankers. Jeddah was flooded with bankers who wanted actually to see SAMA, because telexes from outside world were rarely answered and phone calls were impossible to complete. So hundreds of bankers obtained visas, boarded planes, and braved the uncertainties of accommodation in Jeddah, the risks of bad food, isolation from outside markets, and the problems of getting out of Arabia again. These bankers then descended on SAMA. There were no appointments, so they stood in line to be received in due course in Ahmed's very small third-floor office.

In these early days the Saudis at SAMA were open to receiving visits and tolerant beyond our understanding of the long-winded presentations of one group after another of self-promoting bankers. In the hallway outside, the line of waiting bankers trailed down two or three flights of stairs. Ahmed would listen to politely each group until they had finished, with the result that we often did not break for lunch until nearly four in the afternoon. This experience cured me for life from making lengthy, puffed up presentations to clients. It was patently clear, even to the inexperienced Saudis, that not all the bankers winding down the stairs could each be number one in all the financial market league tables.

In the evenings we started getting access to the sole SAMA telex machine. This was a manually operated machine in a narrow corner in a tiny triangular room wedged into where two sections of SAMA's building came together. There was one small window giving directly out onto a large rusted iron smokestack coming out of the furnace in the basement that burned old Saudi riyals turned in by the banks. When in use the smokestack gave off enormous heat, and the little room in any case was not properly air conditioned.

Under the counter were stacks of old telexes in which hundreds of mosquitoes hid in the dark, coming out to harass us as we operated the telex machine. Making a call on the machine involved dialing the central operator somewhere in downtown Jeddah and requesting a number in New York, London, Tokyo or elsewhere. One then waited anywhere from ten to twenty minutes. Then all of a sudden, as we sat nodding in the heat, the machine would come to life and one was connected to someone in the outside world.

Access to the telex was carefully restricted in these early weeks. We were permitted to use the machine only for a specific purpose, such as communicating with the Federal Reserve in New York about a Treasury auction, or to convey a particular instruction to one of SAMA's banks, or occasionally to make a deposit.

The evening meetings we had to discuss our future contract were long and often mysterious in their result, or their failure to produce a result. Their aim was for us to establish the basis for a team of what they always referred to as "real investment bankers" who would commit to remain at SAMA for long periods and who would help them create a diversified investment program.

They expected these people to bear their first loyalty to SAMA and not to their home firms. They would be "seconded" from their home firm (a term Americans did not commonly use), that is, they would be paid by their home firms and retain their existing firm benefits. SAMA was prepared for these arrangements to operate under a lump sum contract jointly with the two firms.

In our discussions it soon became clear, however, that SAMA wanted us to be accountable under the contract for every individual expenditure and that there would need to be detailed accounting in line with Saudi bureaucratic practices for every expense item. This they said was the law of Saudi Arabia and explained that we would need to comply in all respects to the last detail. In effect, they would need to approve every expenditure, and presumably the big ones, such as housing, in advance.

This resulted in a standoff between us. They disagreed with the projected expense amounts that our research of each day generated. Sheik Abdul Wahab, controller general of SAMA, opined, for example, that a rent of 20,000 riyals per year with two or three years paid up front for a house was ridiculous; that anything over 5,000 riyals was unacceptable. We had never seen a house for less than 20,000 riyals and prices were rising quickly on the few houses available.

How, we asked, could we manage the daily or weekly costs of facilities and the expenses incurred by families if all these items were constantly subject to review? Their response was that there had never been a contract for Westerners to work within the Saudi government bureaucracy and that therefore the procedures had to match exactly the standards imposed by the Saudi format.

My reaction to this utterly unworkable demand was to return to ground zero: their desperate need for bringing order to their financial situation and their stated desire to bring a team of "real investment bankers" who would undertake with their families the commitment to work in the austere conditions of Saudi Arabia. We were now nearing the end of the month we had agreed to stay on in Jeddah, and the hajj was now only days away.

This first serious battle with Saudi bureaucracy was engaged a few nights before our scheduled departure. If we were expected to bring and to keep for long periods a team of high-quality people and their families, we would need the freedom to run our own affairs, make our own spending decisions as needed, freely select our own housing, cars, staff, and schools—in short, we would need to create our own lives in Arabia free from the daily angst of keeping and presenting to SAMA chits and receipts for the smallest and, not to mention the biggest, outlays of daily life in a chaotic cash economy.

An ominous silence was the immediate result of my declaration, followed by two days during which meetings were not resumed. Leonard and I continued to scour Jeddah for housing possibilities and information on the cost and or availability of every conceivable need for setting up family households in Jeddah.

Two nights before leaving the Saudis called us together. In a few minutes it was obvious that we were going to go ahead. The usual back and forth sparring had disappeared. We were told that the arrangement would be a lump sum contract, negotiated to cover all costs, including our fees. The contract would specify that our first loyalty would be to SAMA, that we would not be permitted any reporting relationship with our home firms other than contract related issues, that we would assemble and bring the team members needed for an extended stay in the Kingdom, and that finally we would be back in Jeddah with our teams in three weeks. We would be expected to identify and justify every expenditure item in the composition of the contract, but that once agreed we would receive quarterly lump sum payments with no presentation required for individual items of expense. Negotiations would resume upon our return to SAMA and would be completed while we worked.

With this thunderbolt of practical reality delivered, our passports were returned to us complete with new exit and reentry visas. That night as I tried to sleep I reflected on the hectic uncertainties of the past four weeks. I now knew the magnitude of responsibility we would face in this remarkable country. I found the realization humbling, yet at the same time inspiring. I was proud to have passed some sort of test, namely to have established with the Saudis a basis on which a credible and sustainable investment advisory service could function in Arabia.

I also reflected on the extraordinary scene around me, for the hajj was now upon us. Hajjis were materializing everywhere: Arabs, Africans, Indians, Pakistanis, Afghanis, Indonesians, Iranians, and many others. Some wore the simple white wrappings that denoted their mission. Others were in colorful national dress. Jeddah airport, only three hundred meters away from SAMA and directly across the road from the Kandara Palace Hotel, was said to be the busiest airport in the world, landing a flight with a great roar every few minutes day and night on its single runway. The city was thronged with visitors, many elderly and obviously very poor, taking their once-in-a-lifetime pilgrimage before death could claim them. Treasures were on offer everywhere—on the streets, in alleys, in the souks. Many hajjis carried bags of goods or carpets under their arms or slung across their backs. Out of the bags came jewelry, baskets, blankets, precious stones, fearsome knives, pots, pans, scarves, gold, and incense.

The evenings were now cool and delicious, and the color and diversity of this vast crowd of visitors to the holy places from the Muslim world at large was utterly captivating. Christmas, now only days away, seemed a world apart, especially as I pressed through the mayhem of the souks and Jeddah airport. It wasn't just the people.

I had never seen such piles of bedrolls, bags, and sleeping families sprawled on the floor and on the sidewalks outside. Here and there were small fires, tea brewing, food cooking, stacks of carpets, pots, pans, treasures, and people with turbans, white towel headdresses, blankets, gowns, masks, beards and beautiful eyes in hidden faces.

The London flight was hours late leaving, but the time of night made no difference to the scene. I would be back in a few weeks and strangely enough was already looking forward to my return.

Two days later I was back in New York. How to compose a SAMA team? Who would accept the challenge, who would commit to years in this isolated kingdom in the desert? How would they and their families be incentivized? What types of expertise and personality traits were essential for the task we faced and the limitations imposed by life in Saudi Arabia?

I settled on two investment bankers, one a man who would be able to take over from me in a few months' time, and the other a markets person with fixed income as opposed to equity or banking expertise. The recruiting process was easier than I thought it would be. My friend and colleague in New York, David McCutcheon, a Canadian, unmarried, a man with an open, laid-back disposition, accepted to come as our number two. The other recruit was Joe Huber, a young bond salesman from our Philadelphia office. I didn't know Joe, but I soon learned that he was one of the most focused, disciplined, and loyal people one could meet. Joe was ready to come to Jeddah and marry his fiancée, Louise, in a matter of days to make the big move to the Kingdom of Saudi Arabia. I had our team together before New Year's Day, so early January was a time for rest and rising anticipation.

Contract negotiations continued with the Saudis in the first months of 1975. Somehow, I seemed to have become part of the negotiation, without formally saying so. It was simply assumed that I would stay on in Saudi Arabia when our contract was finally agreed.

This was accomplished in April, four months after our "handshake" with the Saudis. We advisors were now settled in Jeddah, though not fully acclimatized to the sometimes harsh and frustrating life we faced: getting our houses set up; building in kitchens; installing wall-unit air conditioncrs; finding watcr supplics in the desert on the edge of town and bargaining with tanker truck drivers every three or four days to bring the water to put in our cisterns; shopping for clean, dependable food; what to do for family entertainment in a city without cinemas, safe restaurants, clubs, or, indeed, any recreations that men and women could enjoy together. These were major challenges. Meanwhile, the weather was getting warmer and warmer, with thickening humidity and intermittent dust storms that swept up from the south and across the city of Jeddah, with its open sewers and piles of refuse. Sickness was common, especially following dust storms.

My house stood in the desert, half a mile from the more settled neighborhoods. Jeddah was growing so fast that houses simply popped up across the desert, which we drove across to reach the house since there were as yet no streets, sewers, city water, or refuse collection. We tossed our daily garbage over the wall into the desert, and each day Bedouin women in headdresses and black abayas brought their herds of goats, which would scour through the refuse, devouring most of what might give rise to smells and much that was inedible as well.

We discovered that electric bills came in the form of a small slip of paper placed under a rock outside our gate on the cement lip of the driveway. If it blew away in the perpetual wind off the Red Sea, some five hundred yards away, the electric company showed up without warning and took out the main fuse on the outside of the house. Getting electricity back meant a long trip downtown, paying the bill in cash, and waiting several days for a man to come to put the fuse back in place. Meanwhile, no air conditioning, no working fridge or house lights at night. A bribe, of course, shortened the waiting period, and it took only one such experience to gladly pay the necessary riyals.

Cooks and food preparation were constant problems. One cook I recruited down in the souk was to prepare a lunch on his first day for visiting bankers at my house. When after an hour drinking Saudi champagne (orange juice and soda), no lunch appeared, I went in to the kitchen to find that nothing was prepared. "I'm not really a cook" the man said as he shuffled back and forth uncomfortably. "I took the job for my cousin, who is coming into town from an oil rig in the desert." His cousin, Norman the cook, did come in from the oil rig crew a week later, but it turned out that Norman could only cook multiple dishes for a minimum of 40 people. And so it went.

In March King Faisal was assassinated by a young religious zealot whose brother had been killed by security forces in a riot some years earlier over the introduction of television into the kingdom. It was late evening and I was driving to my house when the news came through. I stopped the car to reflect on what I should do. We worked for the Saudis, we had been brought to the kingdom by King Faisal, and we occupied a position of special trust. I turned the car around and drove back to SAMA, not knowing exactly what I should do. After going up to our empty office, I went downstairs to the office of Deputy Governor Sheikh Khaled Al Ghosaihbi. The deputy governor's Secretary motioned me in, and when I opened the inner office door the vice governor and several colleagues were grieving. I took a seat and stayed for several hours. From time to time someone would make a comment about the greatness of King Faisal, to which the others, including me, would nod in agreement. Not knowing what to say, I said nothing, but I waited, hoping my presence would convey my shock and sorrow for the kingdom of Saudi Arabia. That night made a difference for me, and although no one ever thanked me or acknowledged my visit that night, I could tell it had made a difference with them.

The work continued. We wrote papers and explained their content to the Saudis. We were teachers, attempting gradually to establish trust with our masters. The Saudis were intelligent and shrewd, but they were inexperienced in international financial matters and the instruments and practices that constitute the daily fare of financial markets. One day I was called by the governor to be told that SAMA wanted to buy $300 million of that day's U.S. Treasury auction by the Federal Reserve in New York. I had written a paper shortly before explaining how the Fed auctions worked, particularly how bids were made for bonds at various rates which the Fed then used to fill its needs, working from the lowest bids up to the level at which it was able to fill its needs. A line was drawn at that rate and all bidders below that rate were accorded the same terms on their bond order at the highest bid rate accepted by the Fed.

I went to the telex room and went through to the Fed desk to place our order. I do not recall the rates that had been set that day, but let us assume the Fed drew the line at 6 percent. I had been authorized by the Governor to bid 6.1 percent, which would mean that SAMA would not be allotted any bonds, so I asked the Fed to wait while I went back to the governor to explain that if we wanted a $300 million "add on" for SAMA we would have to accept 6 percent. The Governor looked at me and reflected on this dilemma. Then he said, "Can't you do better than 6 percent?" to which I referred back to my paper to explain that it would have to be 6 percent or nothing for us. Then he smiled and said, "Go back at 6.01 percent."

We did not get our $300 million of Treasuries, but two lessons were learned that day. One was that the Fed system was the Fed system, and it was not subject to negotiation as if we were in the carpet souk. The other was that all transactions not governed by the strict rules of the Federal Reserve were negotiable down to the finest details. This was the true nature of Arabia, and I would come to live by that rule, while with the Federal Reserve we followed their rules.

If we the advisers were to be trusted we would have to abide by Saudi practices. Negotiations took on a whole new meaning for me. There was no such thing as a simple act. One learned to think ahead, to imagine and to plan how a given transaction, deal, or simple request might unfold. I also had to learn how to live with being seen as unreasonable in the eyes of bankers, friends, foreign government delegations, landlords, merchants and our masters when it came to contract renewal negotiations, which became annual affairs of several months' duration. Negotiation was expected, and one learned the value of thinking before speaking at all times.

Our office and working arrangements placed all six advisers together in one long, narrow room with a single window at the far end. Leonard and I occupied desks just beneath the window, and each of us had a wall air conditioner behind us, which when we stood up blasted the back of our heads. Our other team members sat at desks facing one another a few feet away from us, and a wall partition with frosted glass and a single doorway divided the room. At the front of the room was a small area for receiving visitors. This was furnished with a red leather sofa against the front wall beside the door, two red leather easy chairs, and several low black chairs with thin silver legs. These were the chairs that the advisers used, because the thin silver legs turned under the chair if one didn't sit correctly, with the result that the occupant would be pitched forward onto the carpet. On the other hand, the red leather sofa was notorious in hot weather for leaving a pink shadow on the light-colored jackets of our perspiring visitors.

Visitors came in constant streams, partly because no business was done by telephone. Thus, there was no substitute for visiting SAMA, but after the first few months the visitors were restricted mainly to us. The Saudis came to the conclusion that such visits were rarely necessary for them to grant, unless the visitors were senior bankers, official government delegations, or other prominent persons. Sweet tea and sometimes Arabic or Turkish coffee was served by Gafar, the small elderly ex-solider who camped in a small closet just outside our door with a pallet and a gas fire ring on the floor for boiling the tea and coffee. Gafar was a friendly fellow, whose first loyalty was to Mr. Ahmed Abdulatif, head of the International Department and our immediate boss. Later, after some two years, we were provided with our first copy machine. This was put under the charge of Gafar, who managed the process of copying papers for us with the strictest discipline. We would approach him, for example, with a few pages we had prepared and ask for six copies. Because Gafar spoke no English we would hold up six fingers to signify our request. Invariably, Gafar would respond by only holding up three fingers. Rather than constantly trying to override him by appealing to Ahmed we would accept our three copies and come back an hour later with a new request for six copies, and go through the same negotiation. Hence, the constant presence of negotiation in everyday life.

At about the same time, we were provided with a separate conference room with a new table and chairs. It also had two air conditioners, which kept the atmosphere in the room frigid and drafty on the hottest days. This had the effect of giving perspiring visitors from outside the shivers and drying their damp suits in a matter of minutes. The other effect of the air conditioning was to slow down the numerous flies that populated our rooms, making them easy targets for the slap of a hand on the surface of the table, a constant feature of our conference meetings. I held the record for killing flies, with thirteen killed in a succession of eleven consecutive blows. Across the hall from our rooms a simple toilet was set in a long, deep room with an open drain behind it. This was used by our section of the building and flushed once a day at three in the afternoon. Needless to say, visits there were kept as short and infrequent as possible.

One of my earliest assignments was to find out why deposit offers from major banks were not honored when SAMA responded favorably to what appeared to be a firm offer. We were just beginning our live telex calls to banks in New York under guidelines that limited us to $5 million per deposit and required us to obtain two other comparable bids before accepting a deposit. Given the fact that we had only one manual telex machine and that each call had to be made through a central telex operator in Jeddah, it was perhaps not surprising that often after hours of effort into the late evening we were only able to accomplish $30 to 50 million in deposits in any given night. With roughly $100 million new money coming in each day, we were clearly falling behind.

The telex offers we received from the banks during off hours were therefore important to Mr. Abdulatif and the senior management of SAMA. The fact that banks did not honor these offers was a matter of considerable frustration. The first thing I discovered was that most of these deposit offers sent by banks as a telex from their end were received during the night by the central government telex office in Jeddah. These were then transferred onto yellow telegram forms with the message posted on the form in blocks of white strips in much the same way as Western Union telegrams used to be done in the United States in earlier days. These messages were then collected in large bags, which every few days would be given to a taxi to be dropped off at SAMA. A few times, I actually watched a taxi pull up in the parking lot in front of SAMA, the driver lean across the front seat, open the taxi door, and push out the bag, which landed with a dusty thump at the bottom of the stairs leading up to SAMA's front entrance. After a while, the Bedouin guard on duty would shoulder his rifle, amble out, and pull the bag up the stairs into SAMA. In another day or two the telexes and telegrams would arrive in the accounting department in a box. By this time, the deposit offers were up to a week old and no longer regarded as valid by the banks. The mystery had been solved and thenceforth all deposit activity was carried out live on our telex machine.

The rising cash balances generated by the limitations on our deposit operation made U.S. Treasury and Agency auctions more important to us because we could achieve greater volume through an auction process that assured the Saudis that prices were fully reflective of markets. Private placements negotiated directly with leading foreign governments were another source of diversification at rates substantially above those that applied to marketable government securities. In addition, the eighteen banks with whom we were authorized to make deposits showed signs of concern over their increasingly large exposures to SAMA.

With new cash of $5 to $6 billion arriving monthly, paid in the first instance in equal dollar amounts to Citibank and JP Morgan, our first challenge was to move these funds away from the two banks, either as deposits to other banks or into marketable government securities in the major country markets. This was much less simple than it sounds. Not all banks wanted new deposits, having already assumed sizable deposit exposures to SAMA. Purchasing marketable government securities in the U.S. market was easier, but there were limitations imposed by our dealing procedures, which required us to secure comparative bids for each transaction in the U.S. Treasury and Agency secondary market in order to document that we had always made competitive purchases. All such purchases were carried out by telex with a limitation of $25 million for any one purchase of Treasuries, and smaller amounts for Agencies.

In order to buy government securities in other national markets that were very much smaller and less liquid than the U.S. market we first had to buy the national currencies required. This too sounds easier than it was in practice. In most markets outside the U.S. in those days a currency trade of $5–10 million was enough to move markets, so there were practical limitations on the amount of currency diversification that we could achieve over a period of days. Add to this the fact that purchases of German Schuldschein (promissory notes), the most practical option for us in Germany, or Japanese yen bonds, or Dutch guilder bonds, or Swiss franc notes were just not possible in the sizes common in the U.S. market.

Finally, there was the problem of time, the number of dealing days each month available for currency diversification operations and investment in national government bond markets. Very simply, although we worked six or more days per week, we never had more than sixteen dealing days each month when outside markets were open to deal with us. Friday in Saudi Arabia was holy day and SAMA was for the most part closed.

Thus, taking a step back, if we wished to achieve a 30 percent diversification of our monthly dollar revenue payment of, say, $6 billion, this would necessitate buying non-dollar currencies aggregating $1.8 billion. If this was achieved in currency purchases of $10 million per transaction we would face 180 executions carried out against 360 comparative bids. Every currency purchase would require a dozen follow-up actions, and we would still need to deploy those new currency holdings in marketable government securities in each country market. These would have to be bought competitively, and the transaction size might be smaller than $10 million equivalent. Each of these purchases would also require a dozen follow-up steps. If we attempted an equivalent target for U.S. government securities, we would face another seventy-two transactions, each with two competitive offers and a dozen follow-up steps. At that point we would still have nearly $3 billion of new money remaining to be distributed to banks or held for the closing of private placements. And finally, these figures take no account of the funds flowing back each month from maturing investments in our short term portfolio. Once again, it must be borne in mind that to accomplish these limited objectives we had to conduct all transactions with outside markets in sixteen dealing days, assuming no public holidays that closed markets.

We worked under substantial practical limitations. We began the day in early morning trading in the Japanese yen market. Then we shifted to the European markets, and in the evening followed the sun to America. Every transaction was explored and executed by telex, and for every execution there had to be evidence that we had engaged others in the market to demonstrate that our executions were competitive. Beyond this, we did not use computers, so that all trades, records, confirmations, payment, and delivery instructions had to be done by hand with carbon copies. It is my recollection that every trade required thirteen separate follow-up actions and telexes to complete, all by hand.

The year 1979 was one more year in a long progression of years of inflation, high dollar rates, and weakness in the U.S. currency. Our investment committee, chaired by the governor of SAMA and often attended by the minister of Finance (both Leonard Ingrams and I attended as ex-officio members and made the necessary presentations), had sought to accomplish a 30 percent diversification away from the U.S. dollar. Thus, taking the sum of $3 billion from each month's incoming revenues (by now $10 billion each month) and adding to it an amount representing a similar share of maturing dollar investments, one can see the difficulty of achieving the goal in sixteen dealing days with Western markets and with the transaction sizes and dealing limitations with which we had to cope. No wonder we worked long into the night with our group of eight team members and a few Saudi clerks. At times I observed that we were the busiest clerks in the world.

So, the facile views expressed in the international media, and I suppose think tanks, though I was not there to hear, which claimed that SAMA could exercise undue influence over the U.S. and other markets took no account of the realities on the ground. The Saudis could not easily and effectively diversify out of the dollar. The rate at which they could diversify from the banks and from the government markets was also clearly limited. Private placements were an effective option for making direct government loans and to denominate each of those loans in a mix of currencies (Dutch guilders, Swiss francs, deutschmarks, and dollars). But any such loan took days to negotiate and weeks to document. Documentation requirements were intelligently conceived but time consuming to realize: formal loan agreements and currency tranches documented in the equivalent of $1,000 pieces might be theoretically marketable in accordance with widespread market practices, but in reality would be difficult to liquidate.

Private placement negotiations through intermediary investment banks varied widely from those conducted directly by us with representatives of governments. Direct negotiations, which were conducted at our headquarters in Jeddah and later Riyadh, could be quite difficult. When we agreed to do a direct deal, it was large, totally private, and off-market. We, the advisors, were both loved and loathed because we controlled the negotiations but were only the first line in the process. We were backed invisibly by our masters, with whom we would have to clear any final agreement. If we made a positive response, usually by telex, to an intermediary bank that had submitted a mandated proposal, we were loved. When it became clear what the rate margin would be above market rates for that particular credit in its home market, and that we were unlikely to be moved, feelings were very mixed indeed. Negotiations often came down to very small spreads, and we therefore often made ourselves the object of exasperation and as a result unpopularity and charges of arrogance, which I find still lingers with friends and colleagues to this day.

Private placements submitted by intermediary investment banks were prepared for and considered by the SAMA Investment Committee, which usually met late Thursday evenings. At the end of such a meeting, perhaps around midnight, we would return to our office downstairs and prepare our offering proposals to be sent, usually to Wall Street, that same evening. These proposals would specify the terms, including the interest rate to be set, and usually require a yes or no response in twenty-four hours. Since we were closed on Friday, and most of us did not have telephones in our houses, the intermediary firms were forced to accept or reject our terms without the benefit of negotiation. Our policy was that if a proposal was not accepted we were under no obligation to negotiate or to receive and consider a counter offer. Most of our deal proposals were therefore accepted: they had the benefit of size, simplicity, and the tapping of a discrete and unique source which was unlikely ever to sell the paper, plus in the end the downside of rejecting a proposal from SAMA. So on Saturday mornings we usually had acceptances for hundreds of millions of dollars of financings, but without warm feelings of gratitude, which I am still reminded of from time to time by bankers I run across these many years later.

There was always excitement in doing these placements. The direct government-to-government placements, however, were a different story. They began with the arrival of a delegation, who also met our Saudi principals. We, the advisors, would then take over the negotiations, which were usually fierce. Our practice was to draw the line at a maximum justifiable rate that was well above market rates and usually considered unreasonable by the delegation, who had no further access to the Saudis to remonstrate against the last bit of margin spread on their deal.

The only exception was a remarkable negotiation in 1978 with France, where a single French government official, as opposed to a delegation, had come to do battle with us. The deal was to be for Banque française du commerce extérieur (BFCE), the French government's export financing agency, guaranteed by the Republic of France. The man who came to Jeddah was a certain Mr. Witkowski, a mid-level official in the French Treasury who had served at some earlier time in Egypt.

Mr. Witkowski was a friendly and charming fellow, who in the great French tradition could talk with a lighted cigarette stuck onto his lower lip that would go up and down with the flow of conversation. It was midsummer, very hot, and many of the senior SAMA people were away on break. The Saudi who would oversee this negotiation was Controller General Sheik Abdul Wahab, an imposing figure with a coal black beard that might have been painted on his intimidating visage. Sheikh Abdul Wahab was not comfortable in his role as the ultimate commander of the process from behind the scenes. When we ran into resistance from Mr. Witkowski, the frustrated and impatient Sheik Abdul Wahab made the mistake of engaging directly with Mr. Witkowski. I forget what the spread difference was at this point in the negotiation, but from memory we were at 6.875 percent and Mr. Witkowski was at 6.5. Since there was no movement and Mr. Witkowski was staying at the Kandara Palace Hotel just across the road and up a bit toward the airport, Sheikh Abdul Wahab took matters into his own hands.

Mr. Witkowski was summoned into the controller general's office. Sitting on the low sofa, his cigarette (Sheikh Abdul Wahab did not smoke) bouncing up and down on his lip, his hands and shoulders moving in ways to express the utter hopelessness of his position, Mr. Witkowski refused to accede to our rate proposal. Sheik Abdul Wahab, frustrated with this show of resigned inflexibility, reduced our rate by 0.125 percent and Mr. Witkowski agreed to consult his superiors in Paris and return the next day. When he returned early the next afternoon Sheikh Abdul Wahab asked whether he had consulted his superiors and whether he had a favorable response to our improved proposal.

Mr. Witkowski shrugged and said that, alas, he had no counterproposal and could not accept our improved rate proposal. Had he consulted his superiors, asked Sheikh Abdul Wahab. "No, of course not," responded Mr. Witkowski. "Why not?" Sheikh Abdul Wahab asked in a strained and somewhat rising voice. "Because," Mr. Witkowski answered, "if I did that I would be fired, my children would have to be taken from school, I would have no future and would have to take early retirement," and so on. With outstretched hands, turned palms up in total subjugation, cigarette dangling from his lower lip, Mr. Witkowski placed himself at the mercy of Sheikh Abdul Wahab. Mr. Witkowski repeated this performance for two weeks, each time with a slightly lower counter proposal authorized by the frustrated sheikh until Mr. Witkowski finally won the day and disappeared back to France with his signed letter of agreement.

This, however, was not the end of the matter. Weeks later, as the legal documentation made its way through the London lawyers, the French government indicated by telex that it expected the loan agreement to be in the French language and to be governed by French law, instead of our standard practice of English documentation governed by English law. We were instructed by Ahmed Abdulatif to make no response to the French message. They sent a repeat of the message and still we did not respond. Meanwhile, interest rates were rising, and after three months of silence we could feel the rising concern of the French that the deal they had so vigorously struck with us might never be closed on the terms we had agreed. When after a few months bond rates had risen by 0.5 percent, Ahmed instructed us to draft a gracious message to the French government in which we were to apologize for the delay, indicating that it had been caused by our or deep reflection on the request they had made regarding the language of the agreement and the law to be applicable to the transaction. We wished to inform them that their proposal was acceptable, provided that there would have to be a text of equal standing in Arabic which would be governed by Sharia law. The next day, the French conceded to a standard English text governed by the laws of England.

We were pushed by these developments toward a more sophisticated and diversified investment program. The new governor, Abdul Aziz Al-Qureshi, clearly intended to expand and diversify our investment operations. We began to receive government delegations from leading developed countries seeking to establish borrowing relationships with SAMA. Apart from the U.S. Treasury market, the gilt market in the UK, and the government of Japan yen bond market, there were few sources of marketable government securities for us to tap into to diversify our credit and non-dollar currency exposures.

Most countries in the West, as well as Japan, had been hit by recession following the massive oil price increase of 1973. Recycling petrodollars became the world's catch phrase for SAMA's investment activities in world markets. Country delegations came to Jeddah one after the other for discussions about how they could gain access to the vast pool of funds that was clearly building up in Saudi Arabia and would help them finance their balance of payments requirements. The attitude of the Saudis was to invest only in top-quality sovereign credits and to keep maturities short in order to preserve the liquidity that Saudi Arabia anticipated would be required to finance their own internal development.

Virtually every week we opened a new flow of credit to a sovereign borrower or to entities designated by the sovereign and enjoying its full faith guarantee. Our earliest deal was a $1 billion, five-year certificate of deposit placement with the Bank of Tokyo, which was the government of Japan's designated borrower. This was followed by private placements with British designated borrowers, France, Germany, Norway, Sweden, Austria, and leading Canadian provinces. Most issues were for five years, or sometimes seven, usually for $200–300 million, and as time went on they were composed of a mix of non-dollar currencies. All placements were documented under English law, and SAMA sought to create at least a theoretical liquidity by insisting that all placements be in the form of securities in $1,000 denominations or some near equivalent in other currencies. This policy represented the Saudis desire to have some measure of theoretical liquidity if they should wish to raise cash for their own development needs.

Maintaining adequate liquidity, of course, was a problem the Saudis never faced. New revenue poured into SAMA every month, and the average life of the growing portfolio hardly reached one year. Private placements were a welcome diversification from bank deposits and the relatively small purchases we made of marketable government securities, but private placements took days to negotiate and weeks to close with the appropriate documentation, not all of which were easy to negotiate with borrowers.

SAMA's next move was into equities, which marked a major departure from its established preference for deposits, government market obligations, and fixed-income private placements. When we began work in 1974, SAMA was responsible for only one small equity portfolio set up years before and managed by Chase Manhattan Bank for the government's social security administration. The funded amount in the account was only $4 million and its value had fallen to approximately $3 million under Chase's management.

In 1976 we began considering proposals from banks and some nonbank investment managers. In each case, SAMA wanted its prospective managers to provide discretionary management under strict guidelines for both equity and fixed-income accounts. After numerous presentations, we selected Citibank, JP Morgan, T. Rowe Price, State Street Research and Investments, and Alliance. From this base we expanded the list of managers to other national markets and currencies. Chase, despite its strong interest, was not granted an equity account then or later, because, not surprisingly, they refused to meet SAMA's demand to make up the million-dollar book loss in the existing social security account.

Eventually, we established equity portfolios in all the major markets, including Japan. SAMA was extremely sensitive about the management of equity accounts. Discretion and total security was required of managers, who were required to provide detailed reports on performance and market expectations twice each year. One of our responsibilities was to monitor all individual equity holdings in all accounts to make certain that SAMA's equity holdings of any given company never exceeded 5 percent of its outstanding shares. This policy was strictly adhered to because SAMA wished to avoid having to comply with the U.S. SEC requirement to report the fact of 5 percent ownership and with it SAMA's intentions regarding its future interest in a particular company. As so often was the case, SAMA took pains to avoid publicity and any prospect of being seen to be aggressively acquisitive in national markets.

In no country was SAMA's caution more amusingly demonstrated than in Japan. The last equity and fixed income portfolios awarded were in the Japanese market—one to Robert Fleming in London and the other to Daiwa Securities in Japan. Daiwa was seen as a major risk in terms of maintaining strict confidentiality. I was, therefore, instructed prior to opening the account to telephone the senior Daiwa account manager for Saudi Arabia and strongly impress upon him the absolute necessity of maintaining total secrecy.

Two years later the governor visited Japan, and among his many formal visits was a meeting with the chairman and president of Daiwa Securities and members of Daiwa's SAMA account team.

When the governor expressed his thanks to the chairman for Daiwa's excellent performance with SAMA's managed portfolio, there was a great stir in the room. Several members of the SAMA team left their seats and gathered around the chairman for a brief but active consultation. When this was concluded, the chairman cleared his throat and said, "Apparently, you have an account with us that is so secret that even I and the president have not been informed."

I have never known whether this revealing episode was genuine or staged by Daiwa to make an impression on Governor Qureishi. Whatever the truth of the matter, it certainly made a deep and amused impression on him.

By 1982 our continuing relations with SAMA's various portfolio managers was both friendly and constructive, with some $25 billion of SAMA's assets managed in large equity and fixed-income portfolios.

These developments of course took time. So did the process of creating a relationship of trust with the Saudis. It is often said that in Saudi Arabia time doesn't matter. In a sense, over time one came to accept the truth of that observation. Before leaving for Jeddah after Christmas 1974, John Meyer, Chairman of JP Morgan, had advised me that living and working in Arabia would require only three things from me: patience, patience, and patience. How true, both in the beginning and throughout the full nine years.

But I also discovered that other qualities were equally important. Foremost among these was learning to live with the isolation and restricted nature of life in Saudi Arabia. In the early years I left Saudi Arabia only once every nine months or year. In the meantime, there were only two broad themes of life. One was work, six days a week from early morning until often late at night. The midday break might last two hours, but as often as not there was a flood of visitors to receive in the office throughout the day. The other was the feeling of remoteness from the world and the need to accept in daily life the limitations that Saudi Arabia imposed.

We had a small team totaling only six professionals confronted by a mountain of work, no modern technology that enabled us to reduce hand-done clerical work, and a portfolio growing at $5 and later $10 billion every thirty days. From the beginning I was struck by the importance of our daily work to world financial markets and the "becalmed" Western nations. This is what changed my initial personal commitment to remain in Saudi Arabia from only a few months to a stay that lasted nine years. As time passed and our portfolio grew by tens of billions of dollars, it was clear that we were "managing" (however one might judge that term) the largest, most rapid transfer of financial resources in the history of the world. Moreover these vast flows were to a kingdom of only a few million people with no body of open fresh water and little capacity to spend its surplus on imports that could restore growth in the West and reduce the huge and growing financial imbalances that threatened world stability. I felt a sense of responsibility far exceeding anything I had known before. It was essential that the recycling of petrodollars should continue on a large scale that was both efficient and nonpolitical. On the other hand, the time and effort required and the sheer magnitude of our clerical work, the need to manage our visitors, and the sense of isolation from the world outside of Arabia made us feel small—clerks engaged at the small end of a vast enterprise.

The reality was that we were truly cut off in Arabia. We did not have telephones, there was only one Saudi TV channel in Arabic, and mail had to be carried to Europe and the United States by visiting banker friends. Our passports were held by SAMA and could be retrieved only with the agreement of SAMA when one of us took an agreed holiday break. This last point however, required us to obtain through SAMA an exit and reentry visa, a process that could take two or three weeks and require a substantial "tip" to the official who dealt with the Foreign Ministry. Travel within the kingdom during our first three years required a permit, and there were few other expatriate workers at that time in Saudi Arabia. For example, at the time of the hajj, the huge influx of airline flight crews were accommodated in a ship offshore in Jeddah's harbor, so there would be no late-night parties unless adventurous souls rowed or swam out and back to the ship under cover of darkness.

We were not able to bring in films, and newspapers were days late and heavily censored, with the objectionable articles or advertisements cut out by censors, so in reading the papers one could see through the windows where items had been cut out. If one fell ill with dysentery or lesser forms of fever and upset stomach, one faced weeks of discomfort and painfully slow recovery. Dining out, therefore, was seldom undertaken, and usually someone in the party ended up sick. One could buy a TV, but programs were in Arabic and heavily censored by the government. The only English offering was a weekly installment of the early chapters of *Gunsmoke*. Religious services were prohibited, except for Christmas and Easter services at the U.S. Embassy, when a priest was permitted to visit from outside the kingdom. Raids by the religious police on shops that carried Christmas or Easter cards were common. Non-Muslims were not permitted to visit mosques or holy places, including the cities of Medina and Mecca. Participation in a private prayer group, if discovered, was punishable by immediate deportation. Alcohol was strictly prohibited, although at an exorbitant cost one could access limited amounts of Johnny Walker Scotch whiskey ($140 a quart) or homemade alcohol sold illegally under the name *sidique*, or "friend" in Arabic. If alcohol was discovered or reported (by staff, for example) one could be flogged and deported. Driving was highly dangerous; accidents were left uncleared for long periods on the roads along with casualties and dead bodies because good Samaritans were often arrested and imprisoned until details of the accident were sorted out. Women, of course, could not drive, work, or venture safely into markets without covering themselves appropriately. Yet we knew that we were participating in a historic venture that would not last and would not come again. While it existed it captured all of us irretrievably in its net. We were admired, even envied, from outside the kingdom, attributed with powers far beyond reality; yet we did exercise remarkable influence, and over time we were trusted intrinsically and fundamentally by our Saudi masters, who knew the system of accounting, supervision, and auditing was less than fully developed. In all nine years we never had a mysterious hitch, a lost payment, or a transaction that could not be defended or explained.

Our link to the outside world was our visitors, whom we saw in the office and often took home for lunch or diner. Sometimes they were ill or covered with bites form staying in second- and third-class hotels. We talked with them about markets, sports, films, and politics, as well as investment issues and the world economy. To this day, however, there are films, hit songs, stars, and music groups that I have no knowledge of, and there are events in the world between 1974 and 1983 that I simply missed. But I remember the two cans of Heineken beer that Joe Huber gave me for my birthday in 1977. As my birthday fell in June, the height of the hottest season in Saudi Arabia, I struggled for several months trying to decide the right time to drink the cold beers. If I came home from playing squash in the heat of the dying day, I would quaff the beer so quickly that it would be a waste. On the other hand, how could I choose an ordinary night to treat myself to a cold beer? Eventually, I placed six or seven glasses in the freezer, opened a beer on two different nights and poured it out one inch at a time into each frosted glass as I watched the perfect red ball of a sun setting through the dust and haze into the Red Sea.

Our remoteness pushed us to establish daily market and investment information flows. Among the various firms, we set up a system in which each day several firms would telex us a full report from their home market. We read these avidly and used them to check our pricing of purchases, currency transactions, and private placements. One day members from a Canadian investment bank came to visit us crestfallen because they had found their firm's five-foot-long market information telex blowing along the airport road when they crossed over from the hotel. In fact, telexes were the most important source of daily information, so much so that several times a week I would walk over to the Kandara Palace Hotel and read through the incoming telexes that the front desk strung on a line for anyone and everyone to check instead of delivering them to the addressees in their rooms. The senders, of course, assumed these were private communications, so as a source of who was offering what to whom the "stringer" as we called it was both useful and entertaining.

More expatriates arrived, many of them hired by private companies in Jeddah as the economy began to boom. Access to Jeddah's port now required a wait of three months, with ships anchored to the north and south farther than the eye could see. Cement was unloaded from ships by helicopters equipped with bright spotlights operating day and night to meet the spectacular rise in construction activity. To us this meant an increase in social activity, usually in the form of dinners that brought together business people of diverse expertise and nationalities. Social dinners became more like those I remembered from Oxford. I called them eighteenth-century dinners, dominated by good conversation on a wide range of subjects, a welcome change from the dreary dinners in Wall Street. If no foreign visitors were present, then the host broke out his best homemade wines—perhaps a nine-month vintage!

The other entertainment was camping in the desert on Thursday and Friday nights. Within easy drive of both Jeddah and later Riyadh there were beautiful dunes, or shacks on the Red Sea, or perhaps just the space and solitude of the desert. One slept under the stars, and I came to love the soft breeze that invariably came up between three and four in the morning and caressed one into wakefulness under the stars.

Several times I went farther afield for more than just one overnight adventure. On one occasion Ali, my driver, drove the three or four hours up the coast to Yanbu. Yanbu was a mud village on a low hill above the Red Sea. Its importance lay in the fact that deep water came right up to the shoreline, making it an ideal deep-water port for the development of the oil and gas industry. When I saw Yanbu there was one large ship anchored a few yards off shore, a handful of mud buildings on the hillock, and miles and miles of steel pipe stacked neatly in the desert. Today Yanbu is a modern, thriving city.

I also drove one week to Amman, Jordan, some fifteen hundred miles north from Jeddah, in order to return into Saudi Arabia's Northern Province. I was a guest of the princely governor of the Northern Province. My friend, Bill Polk, an Arabist of long standing and close friend of the governor, had arranged to have camels and camping equipment available for a four-day trek some twenty-five to thirty miles into the desert. We made the base camp in the first day and stayed in a large goat hair tent on the top of a hill that looked down the Wadi As-Sirhan valley. We dressed in robes, sandals, and *ghutras*, and each day went riding deep into the beautiful wadis, or valleys. In the daytime the wind blew unrelentingly, and I found the ability to pull my headdress over my face an essential protection from the wind and sun. The prince insisted that I should take his Kalashnikov rifle with me into the desert, and on at least two nights he showed up by Jeep around 3:00 a.m. to sit and visit around the fire.

Our diet consisted of dates that we dipped in goat's butter (a white substance with a smattering of black hairs), tomatoes, unleavened bread, cheese, tea, and pieces of lamb meat sliced for cooking off a carcass hanging in the corner of the tent. The black desert tent was extremely comfortable because it let both wind and light pass through its loosely woven fabric. In the event of rain, the wool would swell and make the tent more or less waterproof.

Finally there was the trip to Mada'in Saleh, a desert valley some one hundred miles north of Medina. This valley was closed to Muslims and other visitors unless a permit was obtained from the Ministry of the Interior. Its last inhabitants were mainly pre-Nabatean people who had lived there around 700 A D. Muslims were discouraged from visiting there because it was said that spirits of pre-Islamic inhabitants still occupied the valley. Like Petra in Jordan, Mada'in Saleh's wide desert valley was lined on both sides by large stone facades carved into the rock cliffs that ran along each side. These were edifices of supreme beauty and deep mystery, because little was known of their past. One could often enter the edifices through a front doorway into various rooms, some with light coming in from openings far above.

Even more dramatically running down the middle of the valley were the remains of the Ottoman Empire railway that had run from Turkey to Medina and was the target of T. E. Lawrence's raids during the Arab revolt in 1917–18. The only vehicle access to Mada'in Saleh was to drive the sixty or seventy miles from the main road on the road bed of the Medina railway. Otherwise, one risked becoming immobilized in the soft sand of the desert. Every twenty miles there remained the Turkish-built railway stations and water towers that fed the steam locomotives and served as forts for the Turkish soldiers who protected the railway from marauding bands of Bedouins mounted on camels, often under the leadership of "Lawrence of Arabia." In many places the rails were still in place; in others they had been uprooted and lay twisted along the side of the rail bed. In Mada'in Saleh itself there was a large stone station and next to it an even larger engine house, which at one time had been closed in by glass panes. Now only the structure remained, and inside stood several railroad cars and locomotives, perfectly preserved in the desert's extreme dryness. We walked about viewing these sleeping monsters, reading "Krupp & Co." off the large steel wheels and listened to the perpetual wind that whined through the steel windows and the partly destroyed tile roof.

In October 1978 SAMA moved from Jeddah to Riyadh. This was a development of the first importance. Riyadh was the center of power in Saudi Arabia, the home of the royal family, the political and religious center of the kingdom. King Abdulaziz, known as Ibn Saud, the first king of Saudi Arabia, seized power in Riyadh in 1932. Since then, the capital city had been off limits for foreigners and non-Muslims unless special permission was granted for a visit. The Foreign Ministry and all foreign embassies were based in Jeddah on the Red Sea coast. Aramco, the Saudi state oil company, and its operations that required the help of foreigners and non-Muslims, were based on the Arabian Gulf coast, well away from the Wahabi center of power in the desert. Moving SAMA to a new and impressive modern building in Riyadh acknowledged the rapid change taking place in the kingdom. It was also declared that foreign embassies would be permitted to move to the capital.

Riyadh in 1978 gave the impression of being a low-built desert city. It was spread out, with few buildings of more than two or three stories. Many structures were stone and mud construction. The vast Nafud desert came right up to the edge of town, and the city seemed to be engulfed in a vast cloud of dust.

We advisors had to find housing all over again, an especially daunting challenge. Adequate hotels, apart from the new government-owned Intercontinental, were nonexistent. Fortunately, we were permitted to visit Riyadh before the move to find and negotiate housing, and in late October members of the team and their families set off in several caravans to cross the twelve hundred miles of empty desert that separated Jeddah from Riyadh.

Our new offices on Airport Road bore no comparison with the old Central Bank building in Jeddah. We had ample space for the entire team, though still no private offices. Halfway down our office area an open doorway gave into a large and wonderfully equipped trading room, complete with push-button consoles that put us in direct contact via the Bahrain satellite with the money desks of the major banks. Behind each trading desk chair was a telex machine, which a team member had only to spin around in his chair to use. Our working hours remained the same; SAMA still closed its switchboard during noon, afternoon, and evening prayers. All work stopped during these twenty-minute periods, although if we were meeting in a conference room with outside visitors we were permitted to continue without interruption. Our stature in the eyes of our many business visitors was quietly enhanced by the utter transformation of our tall, elegant and solid building of some twelve stories set back from the road in its own attractive grounds. Instead of languishing in the decrepit old SAMA building in Jeddah, we now matched SAMA's new stature as the world's leading petrodollar recycling agency and the new base of world financial power.

The second oil price increase of the seventies came shortly after our move to Riyadh and substantially raised the stakes for the continued stability of the global economy. In the United States, stagflation, rising commodity prices, slowing growth, rising interest rates, demoralized stock markets, and a disheartened pubic were testing America to the limit. Balance of payments distortions seemed to be challenging the world at large. Inflation in the West and a weakening dollar were also trying the patience of the Saudis. Debate raged in Saudi Arabia about the wisdom of lifting more oil than was necessary to provide the revenues required to finance Saudi Arabia's economy and its major infrastructure plans. The additional oil production required by the West to drive their wasteful economies generated excessive dollar liquidity for the kingdom that was subsequently depreciated by inflation and the weakening dollar. Far better in the Saudi view to leave the oil in the ground, to be pumped up sometime in the future, probably at higher prices, instead of monetizing it now and suffering the attrition of value imposed by inflation and a falling dollar. Thus did Saudi Arabia see itself as serving the needs of the West, chiefly America, at the expense of its own economic self-interest.

We advisors saw ourselves working under a substantially greater burden as a result of these developments. In addition to the $10 billion of new money we now received every thirty days, we were already managing a highly liquid portfolio of some $130 billion, with an average life of only a little over one year. Thus, considering our sixteen business dealing days each month with Western markets, my rough estimate was that we had to invest money at the rate of approximately $500 million per day just to prevent ourselves from falling behind. Add to this the need to diversify away from the dollar and the transaction size limitations in the foreign exchange markets, and one could easily see the pressure and frustration we lived under. Consider that a $300 million private placement, once negotiated, agreed, and properly documented required three or four weeks to close. Transactions in foreign exchange each required yet another decision and action to invest the funds in financial instruments denominated in that currency.

At the beginning of 1981, our need for greater transaction size took a positive turn. SAMA's senior leadership, and by implication the leaders of Saudi Arabia, engaged in discussion with the IMF in Washington about financing the IMF's new enlarged lending facility to assist developing countries suffering severe balance of payments problems as a result of the distortions being generated for them by higher energy costs.

This was to be a $13 billion dollar deal, which, though only slightly larger than one month of Saudi oil revenues, was nevertheless a very sizeable single-shot transaction, the largest private placement on record at that time. The Reagan administration was just taking office in Washington, and Don Regan, the chairman and CEO of Merrill Lynch, currently the holder, with Baring Brothers, of the SAMA investment management contract, had been named secretary of the treasury.

The deal was groundbreaking, not just because of the large sum but because the IMF was traditionally a demanding lender, not a borrower. We advisors were to negotiate perhaps the largest-ever private loan with an IMF team that had always been in the business of setting the terms and conditions of financings.

Needless to say, this was not an easy negotiation. The attitude of the IMF team was that they were doing SAMA a favor to borrow from them, whereas over the previous six years we had created a strong, disciplined, well-documented lending program that set and obtained the aggressive terms insisted upon by our Saudi masters. The negotiations took time and required an attitude adjustment on both sides. Gradually the terms were worked out and agreed in principle, but as it turned out this was the easier part of the deal.

One evening after the IMF team had returned to Washington, Governor Quereshi called me up to his office for what proved to be a surprising but extremely interesting conversation. In confidence he explained to me that there was a separate unwritten agenda tied to the IMF loan. Although the terms of loan had been set and agreed in principle, Saudi Arabia would not complete the transaction without certain other conditions being met. These other conditions applied to the position of Saudi Arabia in the structure of the IMF. Saudi Arabia's present ranking in the fund by quota share (effectively its share ownership position) was number thirteen. Saudi Arabia was a member of one of the multicountry constituencies, which together with the large member nations, each had one seat on the IMF's twenty-two member executive board. Countries in the multicountry constituencies took turns occupying the constituency's board seat for limited periods; while holding the seat, that director was required to negotiate all positions with constituency members in order to vote for an agreed position at executive board meetings on any particular issue. This process could be both cumbersome and frustrating.

The principle countries of the IMF, the large G-5 members, were permanent members of the executive board, which, together with their larger quota positions, allowed them as permanent board members to exercise effective control over the board in most voting situations. The governor explained that for Saudi Arabia to close its loan to the IMF its ranking in the fund would have to rise from number thirteen to number six, and Saudi Arabia would have to become a permanent member of the executive board in its own right. Quota positions in the IMF were set by an elaborate composite of considerations, the chief of which was the size of a country's economy, and were jealously protected prerogatives. Because the IMF's charter guaranteed that no member country could be forced to concede a reduction in its quota position, this made quota revisions next to impossible to accomplish. As far as I could recall there had never been a significant revision of country quotas, and certainly never one in which a country with a modest GDP and relatively small population leap-frogged seven places over other member countries and by doing so seized a permanent seat on the executive board. It was a breathtaking proposition, all the more so for surfacing, as it were, so late in the day.

There was more to come. The governor explained that these conditions would not be part of the loan agreement and indeed, would not be put in writing. In fact, they were not even to be negotiated with the management of the IMF with whom we had just finished negotiating the terms of the loan. Instead the conditions were be to taken up with the U.S. secretary of the treasury, who in turn would discuss them with other leading member countries of the IMF, in effect with the other G-5 countries: Great Britain, Germany, France, and Japan.

The governor then turned to the method by which this was to be accomplished. He said that they were aware that I had a good relationship with Donald Regan. My instructions were to travel to Washington, take a hotel room there, and engage Secretary Regan for as long as it took to work out this dramatic upgrading, or restructuring, as he put it, of Saudi Arabia's position in the IMF. Secretary Regan would be advised through official channels of the conditions which, although not formally incorporated in the loan documentation, would be essential to the loan's consummation with the IMF. I presumed that the communication would be carried out verbally by the Saudi ambassador in Washington. My job would be to ensure that a solution would be found by the U.S. Treasury in its dialogue with the other G-5 countries.

So I went to Washington, took a room in the Sheraton Carlton Hotel, now known as the St. Regis Washington DC, a short walk from Treasury, and made arrangements to meet Secretary Regan. It was true that since late 1978, when Merrill Lynch was confirmed as the firm assuming the contractual relationship of White, Weld & Co. with SAMA, I had come to know Don Regan and also to admire his energy and vision as a leader. But seeing him as the secretary of the U.S. Treasury under the new Reagan administration was an altogether more daunting business than sitting in his office at Merrill Lynch in New York for an informal chat about Saudi Arabia and global finance affairs.

Secretary Regan explained the extremely difficult position the conditions placed him in with the IMF and the G-5 countries. He acknowledged the very great importance for the IMF and the world at large of completing the creation of the enlarged access facility of the IMF, which was to be funded by the Saudi loan, but he was not at all certain that the very demanding conditions could be achieved.

I stayed in Washington for close to two weeks, seeing Secretary Regan every few days for a progress report on the state of negotiations. I knew Secretary Regan well enough to know that he was having a very difficult time, but of course he did not reveal to me which of the G5 countries were being the most difficult, nor did he explain, when he had successfully concluded the negotiations, what final quota concessions were made by individual countries to achieve agreement to Saud Arabia's "informal conditions."

I was deeply impressed that Secretary Regan had managed to achieve the agreement that ensured the consummation of what was clearly a historic financial transaction, urgently needed to provide emergency financing to the developing world. These resources were important for the international financial system to assist developing countries to adjust. Saudi Arabia claimed to represent the developing world. I favored this and other changes at the IMF that would empower emerging market countries. My admiration only increased over the intervening years, during which, as undersecretary of treasury for international affairs, one of my primary responsibilities was U.S.–IMF policy, including subsequent quota negotiations. Don Regan accomplished a remarkable transformation within the IMF; nothing like it had been done before, and nothing like it has been done since, despite the fact that we are now in the new post-crisis world of rising emerging nations and need a new alignment more than ever.

The Saudis, despite their deeply conservative approach to personal relations in the world of finance, were ecstatic. When I returned to Riyadh, the governor called me up to his office to express his thanks for an outcome that would transform Saudi Arabia's position in the world. Its valuable role as the chief recycling agent in the world after the oil price adjustment was now formally recognized in the world's premier international financial institution. Saud Arabia was now the leading representative of the developing world, and its position and constructive role in the emerging global market was recognized and institutionalized in the IMF. I was taken aback by the strength of feeling expressed to me and by the open gratitude the governor conveyed for my role in this historic transformation.

A few days later, I was asked to go to the office of Minister of Finance Sheikh Mohamed Abakhail, who expressed similar views and thanked me profusely for my efforts. I still remember with particular feeling his remark that Saudi Arabia would not have achieved this without me, that they would be forever in my debt, and if there was anything I ever needed I was simply to say so. I walked out of the minister's office with an overwhelming sense of pride that the years of patience, austere living, isolation, and sometimes frustration had come to this moment of deep personal satisfaction. I have never repeated this story until you, the reader, read it today. I knew that like the "informal conditions" of the loan, these sentiments would never be written down, never repeated. They were and remain mine to have and to hold.

There was yet another chapter to this story of the SAMA–IMF loan, one that was harder to accept, but which in no way detracts today from my positive memory of this important event. In late April the governor called me to his office to explain that with the closing date of the loan rapidly approaching, (May 1), he felt that I should return to Washington, take a hotel room, and simply stand by in case any last-minute hitches should develop in the days leading up to the closing. Once again I took up my position at the Sheraton Carlton. I stayed in touch with Treasury, though not with Secretary Regan, and with the IMF management staff to check that the loan documentation was being finalized as agreed. Mr. Fritz Link, partner at Davis Polk in New York, which acted in those years as SAMA's chief U.S. legal advisor, was also present in Washington.

In the course of my visits to the IMF I became aware that the closing of our loan was to be a very big occasion. Governors of the IMF were congregating for the event (and also for the spring meeting of the IMF and World Bank), and I learned from junior members of the IMF staff that there was to be a black tie dinner extravaganza to celebrate the enlarged access facility and the closing of the Saudi loan. The governor of SAMA and the finance minister of Saudi Arabia would be attending, and so it seemed would IMF staff down to the most junior levels.

I had not brought a black tie. Should I plan to rent one? The great day approached, the governor and minister arrived, and I waited, along with Fritz Link, who had done the legal work, for our invitations. The invitation didn't come, and the governor did not contact me when he arrived in Washington. Should I call the governor to remind him I was still in town? On reflection, I thought better of it, reminding myself of both my experience in Saudi Arabia and the nature of our assignment in Saudi Arabia. We had been hired six years earlier as advisors. We were to be neutral advisors insofar as business relations with the finance industry were concerned. We were to maintain absolute confidentiality and though never asked in so many words, I had understood that we were to remain in the background, that it would be damaging to the Saudis and to us to court the publicity so easily attainable in those days because of the secrecy, mystery, and financial power the world's media had come to associate with Saudi Arabia and its billions of dollars of wealth.

The call from the governor never came. The gala dinner was held in the giant atrium of the IMF on 19th Street, and even the junior staff of the IMF attended with their spouses or friends. Fritz Link and I had dinner together in a K Street restaurant, sharing a couple of good bottles of wine for our own rather subdued celebration—the hired hands for the largest private placement the world had ever seen. No explanation or apology was ever made to me by SAMA's senior management, despite the glowing statements of gratitude expressed six weeks earlier.

Those glowing statements, I realized as soon as the closing event was past, were truly private, like almost everything else in Saudi Arabia. There could be no public acknowledgement of my role, or even a private reminder. I had learned in graphic terms the lesson that lay at the root of Ronald Reagan's well known adage, "There is no limit to what a man can do or where he can go if he doesn't mind who gets the credit." I would repeat this lesson again, many times while serving in government and working in the "cut and thrust" atmosphere of investment banking. I had discovered that for me the thrill of hard work paying off was to see an important idea or an initiative succeed, to make its mark at an important moment in the real world.

During my last several years in Saudi Arabia, some friends offered their view that I was staying too long in the kingdom. I could see and feel their point, especially in the last two years; yet I stayed on, fascinated by the continuing building process at SAMA. With some changes in the members of the team, the growing confidence of the Saudi leadership, and the diversification and far greater efficiency of our investment operations, the odyssey of the years of vast liquidity, of careful, disciplined living conditions, and hard work, together with the growing ease of working with the Saudis, brought me a continuing and special incentive to see this great enterprise through.

In Riyadh I lived in the village of Diriyah, some nine miles out into the desert. Diriyah was set in Wadi Hanifa, a draw cut into the flat surface of the empty desert. Diriyah was in an oasis with thousands of date palms that only became visible as one approached the lip of the wadi, the dry stream bed that separated the ruins of the palaces of the ancient House of Saud from the village, which itself was chiefly constructed of mud.

I had found the empty structure in Diriyah that became my house in 1978 when SAMA moved its headquarters to Riyadh from Jeddah. The house itself was of cement construction and set in approximately ten acres of closely planted date palms. Some fifty feet across an open courtyard was a tall mud house with two-foot-thick walls and two large, high-ceilinged rooms. These rooms had shuttered windows that looked outside into the palms and interior shuttered windows and an old double door that joined the two rooms together in an attractive way. The rooms had beamed ceilings with palm fronds laid across the beams to hold in place the mud and plaster surface of the flat roof.

If one loved the pastel colors and clean lines of the desert and the whole idea of the remote desert kingdom, this was the perfect place to make a private refuge. After difficult negotiations with the emir of the village, an aged Saudi who had, it was said, fought with King Abdulaziz when Riyadh was taken and Saudi Arabia unified in 1932, the house was mine. Working with local tradesmen, I set about the renovation of the two buildings. In the house, we removed the wall that divided two of the large sitting rooms to make a fifty-six-foot living room. The house was built in the shape of a U with the living room forming the top of the U. By placing large French doors at virtually all the main window openings of the house, one could look out from anywhere in the house into the rows of date palms that ran right up to the house on three sides. One could see and walk from the rooms out into the courtyard that joined the main house to the mud house in which were placed the dining room, kitchen, and a reception room furnished only with carpets and pillows for informal lounging in the Saudi manner.

I lived in Diriyah for five years, and the house became a central part of my rather isolated private life in Arabia. Immediately across the wadi, just beyond the palm grove that surrounded the house, stood an old deserted village on a slope that rose to the surface of the desert. The old village lay in ruins, the houses and palaces partly fallen down. The village lanes were of fine-packed sand. There were alleys, courtyards, tall sections of palace walls, and wooden doors that creaked open and closed in the evening winds that seemed always to precede sunset in the great Nafud desert. Each evening at sunset I would jog across the wadi up through the deserted village and out into the open desert with its limitless horizon. I could run toward the horizon, across the gravel surface of the desert, with the feeling that apart from my breathing and the passing gravel surface beneath my feet, it could seem that I was not moving at all, so great was the infinity of open space. I made these runs shortly before sunset to minimize the effect of the blistering sun and desert heat, but I was treated each evening to the perfectly round sun setting soft red through the dusty haze of the desert evening. On the return leg of my run, in the softening heat of the day, the call for evening prayers spread out over the village from several small mosques just outside the garden walls of my house. Then it was back to work in Riyadh, listening during the drive to books on tape, and coming home late to a Scotch and Perrier and a solitary dinner prepared and left for me by Hassan, the cook. So went the six days of the week, with Friday set aside for reading and the preparation of our team's expense accounting to be sent each month to New York.

I paint this picture to convey the austere isolation of my life in Arabia. During the day there were many visitors and negotiations, meetings, and the daily action of markets to be observed and understood. There were dinner parties, too, with team colleagues and visitors, complete with homemade wine and beer. But there was a great deal of time alone—to read, think, and reflect on my participation in the historic transformation of the global economy, on its personal cost to me and my family, and on developments in the outside world.

It was clear to me from the distance of Saudi Arabia that the Carter years had been a disaster for the United States, but I was focused on a different phenomenon, which with each passing month was becoming increasingly clear. A revolutionary transformation was unfolding in world financial markets. It had been gradually building since the shock that followed the 1973 and then the 1979 oil price increases. We at SAMA had ceaselessly applied our efforts to broadening SAMA's investment footprint in the world, unaware in the initial years of the impact that we and the petrodollar recycling process were having on world markets. The access privileges SAMA enjoyed with the leading governments of the world had permitted SAMA to become a truly global investor in virtually all the major markets of the world. In the aftermath of the oil price shocks and the need for developed countries to finance their severe balance of payments problems and seek to restore growth in their depressed economies, national authorities in country after country began to embrace deregulation of their financial markets, opening their national markets to cross-border investors. The effect was that over time the various national markets had joined themselves to the spreading global market.

Meanwhile, vast flows of dollars had been accumulating in Western banks, rendering them flush with liquidity they could not easily deploy in their home markets, where low growth and stagflation still dominated economic expectations. The big banks found new markets for their liquidity in the developing world, especially in Latin America. SAMA's large-scale lending had been confined rigorously to relatively short-term deposits with thirty-five of the world's largest banks; marketable government bonds in the world's leading developed country markets; medium-term private placements with leading western governments and triple-A-rated international corporations; and finally to a growing number of equity and fixed-income accounts in the leading financial markets of the world, managed under conservative guidelines to limit excessive risk. Currency diversification away from the U.S. dollar, although a constant priority in these years, never exceeded 15 to 20 percent of total holdings. One result of this investment profile, pursued assiduously over some seven years despite huge current spending by Saudi Arabia on its own development, was a portfolio by 1980 of over $130 billion, invested consistently in accordance with the broad investment profile. SAMA was a conservative investor. In fact, we advisors had a private slogan that perfectly defined the limits of our investment philosophy: "No lending south of the Rio Grande." And certainly not to Africa or other marginal areas, such as Korea or even southern Europe. Financial flows to other countries in the Middle East or to Pakistan and Indonesia were viewed as political operations, essentially grants dressed up as loans, and not included in SAMA's main investment portfolio.

Yet another result of this profile and its associated policies was that in SAMA's view it was the responsibility and the business of the leading banks themselves to assess the risks of Third World and other types of more exotic lending. It was SAMA's mission to protect its liquid financial resources from credit risk, market risk, and, to the extent possible, from the vagaries of inflation, which by 1980 was one of the western world's greatest challenges. Thus we watched the competition among the big banks of Europe, North America, and Japan to deploy the liquidity provided by us for their lending business in the developing world. Many countries of dubious credit quality were able to negotiate massive loans from large syndicates of international banks at spreads which over time appeared to us to border on the ridiculous. I recall our amazement when Brazil managed to put in place a multi-billion-dollar medium-term credit facility at an interest rate set only three-eighths of one percent above the London Interbank base rate (LIBOR).

SAMA was constantly approached by banks to participate in these syndicated loans but consistently declined to be drawn in on the argument that we made deposits with the banks, and it was up to them to make the complex credit judgments that we had neither the inclination nor the expertise to make.

In August 1982, after seven years of the growing LDC financing boom by the big banks, Mexico defaulted on its sovereign debt, and Brazil followed into the abyss a few weeks later. In the short space of a few months, virtually the whole of Latin America was in crisis, as were other heavily indebted developing countries, such as Korea. The IMF, the World Bank, and the leading finance ministries and central banks around the world were suddenly faced with a global financial crisis that threatened to destabilize world markets and break the world's banking system.

In the case of Brazil, SAMA was approached by the Bank for International Settlements (BIS) in Switzerland and by the U.S. Treasury to participate in a large syndicated bank loan to support Brazil in its moment of crisis. This was our first, and as I recall, only loan directly to a South American country. SAMA agreed to put up $250 million and to take the longest maturity tranch of the loan, in short, to be the last participant to be repaid. This seemed to me to convey an exploitive attitude by the other lenders. Likewise, I was not impressed by the condescending attitude of the BIS. We had asked that loan documentation be in line with our established practices, including the issue of potentially marketable securities. This request riled a senior British staff member of the bank, who telephoned to say in the best dismissive English: "You don't understand, old boy—we do these things on the back of an envelope." My answer was that we do them with appropriate documentation and in accordance with established SAMA practices. In the end we did the Brazilian loan participation our way.

The international debt crisis, as it was soon called, the peaking of dollar interest rates, the collapse of global commodities prices, and the U.S. recession that followed the election of Ronald Reagan all served to crystallize for me the extraordinary fact that we were witnessing the emergence of a truly global economy underpinned by an embryonic global financial market that began to greatly enhance free capital flows across national borders. Regulatory oversight could not keep up with the speed and magnitude of this transformation. It could also be argued that bank management and risk managers also could not keep up. This market had at first appeared to be available only to SAMA, with its special status as a central bank of issue, or as one might say today, the world's largest and most global sovereign wealth fund. In fact, a far larger market had been following SAMA without the visibility and publicity that had attended the OPEC petrodollar recycling process. Press articles that speculated on the threat that Saudi Arabia might withdraw its money from the U.S. Treasury market clearly had no idea of how global markets were actually functioning.

These changes seemed to bring about yet another development

for me in Saudi Arabia. During my last four years there was greater interest shown by top levels of the Saudi government (royal family) in the broader geopolitical issues that the growing influence of Saudi Arabia was having in the world. Saudi Arabia's own development was now proceeding on a large scale. The $25 billion gas gathering project on the Arabian Gulf side of the country, the new port and city at Yanbu on the Red Sea coast, new airports in both Riyadh and Jeddah, and road and general construction all over the country drew attention to Saudi Arabia's ambitious drive for development and also brought countless large-scale business opportunities to international companies. Military equipment purchases by the Saudi government also exploded in these years.

A result of this growing confidence and openness in Saud Arabia was that I began to have periodic one-on-one meetings outside SAMA with a senior member of the Saudi royal family. These private visits were very interesting, because our discussions focused on the broad economic and political issues of the day as they impacted Saudi Arabia then and in the future. We also discussed SAMA investment policies, currency issues, and other financial themes, which conveyed to me the care and strong interest that the Saudi leadership took in their investment policies. I had always found in my years at SAMA that the Saudis wished to be seen as constructive global investors, in addition to looking after their own particular interests. These meetings confirmed that view, so that even today after years of new financial history I always take care to explain the responsible and sensitive attitude the Saudis displayed toward international investment in the nine years I served at SAMA.

Finally, the most important development for me was a rendezvous with God's great good fortune. Returning to Saudi Arabia from a vacation in the United States in 1979, I boarded a flight and met Jeannie Simmons, who became my wife and loving partner of now thirty-five years. It was love at first sight. Though our conversation on board the flight was brief, when I returned to the United States after four months in Saudi Arabia I called her. She answered as if we had met only yesterday. As we were both in the process of divorce, there began a lengthy long-distance courtship that ended in marriage some five years later. I stayed on in Saudi Arabia and met Jeannie from time to time outside the kingdom. An unmarried woman could not obtain a visa at that time to visit Saudi Arabia, so we remained separated for long periods of time. Telephoning was difficult, expensive, and not very private, and mail was not a practical alternative for regular communication.

Work continued. The Reagan administration, then in its third year, began to find its feet and I began to give serious thought to leaving Saudi Arabia. It seemed inevitable that I would have to reenter the investment banking business by returning initially, at least, to Merrill Lynch. I had been treated very well by Merrill Lynch, but it was a huge firm, quite unlike the small international investment bank I had started with in London in the eurobond days. Once again, I was looking for a transition back into America after years away and being out of touch with the most elemental things going on in American life.

Once again, passing opportunities intervened. When Secretary of Treasury Don Regan heard I was leaving SAMA, he asked me to stop in Washington. His assistant secretary for international affairs, Mark Leland, was leaving Treasury to manage the investment funds of the Getty family. Don asked whether I would come to Treasury to do the international job. He flattered me by saying I knew more about world capital movements than anyone else, and in any case I should come and help solve the Latin American debt crisis, which to some extent was a result of the liquidity provided to Western banks by the OPEC countries.

I admired Don and, perhaps more important, had become very impressed by President Reagan. From my White House Fellowship days I knew the job at Treasury to be challenging and important. But I would be entering the Reagan administration at the beginning of his last year in office before the election of 1984. Could I make something of the job in that short time? What were the chances that he would be elected for a second term? The outlook in late 1983 was not particularly favorable. How could I move from a short stint at Treasury back into investment banking? Should I be trading on my fresh background at SAMA now for a top job in investment banking? Was I throwing away leverage that would carry great weight in Wall Street? Could I get confirmed by the Senate in view of my long service in Saudi Arabia and unfounded rumours that I had enforced the Arab "blacklist" against investment that might benefit Israel? Would I survive public scrutiny with my unusual, possibly sensitive background to achieve Senate confirmation?

Once again, I referred back to my base of practical experience and my willingness to embrace the unknown and confidence that I could take on any new job and make a reasonable success of it. The passion for learning that I had discovered at Lawrence, expanded at Oxford, and exploited in Africa, the White House Fellowship Program, and in Arabia and international finance took over. Here was an opportunity to transition back to America after nine years in the desert, a chance to learn, to grow—possibly a short-lived chance because of the election just eleven months away, but a real chance nonetheless. Besides, I felt I had a duty as a former White House Fellow to serve if asked. That, after all, was the essential idea of the White House Fellowship Program—I would be serving my country; what higher calling could there be?

I told Don Regan I would be honored to be named Assistant Secretary of Treasury for International Affairs and went to Washington to obtain the forms to be completed for the clearance process. Over the years many friends and colleagues had said to me, "How will you ever adjust from the huge numbers you handle in Saudi Arabia to the small numbers of Wall Street?" Now I had the answer: "I'm going to Treasury, where there are just as many zeroes—even though they are on the other side of the balance sheet!"

In October 1983 I advised the Saudis that I would be leaving at the end of the year to take up my new position at Treasury. They were impressed and extremely pleased. Among other things, this was the position at Treasury that oversaw the functioning of the U.S. Saudi Joint Economic Commission. I labored over the White House and FBI forms for weeks on end to reconstruct my previous life back to the time of my birth and all my global movements. I was both amused and irritated by the requirement that I provide all the addresses at which I had received mail back to 1930 (I was born in

1937) and the dates and periods of every visit to every foreign country I had ever made. I also had to describe the nature of my employment at SAMA over the past eight years. As I was an employee of White, Weld and later Merrill Lynch, "seconded" to SAMA, it was not easy to describe my status to an institutionally suspicious FBI.

I knew it would be difficult to leave Saudi Arabia, despite the many limitations on my life and the frustrations of working in the kingdom. But in my final three months there was a very happy, deeply memorable experience that made leaving easier.

At my periodic meetings with the senior member of the royal family, our meeting always concluded with same exchange: "Remember, David, if there is anything you need please let us know," to which I had always responded that there was nothing that I needed, thank you. On this occasion I suddenly responded differently to my friend.

"There is something I would like," I heard myself saying. "There is a lady I am going to marry. She is single and I know single women almost never obtain a visa to Saudi Arabia. I need help packing up my things of these past now nearly nine years, and I would like her to see the Kingdom of Saudi Arabia and how I have lived here these past years."

My friend smiled beneath his spotless white *ghutra* and said, "Please give her name to my secretary outside and a visa will be ready at the New York consulate in the morning." This was the kind of grand Saudi statement that I loved! But bear in mind that for all my years in Arabia, obtaining a visa to visit for anyone was always a difficult and uncertain process. I had never heard of a visa being issued overnight, let alone to a single lady. There was, he said, one condition that I would have to agree to, namely that Jeannie could not stay with me and that she would have to be delivered each evening by 10 p.m. to her room at a government hotel. I agreed at once, and he said, "I will write this visa tonight myself, though it will be in the name of my private secretary as sponsor. I hope you understand that it should not be in my name."

"Can you imagine!" I said to Jeannie that night on the phone.

"You must call the consulate in New York tomorrow to see if it is there." She did, and to our astonishment the visa was there for Miss Jeannie Simmons, ready for collection at her convenience!

Jeannie came to Riyadh twice in those last three months (the visa was multiple entry) and arranged the packing and shipping of all my possessions and papers, including the two Mercedes automobiles I had acquired. She stayed in the government hotel, was there every night before 10 p.m., and was given a room only a few yards away from the front desk. We shared Thanksgiving together in Diriyah on the veranda that opened into the palm trees, and I bought three perfect giant white chrysanthemums, imported at $50 each to decorate our table. Jeannie, appropriately wearing a black abaya, moved around Riyadh, dealt with Saudis to arrange shipping and closing up the house, and saw my life that we had so often spoken about during the years of our courtship.

7

Treasury

The move from Riyadh to Washington took place over a long weekend in early January 1984. It was like stepping into a beehive from an isolated glade. On my first day I met Deputy Assistant Secretary for International Monetary Affairs Charles Dallara, a life-long friend ever since who has enjoyed a distinguished career in both government and the private sector. It was Charles's job to begin my briefing while I awaited clearance from the FBI, formal nomination by the White House, and confirmation by the Senate Finance Committee. Charles was a mine of information and provided me with six thick briefing books. I was amazed by the breadth and diversity of subject matter that lay before me, and Charles, to his great credit, was as good a listener as he was a teacher.

I spent nearly nine years at the U.S. Department of Treasury, serving as the senior international economic policy official under two presidents and three secretaries of Treasury. At my departure reception it was said that I was the longest-serving presidential appointee at Treasury in the twentieth century. I am not sure of the accuracy of that record, but serving first as assistant secretary for international affairs and then as undersecretary, I was at Treasury for what by U.S. government standards was a very long time. January 1983 to November 1992 was an important period in U.S. economic and financial affairs; I saw a lot and made my mark.

President Reagan in his first term accomplished a complete turnaround in America. Pride and patriotism replaced humiliation and abasement. Growth replaced stagflation. Job creation replaced layoffs.

Hope and optimism replaced disillusionment and demoralization. America and the energy and productivity of American life challenged the Soviet Union to a test of sustainable productive power. America was back as the leader of the free world.

We weren't in paradise. There was arrogance and ignorance about the world. There were overbearing attitudes and policy shortcomings. But without doubt there was energy and vision. One could feel the energy of America's recovery, and at Treasury one could find no greater optimist for America's future than Secretary Don Regan. He held all-hands staff meetings several times a week. He was bouncy, combative, demanding, and inspiring. I quickly learned about the full range of Treasury policy areas and initiatives. When Don Regan left a year later to become chief of staff for the president I presented him with a cartoon that portrayed these entertaining staff meetings with the caption, "All firearms to be checked at the door."

Opportunities and challenges lay in all directions. The debt crisis in Latin America now included virtually every country in the region, and its fallout risk to the world's banking system was a shared concern to the governments of all the leading developed countries. Argentina and Peru were the poster children for bad behavior in a continent of bad behavior. President Reagan's dialogue with Japan was just being launched in the form of the yen-dollar talks, which I chaired for eight years. Plans were underway for the Treasury to sell special Treasury issues in Europe, and the G5 economic policy dialogue sought to reconcile widely different economic policy regimes among the leading nations that were thought to be driving the growing misalignment and volatility of currencies.

It was an exciting moment, a bright revelation and confirmation of the growing global market I had seen developing during my years in Saudi Arabia. We had moved across the edges of national boundaries into a budding world economy with growing markets for both goods and finance. A new or strengthening trend somewhere in the world had a result that mattered somewhere else.

Saudi Arabia's liquidity had flooded Western banks, who, in turn, had over-lent to a capital-hungry developing world. Recession in the West was followed by a collapse in commodity prices. Interest rates and inflation peaked at record levels in the United States in 1981, but after a painful recession, growth in America returned in high gear, and we began importing virtually everything under the sun. Japan prospered, building a massive trade surplus, and Germany was attacked for having inadequate domestic demand-led growth, importing too little and tolerating too easily a high structural unemployment rate. Stock markets, currencies, commodities, syndicated bank loans—all were now cross-border businesses whose global implications were not generally understood by either the man in the street or by the political class in Washington. If one wanted to know what would happen next in the American economy and its financial markets, one had to study and understand what was happening in other parts of the world. It seemed to me we had arrived at a new place: the beneath-the-surface global market I had worked in the past fifteen years was breaking into the open, establishing itself as a political as well as a financial reality. I felt in my element, ready to participate and to make my mark in this fast-moving transformation.

The opening economic dialogue with Japan was an immediate case in point. My experience with Japan at SAMA suggested that the way to change Japan was not to engage them endlessly on trade issues, but instead to convince them to expand and liberalize their financial markets and to push them to permit wider international use of the yen for both trade and investment transactions. At the same time we would need to seek broader and deeper access for foreign financial players in Japan's financial markets. The structure of Japan's very successful economy and its ability to manage—some said to manipulate—its currency was closely tied to its strict and comprehensive control of its financial markets and currency.

What had struck me while working at SAMA was the speed with which Japanese commercial and investment banks had evolved their attitudes and approach to SAMA in order to establish and develop new business relations. The first large transaction for Japan's government with Saudi Arabia, a $1 billion-dollar five-year Bank of

Tokyo CD, with the bank acting on the government's behalf, was completed in early 1975. Afterward SAMA's relations with Japan's commercial banks expanded dramatically, including direct access for SAMA to the Japanese government's Yen bond market. Japanese investment banks then besieged SAMA to open transactional business relations. They were constant visitors at regular intervals and clearly had instructions to break into SAMA's business flow at all costs. Leonard Ingrams, our colleague from Baring Brothers, possessed an extremely sharp wit, reminding us from time to time that the thumping sound we sometimes heard on our building was nothing less than Japanese bankers parachuting by the dozens onto our roof.

There was an obsessive interest in winning an equity or fixed-income managed portfolio mandate from SAMA, similar to the ones we had established with several U.S., UK, and European asset management groups. At first, the Japanese presentations and booklets were poorly prepared and presented, but gradually this changed over several years, with the Japanese firms submitting presentations and proposals more comparable to those of the big Western banks' fund investment mangers.

At Treasury, our early yen-dollar meetings with the Japanese vice-minister of finance and all the Ministry of Finance's director generals were very formal and somewhat stilted, producing little beyond repeated explanations of why they could not agree to make changes to their system. Yet with patience and by highlighting their own potential self-interest in change, it seemed we could make progress with Japan. After all, if there was one thing I had mastered in Arabia, it was patience.

And so began a process of engagement with Japan that went on for eight years. Essentially, we had a three-point agenda with Japan:

1. Encourage Japan to permit the broader use of its currency for international financial transactions.

2. Get Japan to agree to authorize the inclusion of foreign financial firms, banks, investment banks, and institutional money managers in Japan's markets and in yen-denominated international transactions. We also sought agreement with Japan that foreign firms doing

business in Japan would receive more liberal treatment to enable them to participate more fully in Japan's domestic capital market.

3. Press Japan to liberalize and promote the restructuring of its domestic capital market.

If through these negotiations we could achieve a more level playing field for U.S. financial firms with and inside Japan, broaden the use of the yen internationally for trade and investment, and free up and diversify Japan's internal financial markets, Japan would grow more quickly and become more closely linked with world markets.

These changes would also provide Japanese citizens many more options for the investment of their very substantial savings rather than restricting them to Japan's massive one-size-fits-all low-paying postal savings system. The theory was that if domestic investment in Japan could be strengthened and diversified, and if the yen could be more widely used internationally, this combination of change would over time work to soften Japan's export-driven, surplus-building economic model.

Meetings were held every six months, usually in Tokyo, where we had concluded that by facing off with a wide range of officials at the director general level in the Ministry of Finance (MOF) we could make better progress. Meanwhile, our homework in the Treasury's international department was extremely thorough. We needed to master our understanding of their system in order to counter the micromanagement approach of the MOF. We needed proposals and reasoning for permitting greater freedom in Japan's financial markets. We proposed that Japan's restricted bank certificate of deposit market should be liberalized to remove the requirement that banks had to endorse the transfer of their CD's from one owner to another in the secondary market. We also advocated for smaller, more tradable denominations for CD's.

Japan's treasury bill market was reserved only for the very largest investors. We pushed for denominations to be reduced from the minimum ¥1 million denomination to something closer to the $1,000 denominations in the U.S. treasury market. Eventually the Japanese agreed to introduce commercial paper but initially only for long maturities of 180 days and in very large denominations. By way of comparison, the bulk of the highly liquid U.S. commercial paper market had maturities of approximately 30 days and was available for U.S. investors in small denominations. We urged that Japan introduce banker's acceptances, again in small denominations and relatively short maturities to improve liquidity to support product trade in yen.

There were negotiations to permit foreign firms to act as comanagers and even lead managers of samurai bond issues, the equivalent in yen of eurodollar bonds. No restrictions existed in the eurobond market regarding the nationality of lead management firms for issues in different currencies. The Japanese restricted leadership only to Japanese investment banks. Likewise, foreign investment managers were not permitted entry to Japan's large and lucrative market for pension fund and other institutional investment management.

Each of these proposed innovations had to be painfully negotiated with Japanese officials, who often were obstructive in their approach, giving long and detailed explanations of why these types of liberalizations were neither welcome nor required in Japan. Despite the hard work and frustrations, however, relations between us remained good. We were always treated courteously and shown genuine hospitality. Elaborate dinners were served with delicious Japanese food. Sake, beer, and Scotch flowed freely, and I can remember singing country and western tunes with Finance Minister Hashimoto as smiling geishas looked on.

Early in our negotiations there was a moment of seminal understanding. Undersecretary Beryl Sprinkel was still at Treasury at the time before becoming the president's chief economic advisor. He was leading the first of our meetings. The Japanese side, headed by Vice-Minister Oba, was arranged across the other side of the long table. Dozens of young MOF officers with listening devices held to their ears were seated in the lounge outside the meeting room. The simultaneous translation process conducted from a booth in the corner of the room ensured a long delay before the message of one side was understood by the other. We were always heavily outnumbered, as the international area of the U.S. Treasury was smaller and a much less complicated place than Japan's Ministry of Finance.

Mr. Oba was explaining for at least the twentieth time the importance of the gradual "step by step" approach to change in Japan. Beryl Sprinkel, an outspoken man with a rich base voice, lost his patience with this elaborate system of effective denial.

"I grew up in Missouri on a dirt farm," boomed Beryl. "When we got new pups we had to cut their tails off. When we cut them off we didn't cut them off one inch at a time! This would just hurt the puppies more. We just hacked them off once up at the top and that was the end of it."

We waited for the translation to arrive in the headsets across the table. When it did there was a look of shock and a sharp collective intake of breath followed by total silence. All the director generals looked up the table to Mr. Oba for a response. After what seemed a very long pause, Mr. Oba broke into laughter, which immediately spread down the length of the table. The next day Mr. Oba announced that the Japanese team had understood the story of the "dogs' tails," and that the Japanese approach would now be changed from "step by step" to "stride by stride." This too produced general laughter, but Mr. Oba and later Toyoo Gyohten stuck to this commitment. Over the years, when we reached a difficult impasse requiring decision, a voice from across the table would sometimes come: "Oh . . . we understand—dog's tail," followed by general laughter.

Gradually we moved forward. Most of the changes we advocated were accepted, although often in a form that would not be as fully effective as we had hoped. The one point of the agenda that was not accomplished was our advocacy for a transformation of the structure of Japan's banking system, which strictly divided commercial banking from investment banking and brokerage. But at least Japanese savers and investors had more options for investing their savings in instruments other than postal savings, the financier of Japan's fiscal deficits. More importantly, we had achieved widespread access and equal treatment for U.S. and other foreign financial firms, which stayed in place and fundamentally altered the playing field in global markets. And finally, through this and other follow-up initiatives that engaged the Japanese on structural economic and trade issues, we saw Japan's giant surplus reduced by approximately two-thirds by the late 1980s.

I describe the yen–dollar initiative at length because it so clearly illustrates how important it is in complex economic and financial relations between sovereign states participating in a global system to analyze carefully the underlying realties in play and then to pursue with imagination and perseverance the solutions needed to encourage change and cooperation.

I applied this approach frequently during my time at the Treasury to a number of major international economic policy challenges. Often we accomplished concrete, though usually imperfect, results. In my view it is precisely this careful analysis of realities, coupled with in-depth engagement and creative policy objectives, that has been so sadly lacking in the U.S. approach to the current global and domestic U.S. crisis. If you can't be bothered to look reality in the face and discipline yourself to address head-on those realities with carefully crafted policies that are right instead of popular or convenient, then one is condemned to flailing about with nothing more than pious posturing. This is what America has been treated to from 2007 into the present. The suffering, chaos, and lack of progress is there for all to see.

The first thing to be said about international economic policy coordination is that it is not quite right for what is required in an increasingly interdependent world economy and global financial system. Nevertheless, the phrase came into use as a term of art, and because it was not entirely accurate it came under easy attack from a number of sources. This falls in the category of angels on pinheads and opens the field to both serious debate and cheap-shot artists.

The fact is that this effort began under Treasury Secretary George Shultz, who created the Library Group in the 1970s. This group comprised the finance ministers of the Big Five nations—the United States, UK, Germany, France, and Japan—which first held its quiet, private, informal meetings in the library of the White House. In the period following the 1971 crisis, in which the dollar's fixed link to gold was severed, George Shultz, to his great credit, foresaw the need for dialogue between the leading economic powers on the deeply sensitive economic and related political issues that were emerging in an increasingly global economy with floating or at least semi-fixed exchange rates. These meetings were between principals only, without bureaucracy present and without public fanfare. Under this format and in this collegial atmosphere, ministers could engage in a constructive exchange of views and explanations of each other's particular problems and limitations.

The spirit of the Library Group was carried forward into the G5, which came to include each country's finance minister, central bank governor, and one finance deputy drawn from each country's finance ministry. In time, the group became more visible. By the time I joined Treasury, its rising visibility was beginning to be a problem. In part, this was because the group was less collegial, and the United States, under Secretary Regan and Beryl Sprinkel, had become significantly more aggressive, with the result that participants began to turn increasingly to the press to vent frustrations or to apply pressure on their counterparts to modify or to embrace particular policies. The stridency of the United States in pushing its supply-side, open-market philosophy created resistance and hostility among members, especially when sensitive issues became public. I was sympathetic with the policy positions of the United States but not to the often overbearing method of advocacy we adopted. Obviously, one could not be soft or excessively diplomatic, but neither could one have the claws out all the time. It was basically a question of the mix of patience, hostility, understanding, acceptance, and aggression that was wanting in the process, plus the need once again to succinctly and patiently present and understand the basic realities. Too often our case was simply "Be like us, do it like we do, and look how successful we are and how good this would be for you." Add a bit of jet lag, some media leakage, and a few glasses of wine, and the problems become pronounced.

In March 1985, after the reelection of President Reagan, Secretary Regan swapped jobs with James Baker, the president's chief of staff during the first term. The swap was accomplished almost immediately, and my first contact with the new secretary-designate was to meet with him in the White House to help prepare him for his

1. My portrait at age twelve in 1949, after my father sent me back for a retake with a crew cut and a V-neck sweater instead of a suit and tie.

2. Robert Lewis Mulford, my father, after his graduation from Lawrence College in 1932.

3. Home from a year at Oxford and Cape Town University, South Africa, visiting my mother, Mrs. Theo Mulford, in Rockford, Illinois.

4. (*Opposite top*) Gaining tough yardage as a Hall of Fame tailback at Lawrence University in 1958.

5. (*Opposite bottom*) Running to win. I was Midwest Conference 880-yard champion and permanent record holder for the half-mile at Lawrence University before starting my career in international affairs.

6. Pedaling out of Glasgow to Edinburgh on the first day of my trip to Europe as a student in the summer of 1958.

7. The day I received my Doctor of Philosophy degree in 1966 at the Sheldonian Theatre, Oxford University.

8. Trekking into Wadi As-Sirhan with a local Bedouin in the northern desert of Saudi Arabia, 1977.

9. With Secretary of Treasury Don Regan following our meeting with Finance Minister Bernardo Grinspun during the Latin American debt crisis in 1984.

10. With Jeannie on our wedding day, October 19, 1985, following our ceremony in historic rooms at the U.S. Treasury.

11. Briefing President Ronald Reagan, Treasury Secretary James Baker, and Secretary of State George Schultz at the Tokyo International Economic Summit, 1986. I served two presidents as a Sherpa for seven economic summits.

12. Meeting with Secretary of Treasury Nicholas Brady and President Ronald Reagan in the Oval Office to discuss economic policy.

13. President George H. W. Bush greets Jeannie and me for a private dinner upstairs in the White House family quarters in 1992.

14. With Secretary of Treasury Nicholas Brady and Federal Reserve Chairman Alan Greenspan as undersecretary of the Treasury for international affairs at the Kremlin to meet with President Mikhail Gorbachev during the crisis that brought about the end of the Soviet Union in 1991.

15. Signing the oath of office after being sworn in as U.S. ambassador to India, at the State Department, January 20, 2004. Also pictured are Jeannie's niece, Kaitlin Lang, and my grandson, David Mulford.

16. Sharing tea with President A. P. J. Abdul Kalam of India on the day I presented my credentials as U.S. Ambassador Plenipotentiary to India, at Rashtrapati Bhavan, New Delhi, February 2004.

17. Holding a child just after her immunization at a Rotary inoculation center in April 2004 during the fight to eradicate polio from India. Photo by STR, Getty Images.

18. With President George W. Bush as he meets Prime Minister of India Manmahon Singh in the Oval Office, July 18, 2005, with Vice President Richard "Dick" Cheney, Secretary of State Condoleezza Rice, and Undersecretary of State for Political Affairs Nicholas Burns.

19. Jeannie in July 2005, twenty days after her open-heart surgery, with First Lady Laura Bush and Gusharan Kaur, wife of the prime minister of India, in the Red Room of the White House during the prime minister's state visit to Washington.

20. (*Opposite top*) Introducing President George
W. Bush at Roosevelt House to begin his state
visit to India, February 28 to March 2, 2006.

21. (*Opposite bottom*) Greeting President
and Mrs. Bush at the state dinner given by
President of India Abdul Kalam in the Mughal
Gardens of Rashtrapati Bhavan, March 2, 2006.

22. (*Above*) Receiving the 2007 Sue M. Cobb
Award for Exemplary Diplomatic Service
presented in recognition of extraordinary
efforts to foster commercial ties with India
and with appreciation for my outstanding
management of Embassy New Delhi.

23. Leading India's first-ever Walk for Life to raise cancer awareness, Jeannie is joined by Mrs. Gursharan Kaur, wife of Prime Minister Manmohan Singh, New Delhi, February 10, 2008.

24. Receiving blessings from His Holiness the Dalai Lama and exchanging views following Chinese provocations of Tibetans in exile in India, June 2008.

25. Speaking with media representatives at the Ministry of External Affairs on November 29, 2008, after a meeting with Indian Foreign Secretary Shivshankar Menon. That morning, Indian commandos had killed the last remaining Islamic militants in Mumbai's Taj Hotel to end a devastating attack on India's financial capital that left 195 dead, including 22 foreigners. Photo by Manpreet Romana, Getty Images.

26. Welcoming U.S. Secretary of State
Condoleezza Rice on her visit to India,
December 3, 2008, following the Mumbai
attacks, which U.S. intelligence blamed on
a Pakistani-based militant group. Photo by
Raveendran, Getty Images.

Senate confirmation hearings. I liked Jim from the moment I met him in his White House office. My job was to ask him questions of the type members of the Senate Finance Committee might ask about Treasury policies, and my brief was that the more difficult these questions were, the better. My first question, therefore, was, "Mr. Baker, what qualifies you to deal with the extremely complex international issues you will be confronted with as secretary of Treasury?" His smiling answer was, "Seven international economic summits with the president of the United States and four years in the Marine Corps." We were off to a good start.

Secretary Baker was an entirely different personality from Don Regan. He was a skilled and experienced lawyer, an outstanding political operator, and very good with people of all kinds. He was always remarkably well prepared for the many and diverse meetings required of a Treasury secretary and seemed able to read every situation in a way to achieve maximum results. In short, he exercised power judiciously but with maximum effect. The more subtle and thoughtful approach to G7 issues was apparent immediately.

In February and March 1985 the long-strengthening dollar spiked to its peak against the deutschmark and the yen. U.S. current account and trade deficits were reported at new historic highs month after month. Strong growth in the U.S. economy and weak domestic demand growth in Germany and Japan, both of which were enjoying the export benefits of weak currencies, were feeding rising imbalances. Traditional U.S. manufacturing industries were being hit hard by the strong dollar, the term "rust belt" began to appear to describe the destructive pressure of an "overvalued" dollar on the manufacturing industries of the American Midwest, and protectionist forces gathered momentum in the U.S. Congress. Work began in Congress on an omnibus trade bill that promised the possibility of a comprehensive protectionist trade regime ostensibly to save U.S. jobs and to protect U.S. industry.

These were alarming developments for the administration and especially at Treasury, the keeper over many years of the U.S. commitment to free trade. Secretary Baker, who was sensitive to and well connected with members of Congress, immediately began to seek an effective means of strengthening macroeconomic policy cooperation with our major trading partners and in particular to bring about a more realistic alignment of global exchange rates to relieve the growing protectionist pressures in Congress.

This was no easy challenge. Previous overbearing U.S. attitudes within the G5 had left a residue of resistance and resentment. Continued strong growth in the U.S. exacerbated the prospect for continuing, if not growing, imbalances, and Treasury's passion for free-floating exchange rates, namely, a policy of no intervention in currency markets, seemed to leave us with little room for creative ingenuity on the international economic policy front.

This is where knowledge of the functioning of markets, their capacity to read and anticipate changing trends, and finally their susceptibility to unexpected surprise becomes invaluable to a policymaker who understands the power of open markets. I was just such a person, and with undersecretary Beryl Sprinkel now removed to the president's Council of Economic Advisors, and with a new secretary and deputy secretary of Treasury who were both deeply sensitive to the forces at work in Congress, the field was open for a new U.S. strategy in the international economic policy area. The components of any such strategy aligned themselves in my mind as follows.

It was obvious to me that we had arrived at the point where the emerging global financial market I had seen developing during my years in Saudi Arabia had now fully emerged. Despite this new reality, which could be seen every day influencing the world around us, the realities of a global financial market were not fully understood in Congress or in the political class generally. To put it in terms of stark simplicity, when Americans began a new day they did not check global exchange rate movements overnight before looking at prices in the U.S. stock market or other U.S. economic data. The Treasury, for reasons beyond my understanding when I arrived in early 1984, had closed down its foreign exchange desk. This meant that the Treasury was not a participant in foreign exchange markets. How, I wondered, could we expect to read foreign exchange markets if we were not a participant? How could we communicate with the market, or even send a message to the market, without the contacts and working knowledge provided by a full-time presence in the market. Even if we were not an active trader and were intent on convincing the market beyond all reasonable doubt that we would never intervene in markets to influence or "manipulate" the value of the dollar, why would we cut ourselves off completely from the market? Within the international area of the Treasury I found that we had neither in-house expertise on foreign exchange markets nor any significant institutional memory of that critical field of activity. Before long I had reestablished Treasury's foreign exchange desk and asked Jim Lister, a bright young economist with an interest in the functioning of markets, to open an ongoing dialogue with the market.

In the first quarter of 1985, Europe suffered one of its coldest winters on record, especially Germany. It was estimated that with construction activity in Germany near standstill in those freezing winter months that Germany would report a significant flattening of its already inadequate domestic-demand driven growth. It was this suppression of growth, which the market seemed to anticipate spilling into the second quarter's economic activity, that had driven the deutschmark to new lows against the dollar.

The yen peaked (reached a new low against the dollar) in April, a month or so behind the deutschmark. By May it could be said that the strengthening dollar had "overshot" any reasonable fundamental value, a statement that was based on market feel as much, if not more, than on fundamental economic analysis. When currency markets "overshoot," just as with any other market, speculative momentum, or herd behavior, may well carry forward for some indeterminate period.

As the second-quarter economic data unfolded in Germany, it suggested that a strong rebound was taking place that was not being fully reflected in foreign exchange markets. This was how I read the market situation in early June when I wrote Secretary Baker a memo outlining a new and dramatically different strategy for the United States to address the over valuation of the dollar.

U.S. economic policy in the first Regan administration was strongly driven by the belief that freely functioning markets were the best allocator of resources and the truest determinant of value. I was in general agreement with this market-based approach to economic policy. Following the debilitating years of the Carter administration, this refocus on market-driven activity as opposed to heavy-handed micromanagement by government was a necessary and welcome change, which in its full range of policy adjustment and change had brought vibrant growth back to the U.S. economy.

I did not, however, share the ideology that markets were perfect and would at all times and in all circumstances bring about correct and sustainable valuations in the shorter run. The Treasury of Don Regan and Beryl Sprinkel maintained a purist commitment to nonintervention in foreign exchange markets. The slightest consideration of market intervention was interpreted as challenging this basic philosophy and revealing a sinister belief that exchange markets, and therefore currency alignments, could and should be manipulated by governments. Intervention in foreign exchange markets by governments would be both damaging and completely ineffective.

I shared the view that markets could not be manipulated by central bank intervention. Daily trading volumes were far too large in modern markets to be manipulated by government intervention with perhaps impressive but essentially inadequate resources. Over time, currency values would reflect underlying economic fundamentals. However, the time element was important for me, and likewise the fact that markets are influenced by short-term developments and are reflective of trends often before a trend can be seen. In my view, one could and should communicate with markets and get on the inside of market thinking as a practitioner, as opposed to being simply an analyst. I also believed it was possible to signal markets as to underlying developments, not to manipulate or direct the market, but possibly to change its focus and priorities. Sending messages or signals to a market by government is an extremely sensitive matter, and if it is to be done must be done infrequently, with great skill, and especially with the right timing.

Given these considerations, I developed a proposal for changing the markets' perception of the currently high valuation of the dollar. When Europe, and especially Germany, reported their second-quarter economic figures and moved into the third quarter with more expansionist expectations, a trend would begin to be formed. Strong U.S. growth could coexist with strengthening domestic demand growth in Europe and Japan. If this pattern were sustained into the future and currencies began to realign, there would surely begin to be some adjustment of the world's large imbalances, which were driving the United States toward protectionist policies in the trade field that would very likely undermine prospects for world growth.

These trends would take time to materialize and become recognized as sustainable by markets. What was needed, in my view, was a message, preferably something of a "shock," to the markets that would significantly and immediately transform market psychology. If the United States was perceived to be in favor of these trends and willing to transform its previous ideologically driven attitudes that had undermined G5 cooperation efforts, the world would respond in due course to this more favorable prospect. More important, if this "message" could be conveyed in some dramatic form, backed up by firm evidence of this new policy cooperation, the effect might be achieved more quickly. If the message came in the form of a shock or very significant surprise, the effect might well be instantaneous. Changing the U.S. policy of many years' standing not to intervene with other major nations in foreign exchange markets would provide a message that markets could not ignore, especially if we achieved the all-important element of surprise.

This was the game plan for the Plaza Accord of September 25, 1985. Work began among the G5 deputies in July 1985 to see how much progress we could make with our European and Japanese colleagues in obtaining or encouraging clear policy commitments for stronger growth. If the United States held out the possibility of cooperative action in exchange markets, which the other G5 countries had been pushing for over the past four years, we might well achieve a credible critical mass of policy commitments from all the G5 countries. The deputies met repeatedly throughout July, August, and early September. It was long and exhaustive work, but for the first time, thanks to the patience, intellectual clarity, and political acumen of my G5 colleagues, I truly began to understand how complex, important, and hopeful the outlook could be if the U.S. could exercise its views more judiciously and with greater imagination. The necessary responses were never going to be all we hoped for, but the willingness to put commitments and expectations to paper for eventual public review was impressive.

Eventually, in September the critical mass of credible cooperative understandings was judged to be sufficient to lay the plan for a G5 finance ministers meeting at the Plaza Hotel at the time of the United Nations annual meeting and just prior to the annual meetings in Washington of the IMF and World Bank. The plan was shared on a "need to know" basis within the administration (a very small number of officials), and rigorous emphasis was placed on secrecy within the small G5 group of finance ministry and central bank officials. In the final weeks we negotiated the arrangements between us for intervention operations in the currency markets, setting the amounts each country was to provide as ammunition for these repeated interventions.

The Plaza Accord that September day in New York was the world's best-kept secret. The element of surprise was complete, the market effect immediate and dramatic, and the judgments of the written policy undertakings and observations were seen as credible evidence of change in markets in the weeks that followed. So stunning was the effect on currency markets that only a modest amount of the war chest resources agreed for market interventions by the central banks were deployed in the days and weeks that followed. The fact that the dollar had begun to move off its peak of the late spring was sharply accelerated into the balance of the year and through 1986. Eventually, the dollar declined by something close to 40 percent from its high against the other major currencies. Cynics and ideologues insisted that the currency adjustment would have happened anyway without the Plaza Accord, but these people did not understand the vital dynamics of markets, the importance and timing of trend identification by markets, and the influence these would have on political attitudes for the prospect of better international policy cooperation. I knew we had administered a successful market shock and that while we would not control foreign exchange markets or manipulate them, we had nevertheless successfully communicated with markets and demonstrated a new direction that in fact strengthened cooperation over the next few years. I was not troubled by the contrary opinions. I had played enough football to recognize Monday morning quarterbacks. Most of them never won a ball game.

The Plaza Accord won a big breakthrough for stronger international economic policy cooperation among the major countries and for the global economy as a whole. The dollar continued its downward adjustment for the next year, at which point as concern grew that perhaps the adjustment had gone far enough, we then agreed on a plan to stabilize currencies within certain broadly understood ranges.

This meeting, which became known as the Louvre Accord, took place at the Louvre in Paris in February, 1987. It was memorable for two developments. One was the successful inclusion in the G5 Group of two additional members, Canada and Italy. The second development was an understanding in the now G7 Group that we would establish certain appropriate ranges for our respective currencies in foreign exchange markets. If our currencies moved outside the consensus ranges, the understanding was that national policies would need to be reviewed.

This could not be a formal agreement announced in detail to the world at large, nor could it be treated as an arrangement to control particular targeted exchange rates. We would be attacked and tested by world markets if we set specific targets for exchange rates. Instead, we had established a general consensus about the value ranges that should be considered by our various central banks to encourage or even defend with joint intervention in markets as we moved forward. The chief value of this accord was that it focused attention on the desired policy objectives of each country, and while implying certain broad value ranges for currencies in markets, it did not provide precise, inflexible guidelines. All markets knew was that at the approximate but unconfirmed edges of these broad and flexible ranges there was a possibility of certain cooperative central bank intervention in markets. Importantly, because of the success of the

Plaza Accord and its aftermath in financial markets, G7 cooperation enjoyed high credibility in world markets.

The exercise in cooperation from Plaza to Louvre and beyond contributed greatly to a significant reduction in global imbalances. By 1991 Europe's surplus with the United States had all but been eliminated and Japan's large surplus had been cut by approximately two-thirds. Ministers and central bank governors now listened to each other and took seriously the group effort to recognize that each country's domestic policies had implications for the global economy and world markets that could not be ignored. Once again, there were many critics of global economic policy cooperation. My own assessment of our success, however, is that we made important progress in a difficult and uncertain world of interdependent sovereign nations, and that as a result the global economy was embarked on a sustainable course where conditions remained essentially benign for over a decade.

Another judgment I was to enjoy came from my mother midway through the Plaza to Louvre adjustment period. She called one day to say that she flew from Tucson to Chicago sitting next to a senior executive of a leading U.S. multinational corporation headquartered in Chicago. When she told the man that her son worked at the U.S. Treasury and gave him my name, she said he practically shouted, "Do you realize your son saved American jobs and the American manufacturing industry by the action he engineered at the Plaza?" She was proud, of course, but, true to form, asked me for a clearer explanation of exactly what had gone on at the Plaza Hotel.

When Brazil and Mexico were unable to meet their indebtedness obligations in 1982, the problems of overindebted nations reached as far as South Korea and to Africa, Poland, and the countries of Central America and the Caribbean. This international situation was frequently referred to as the Latin American debt crisis because over time it settled increasingly and most intractably in the countries of South America.

When I joined the Treasury, Secretary Regan had said to me,

"Come and help us solve the Latin American debt crisis," referring to the concentration of liquidity created by SAMA in the world's leading international banks between 1975 and 1982 that fueled over-lending to most Latin American countries. In early 1984, when I was getting my feet under me at Treasury, it was obvious that the debt crisis would be a continuing focus of concern and attention for some time to come. The total corpus of outstanding government debt in Latin America alone was roughly $400 billion and growing. The debt was held by large international syndicates of banks, running in size from 250 to perhaps 500 banks.

Each syndicate of banks was led by a steering group of some fifteen or sixteen of the largest banks, with two or three firmly in the position of lead managers or agent banks. At the time that the original loans were made these large and diverse syndicates were seen as sharing the country risk on a widely distributed basis, which was advertised as evidence of both prudence and safety in numbers.

As the crisis spread and became more entrenched the international diversity and sheer complexity of the large syndicates began to be increasingly apparent. U.S. banks accounted for roughly 32 percent of total exposure, the balance being spread to banks around the world. Although the syndicate agreements were seen as solid and dependable, the fact that banks of the various nations came under different national regulatory and supervisory regimes, as well as different tax and accountancy practices, gradually undermined the underlying consensus among the banks, even though they remained committed to the common syndicate agreement governing the original loan.

In the early years, 1982 to 1985, the treasuries and central banks of the leading creditor countries sought to keep the syndicates intact and exercise flexibility in their national oversight function with their own national banks. By not forcing a confrontation and instead playing for time, the very frightening threat to the stability of the world's banking system was carefully kept in hand. The chief requirement that governments faced was to ensure that through the common efforts of the IMF, the World Bank, and the banks themselves, the troubled debtor countries would remain current on payment of interest even though they could not hope to meet the demands for payment of principal required by their original agreements. If countries were able to establish an acceptable IMF adjustment programs and to sustain access to the World Bank for project loans and structural adjustment programs and thus be able to negotiate new money increments from the banks, then the countries could be kept afloat to reestablish growth, and the banks would not be forced to face the prospect of massive write-offs of their country loan portfolios.

In early 1984 we faced the first great test of this strategy, when in March it appeared that Argentina would not be able to meet its current interest payment requirement. Were this to happen, the banks would be forced to face the reality of default, and no additional new money flows to Argentina would be possible.

I was attending one of the early meetings of the U.S.–China joint economic commission in Beijing at the time. I was to travel from Beijing to Punta del Este, Uruguay, at the close of the commission meeting to attend the twenty-fifth annual meeting of the Inter-American Development Bank (IADB). This required flying for some forty hours from Beijing to Tokyo, to Los Angeles, to Miami, to Rio de Janeiro, and to Montevideo, with a two-hour drive to Punta del Este, to take part in the debt crisis debate. In the background, with five days until the end of March, stood Argentina as a potentially lethal threat to the ongoing credibility of the "debt strategy."

Argentine Minister of Finance Bernardo Grinspun was desperately playing for time, with stories about how Argentina was on the verge of selling two naval vessels to Iran to raise the funds. If Argentina had an IMF program at the time, I am sure new drawdown tranches had been put on hold, because the country was in a fiscal calamity, with inflation running at levels beyond all reasonable expectation. In fact, I recall buying a handful of one million Argentine peso notes for less than $1 each to distribute to young people in our family with a note informing them that they were now millionaires.

Meanwhile, I began a consultation process with Treasury colleagues, including Secretary Regan, to see if we could put together a bridge financing facility to provide Argentina with funds to meet its first-quarter interest obligations to the banks on March 31, 1984. This would require approximately $500 million to be provided in the next four days. The arrangement discussed was for four leading countries of Latin America (Brazil, Mexico, Colombia, and Venezuela) to put up $300 million for thirty days, supported by a backup guarantee of the U.S. Treasury. In addition, there would be $100 million of new money put up by eleven large international banks, led by Citibank, for 90 days, and $100 million paid by Argentina itself. Argentina was to commit to remaining in compliance with its IMF stabilization program.

It was decided that I should fly to Buenos Aires the next morning to meet with Argentine President Raúl Alfonsín. The meeting was to be arranged by U.S. Ambassador Frank Ortiz, who accompanied me late that afternoon to the Quinta de Olivos presidential residence, well outside of the center of Buenos Aires. The palace was set in spacious and beautiful grounds and had the appearance of an old-fashioned Argentine estancia. President Alfonsin, a small, very charming man, was clearly no economist. He did, however, recognize that Argentina would be in grave danger if it were cut off by the banks, which would also result in the choking off of support from the IMF and the World Bank. He agreed in principle to the terms I had outlined for the month-end bridge loan and instructed Minister Grinspun and the governor of Argentina's central bank to begin working with us at once to finalize the arrangements.

It was now Wednesday evening, and our deadline for completing and documenting the operation was close of business Friday night in New York. We began work that night at the embassy and in the offices of the central bank. Although I had a hotel room at the Sheraton, I never slept in my bed, returning only around 5 a.m. each morning to shave before going an hour later to the home of Minister Grinspun to review the documents we had worked on through the night. Each morning at the hotel, the room maid eyed me suspiciously because my bed was never slept in. Angel Gurria, from Mexico's ministry of the treasury, remained in Buenos Aires and was our critical link with Mexico and the other three countries providing the finance under the U.S. guarantee.

Documents had to be agreed on among all seven parties to the agreement, and the movement of funds to New York prior to the end of the day Friday, the last business day of the month, could not be completed until all details in the agreements had been resolved and each head of state or finance minister had authorized the transfer of funds to New York. As the deadline drew near, pandemonium developed as Citibank negotiated the finer points of the participation for each bank, many of which were spread around the world and with different agendas. Lloyds Bank, for example, resisted participating because it did not want to put up more new money for any Latin debtor country, especially one they regarded as responsible for the Falklands conflict. It was all banks in or no deal for the bank group. Among the four Latin lenders, the last to put in funds was Venezuela, at 2.25 Saturday morning. At 4:30 that morning, we obtained the last signature required in Argentina. In the end, the Clearing House Interbank Payment System (CHIPS), used for accomplishing daily settlements between banks, had to be kept open well into the night to permit the completion of the bridge loan.

I was exhausted, having been up for two full days, on top of more than forty hours of flying from China to Uruguay early in the week. The intensity of the effort left me with a sense of accomplishment. I had prevented a situation in which Argentina would have created unpaid arrears on its external debt, effectively defaulting and forcing what could well have been a far-reaching world financial crisis. On the other hand, I also understood that we had revealed in dramatic fashion the vulnerability of our international debt strategy. We were seeking to play for time for the debtor countries to engage in serious reform efforts and create new growth, and time for the banks to gradually reduce their exposure to indebted countries without being forced to suffer large-scale debilitating losses with highly adverse fallouts to the world's banking system.

Was this the right policy? At the time I believed it was, even though the flexibility permitted to the banks and indebted countries clearly violated sound banking principles and orthodox supervisory and regulatory standards among world governments and central banks. We had bought time but had not begun to actually solve the debt crisis challenge. The effort expended to make Argentina compliant with a technicality at a given moment in time was not a policy that could be applied across the board. We had passed an important crisis point and had demonstrated that governments in Latin America, who were themselves troubled debtors with scarce financial resources, had been willing to support the principle that the priority for everyone was to keep the financial system intact while a credible long-term solution to the debt crisis could be found.

It was this principle that motivated the launching of the Baker Plan the following year. As banks became less willing to continue providing enough new money to enable debtor countries to stave off default, banking syndicates were showing signs of strain. The Baker Plan sought to soften those strains by renewing a sense of commitment from the banks to continue to support the major debtor nations. Equally important in the plan was the renewal of support from the G5 countries to stay the course together, with the IMF and World Bank, by encouraging their banks to continue to provide new money to permit debtor countries to remain current.

The Baker Plan was announced with considerable fan fare at the IMF and World Bank annual meeting in Seoul, Korea, in October 1985, and for the next eighteen months it had more or less the desired effect of renewing the energy and commitment of the global banking community to work closely with their governments and the international financial institutions to avoid a global calamity. The chief objective of the plan was to encourage the large, multinational syndicates of banks to continue to provide new money to support existing IMF and World Bank adjustment programs. The other objective was to encourage all countries with lending banks in the syndicates not to take regulatory action precipitously that would force their banks to recognize book losses and start a flood of tax writeoffs that would shut down possible new money flows.

Nevertheless, the controversy surrounding the debt crisis continued to boil. The image of a U.S. administration and other major governments around the world, together with the international financial institutions, having their collective heads buried in the sands of unreality was an easy target for criticism. Most critics greatly oversimplified the complexity of the problem and through one means or another were advocating large-scale debt forgiveness dressed up as new and creative proposals. Unfortunately, they were neither new nor especially creative. The critical defect in all of these schemes was that debt forgiveness and the harsh losses it would bring to bear on the banks would effectively destroy any prospect of new finance for the debtor countries as they tried to restart growth.

What could be said for the period from 1982 through 1986 was that debtor countries gradually learned that there could be no return to significant and sustained growth without embracing genuine structural reforms in their economies. The short-term-fix mentality of the early days, in which countries thought that some temporary belt tightening and injection of finance from the IMF, the World Bank, and the Inter-American Development Bank would return them to growth had clearly failed. By 1985 some countries, notably Chile and Mexico, were embracing more fundamental reform. The international institutions could also see that conditionality alone or money lent was not enough.

Genuine, homegrown, politically supported reform and adjustment were essential to long-term recovery. Korea proved the point in spades, moving from a troubled debtor to a surplus, building an "Asian Tiger" economy in a few short years of painful transformation.

By the end of 1987, the Baker Plan had lost momentum. It had bought time by providing some continuing new money flows from the banks but created no definitive solution to the debt crisis. In fact, the threat to the world's financial system was again on the rise. The cohesion of the bank syndicates was breaking down, new money flows had slowed to a trickle, and various governments had begun to encourage or to insist that their banks begin to face the reality of realized losses, tax write-offs, and the need to begin reducing their exposure to developing countries. In general, banks stuck to the position that the debt of the troubled countries was still worth one hundred cents on the dollar. Never mind that small amounts of debt that traded did so at deep price discounts. In addition, the discipline that had driven the emergency financing for Argentina in 1984 that permitted Argentina to remain current in the servicing of its debt had now completely broken down. As there was little or no prospect of new money, debtor countries allowed, or indeed encouraged, the building of arrears on debt service requirements. This had the effect of massively increasing the corpus of outstanding debt at an accelerating rate, dramatically enlarging the magnitude of the threat to the global banking system, not to mention the prospect of rising economic and political tensions in the indebted countries.

By late 1987 it was clear to me that we were facing a potential calamity. We had to find some means of resolving the now quite mature debt crisis that we had simply been managing over the past five years with a view to avoiding a blowup in Latin America and among the world's banks. The consequences could also be extremely damaging for the developed world economies. Yet, the conventional view was that the debt crisis was not resolvable in less than a generation, and only then if we could continue to muddle through as we had over the past five years.

It was my belief that the muddling through approach had provided vital time for banks to begin to adjust their exposures and governments to hold off on precipitous regulatory and tax actions. The Baker Plan, however, was no longer a viable option for the future. Despite some impressive progress in the reform and opening of some Latin America economies, prospects for investment and financial support in the region were dismal. I believed that we had to look for a solution that rested with financial markets, where in my experience, the discipline of what I called recognizing reality would be the governing force for resolution.

I took deputy assistant secretary Charles Dallara with me to Wall Street to meet with investment banking firms that we understood had set up small boutique trading desks in Latin American debt paper. We talked with Goldman Sachs, Solomon Brothers, Lehman Brothers, and Bear Stearns, among others, about how they conducted this new trading business. The amounts traded, of course, were small, but the dynamics of the market were deeply revealing to me.

Investment banking trading desks were buying small amounts of bank loan instruments on a negotiated basis from banks seeking to reduce their exposure to debtor countries. These purchases were taking place at extremely deep discounts, some in the range of thirty cents on the dollar. The paper was then resold by the investment banks at sizeable markups, but still at prices nowhere near par, to private investors whose aim was to hold the paper in the belief that they might eventually be paid out at or near par. In other words, investors were buying debtor country instruments that they believed would ultimately be paid out at or near one hundred cents on the dollar, a claim which at some point they would be willing to enforce. Remember, however, this very same paper represented debt obligations that leading and heavily exposed banks around the world still loudly proclaimed to be worth one hundred cents on the dollar, while at the same time quietly selling small participations at massive negotiated discounts to private investors, who inevitably would also claim that the debt must be honored in full.

In this insight of market realities must surely lie the key to resolving the debt crisis. Also, the process, although small at this point, also suggested to me the very unpleasant possibility that over time the indebtedness of troubled countries could be shed by the banks to a new class of widely diffused, aggressively demanding investors. If the IMF and multilateral development banks were to continue lending as the sole source of new money to the debtor nations, one could foresee a situation in which the bulk of the risk would be transferred to governments and a group of aggressive private investors with deep pockets to finance the enforcement of their rights. The debtor countries would still be burdened with debt, the banks would have eliminated much of their loan exposure without providing new lending, and governments would end up bearing the burden of responsibility for dealing with the countries. The debtors themselves would get nothing unless there were to be a massive rich-country taxpayer-financed bailout of the debtor countries.

The realization of what the markets were revealing drove me toward finding a market solution that could resolve or at least substantially dissipate the growing burden of debt. When an oversupply of debt has overwhelmed a functioning market, one must seek the means to force the market to price that debt and clear the market. This is a fundamental principle for relieving markets that are under severe stress. The debt strategy up to this point had encouraged the creation of more debt, which, with the breakdown of the bank syndicates, resulted in a situation where indebted countries could improve their leverage over the banks and governments by allowing arrearages on their outstanding debt to mushroom. The challenge was to find a way, as it were, to lance this particular boil and at the same time create conditions under which the countries could unlock new sources of capital to finance their recovery.

Those principles formed what later became the heart of the Brady Plan. In early 1988 I tried out my ideas for a resolution of the crisis with Secretary Baker. The fact that it was to have some element of debt reduction, or more graphically, debt forgiveness, rendered the proposals unacceptable to Secretary Baker. His objections were understandable. It was the beginning of the 1988 election campaign, and in his view there would be strong opposition in Congress, and debt forgiveness in Latin America could easily become an election issue. The elements of the proposals I put forward would not require legislation, but as Secretary Baker pointed, out there was some $155 billion of U.S. government lending programs (e.g., student loans, small business loans) where the argument might well be raised, "If you are bailing out deadbeat Latin American countries, why not the American people?" There was no doubt that this inconsistency in treatment could be a possible political problem, especially in the midst of a difficult election campaign for President Bush. But so could a major crisis in the banking system that could do serious damage to the U.S. and international economy.

Not long afterward, Secretary Baker was placed in charge of Vice President Bush's election campaign, and after a brief interlude, Nicholas Brady was nominated by President Reagan to become the new secretary of the Treasury. Mr. Brady was an investment banker with a long and distinguished history of working in financial markets. He had headed the commission to investigate and recommend new policies following the unprecedented stock market break of October 1987. He understood markets, and more important, respected the judgment of markets.

Mr. Brady asked me to stay on as underecretary of the Treasury for international affairs. In September 1988 he was approved by the Senate and sworn in as secretary. In the early days of October we attended the annual meeting of the IMF and World Bank in Berlin, and as a part of the trip, Secretary Brady attended his first G7 meeting.

This was for Secretary Brady a new and not very impressive event. He returned to Washington genuinely alarmed by the state of the Latin American debt crisis and recognized immediately that the present U.S. debt strategy was not sustainable. He wanted ideas, and quickly, for resolving the debt crisis before we were all swept away in an international financial meltdown. I dusted off the earlier ideas, arguing that I believed they could form the basis of a long-term solution by introducing the element of market reality and requiring that the banks be forced, or better yet, would decide in their own interests, to choose a more realistic approach to resolving the standoff with debtor counties. Demanding one hundred cents on the dollar while selling their loan participations out the back door for thirty was not a tenable position.

Secretary Brady understood these market realities. He convened a group of top cabinet officials, as well as Chairman of the Federal Reserve Alan Greenspan, to discuss and agree to a process for moving to resolve the crisis. I was the sole sub-cabinet-level official to attend these meetings, for which it was agreed that I would prepare a paper setting out exactly where we stood at that point in time. This paper, which I termed the "truth serum" paper, was to be discussed by the group and possibly revised until everyone agreed that it accurately described the reality we faced. Once agreed, we would pose possible solutions for resolving the crisis. The key condition was that the only solutions considered would be those that complied with our agreed description of the realities set out in the "truth serum" paper. It was amazing how this agreed methodology narrowed the field of potential options for resolving the crisis.

It was from this process in late October and November 1988 that the Brady Plan emerged, although it was not named until much later. Vice President George H. W. Bush was elected president in early November, and the transition to the new administration began shortly thereafter. For me, these weeks were exclusively focused on developing the new debt crisis plan. Its key components were as follows.

Even though debtor countries arrearages were building, the countries had been making significant progress on economic reforms and opening their economies to foreign trade and investment. The banks had demonstrated privately that they were willing to exit from their country exposures at a discount from the face value of their loans, at least on a selective basis. Meanwhile, virtually no new money was forthcoming from the banks, because the banks had begun setting reserves against potential losses or in some cases were already recognizing losses and taking tax write-offs in their own national tax jurisdictions. Loan participations being sold at deep discounts were moving into the hands of a diverse group of other investors, all of whom maintained the expectation of profiting at some point from being paid off at par, or at least at a substantially higher price than their purchase price. These investors represented a new class of investors who would be much harder to reach and to negotiate with than the banks.

Funding from international financial institutions such as the IMF, the World Bank, and the Inter-American Development Bank (all government-owned) were picking up relatively more of the burden of financing the troubled debtor countries. Over time, this trend would continue, leading to more debtor country risk ending up in the hands of governments. When that process had moved far enough, the debt crisis would move exclusively to a government-to-government showdown, with taxpayers in the developed countries left "holding the bag."

To break this relentless trend and to provide some measure of debt relief to the indebted countries, now struggling to implement more pro-growth policies, we would need to induce the banks to accept a write-down of the debt in a form that gave them the benefits of better security, greater certainty of fundamental value in the future, and a realistic prospect of escape from their still-excessive exposure to the troubled debtors. In addition, the relief provided to the debtor countries would have to be sufficient to change the expectations of markets and investors as to the outlook for the apparently ever-increasing prospect of a rising corpus of debt. Unless we could show some positive change whereby debt levels would level off or decline modestly, there would not be a sufficient prospect for re-creating growth that would attract new capital from other non-governmental sources.

This is where the key decision was made for the ultimate success of the Brady Plan: to use U.S. Treasury thirty-year zero-coupon bonds as collateral for a new debt instrument to be offered by the countries to the banks at a substantial discount for the exchange of debt presently held by the banks. At the interest rates current in the U.S. Treasury market at the time, a zero-coupon thirty-year Treasury could be bought at .07 to .09 cents on the dollar. This meant that if a country such as Mexico had some cash reserves to deploy for the purchase of these bonds from the Treasury, the Treasury zero-coupon bonds could be pledged as collateral for the new Mexican government instrument to be exchanged with the banks. Thus, to illustrate the simplicity of the concept, if Mexico had $50 billion of outstanding debt held by banks, and it were to offer to exchange a new Mexican government thirty-year debt instrument with the banks, which was fully backed by triple-A U.S. government thirty-year zero-coupon bonds, and that exchange was accomplished at a discount from par of 50 percent on the outstanding debt, Mexico could buy the $25 billion of collateral required with an outlay of only $1.75 to $2.25 billion. Staying with this illustrative example, Mexico could "treat" a body of $50 billion of debt with $25 billion nominal value of U.S. 30 year Treasury zero coupon bonds at a cash cost of $1.75 to $2.25 billion, depending on where prices for the zero-coupon bonds were set at the time of purchase. As a result, Mexico's stock of outstanding debt would be reduced by 50 percent, and the remaining $25 billion of its debt would be paid off in thirty years by the maturing Treasury zero-coupon bond collateral. The principal amount of the $25 billion of restructured Mexican debt would therefore no longer rest on the shoulders of the Mexican people. In addition, no U.S. taxpayers' money would be required to accomplish the reduction of debt.

Banks would be faced with accepting a loss on their outstanding loans. To continue with the Mexican example, they would take a loss of 50 percent on the nominal value of their Mexican loans. It could be argued that this was a less painful loss than selling out over the years at a price of approximately 30 percent of nominal value. The big benefit to the banks was the certainty of an outcome that "treated" their entire holding of debt and the fact that the new instrument would be fully and easily marketable by them in public markets, thus greatly accelerating their ability to reduce or eliminate their Mexican exposure. If the banks did not accept this new structure of collateral support, they might eventually face total default by countries, which might decide that the advantages of allowing interest arrears to build up could be extended to principal amounts by a full default. We knew the banks would be strongly opposed to accepting any discount on the price of the debt they had contracted with the countries. We hoped that the finality of the Treasury proposal, the creation of top-quality marketable instruments that would permit the banks to exit from future risk, and alternatively the prospect of total default if they failed to cooperate, would be clear incentives for the banks to accept the plan.

Finally, there were two appealing aspects to taking this course of action. One was that the debtor countries would buy the Treasury zero-coupon thirty-year bonds from the Treasury at the same price as all other investors in the Treasury market. There would be no subsidy or use of taxpayers' funds to "bail out" debtor countries. Instead, the U.S. would simply agree to the use of its triple-A Treasury zero-coupon bonds as collateral for the debtor countries' restructured debt. The second advantage was that the level of the discount to apply, and therefore the amount and cost to the countries, in purchasing the needed collateral would be a matter negotiated entirely by the debtor country and the banks. The Treasury or U.S. government would not prescribe the price settlement, but only provide for purchase of the zero-coupon bonds.

In the weeks during which we developed these ideas I was sent by Secretary Brady to Houston to meet privately with Finance Minister of Mexico Pedro Aspe, and Under Minister Angel Gurria. The purpose was to conduct a strictly confidential discussion to test the acceptability and practicality of our proposed thinking. Mexico, a critically important country to the United States, was one of the largest of the debtor countries and had been conducting significant economic policy reform since its devastating earthquake in 1985. The other important consideration was that Mexico had successfully carried out a debt-for-equity swap engineered by JP Morgan some months earlier, which, though a wholly different structure, tested some of the same propositions. The most important of these was the exchange of debt for equity at a price that established a discounted value on Mexico's outstanding debt.

When the principles of the plan had been agreed by the "truth serum" group, Secretary Brady and I met with President-elect Bush. We took him through the plan, the background for the necessity of action, which as vice president he had been fully aware of, and sought his approval to proceed. Secretary Brady proposed to the president-elect that we would like to call the plan the Bush Plan. He reflected for a few moments and then said, "I don't think so. We should call it the Brady Plan if it succeeds, and if it fails we will call it the Mulford Plan." It was the kind of friendly humor that was always near at hand with President G. H. W. Bush, together with his consideration and kindness to all of us who worked for him.

In January of 1989 the action on the Brady Plan shifted to the G7, where the vast bulk of outstanding bank risk resided, apart from the approximately 32 percent of exposure in U.S. banks. The G7 deputies met in Paris and again in February. Gradually, consensus was achieved, and we began working on the means by which the Brady Plan would be unveiled. Because the debt crisis involved virtually the whole developed world of banking, as well as the international financial institutions, we had to reveal the plan well before the IMF–World Bank spring meetings in April in Washington to give them, and the global banking community and the debtor countries, adequate time to consider this radically different approach to the debt crisis.

We knew that there would have to be some changes of rules and policy practices in the international financial institutions, which could not realistically be negotiated with them in advance of the announcement. In the end, we elected to have Secretary Brady announce the Brady Plan at a luncheon meeting of the Bretton Woods Committee on March 10, 1989. This was the day that we addressed reality with a market-based plan that aimed at solving a world problem that Washington pundits had reckoned would take more than a generation to solve.

The reaction to the Brady Plan among the banks ranged from subdued to hostile. In the IMF and World Bank there were the usual voices of academic concern. The IDB, under the leadership of President Enrique Iglesias, was supportive, as you might expect from the multilateral bank for Latin America.

Before we could move forward with the international financial institutions we knew there would have to be a moment of truth with the banks, which would be strongly opposed to accepting any discount on the debt they had contracted with the countries. One could imagine saying in such a confrontation, "You, the banks, are on the top floor in a building with one hundred stories. You get into the building's elevator, planning a modest descent to a lower floor, but the elevator suddenly drops to the fiftieth floor. The door opens and standing outside are representatives of the U.S. Treasury, who offer to provide supports under the elevator that would keep it at this floor. The supports are U.S. Treasury zero bonds. If you reject this offer, the doors of the elevator will close and you will plummet down, possibly to the basement. Take your choice." It never quite came to that, but the finality of the Treasury proposal eventually became clear to the banks. For all we knew the elevator doors might open at the seventieth floor. The final level would be a matter between the countries and the banks to decide, but a refusal to engage would mean that the elevator could be in freefall.

We began a dialogue with the IMF and World Bank, whose spring meeting was only weeks away. Beforehand, Secretary Brady agreed to speak at the IMF annual meeting in Madrid, which would involve a direct conversation with the CEOs and chairmen of the top one hundred world banks. Secretary Brady and I visited Moscow and the Czech Republic prior to the Madrid meeting. I returned directly to

Washington, and Charles Dallara accompanied Secretary Brady to the Madrid meeting, which proved to be a turning point with the banks. In the secretary's speech it was necessary to make clear to the banks that the Brady Plan proposal was the bottom line position of the U.S. government for resolving the debt crisis. We did not incorporate in the secretary's speech the elevator analogy but instead used Charles Dallara's story about Willie the Cook, who, according to the history of the Old West, was part of an early expedition down the Colorado River. After days of fighting through rough water, Willie was so frightened that he elected to leave the river group to scale the canyon walls and proceed overland to meet the group at its final destination. The next day, the river group descended through what proved to be the last big cataract into the gently flowing waters of the lower Colorado. Willie's remains were later found in the desert, where he had been murdered by Indians. There was no misunderstanding the meaning of the story, particularly including the need for solidarity among the banks if they were to reach calm water. Those who chose to leave the group of cooperating banks would be left to the vagaries of the wilderness. The banks understood the message, and despite resentment over what some believed was a crude message, the banks accepted the reality of their position.

The next hurdles lay with the IMF and the World Bank. For the Brady Plan to work there needed to be a change in policy and procedures in both organizations that would permit tranches of finance to be released to debtor countries who engaged in negotiations with the banks under the Brady Plan. This liquidity, which would normally be released against specific policy actions in stabilization or structural adjustment programs, would now be released pending negotiation of a Brady Plan settlement between the banks and a given country. It would be these funds that would provide the liquid resources required for the country to buy the necessary allotment of U.S. Treasury zero-coupon bonds needed to collateralize its new Brady Plan instruments.

This provoked a passionate debate with the institutions, because until now their role had been to provide finance as a part of agreed adjustment programs with the debtor countries and, more important, by doing so to provide the trigger for the release of new money from the banks that would ensure that the country was at that moment fully financed. But countries could no longer be fully financed at a given moment in time. Under the Brady Plan, we accepted that there would be no new money forthcoming from the banks, because they were being required to accept and recognize losses. The static calculations of the international institutions would no longer provide the assurance that countries in negotiations with the banks were fully financed from external sources. Instead, we would be depending on dynamic market realities: the relief provided to countries from a reduction in the stock of their debt and the cost of debt service; the ability of countries to now attract private external investment in the form of equity investment, supplier's trade credit provided by economic agents who believed in the recovery of growth in the debtor countries' economies; and the return of flight capital, some of it under national amnesty programs.

Attracting these private market sources of support was an act of faith by the United States in the power of markets, once it was perceived that country reforms were making progress and countries would have even more appeal once the prospect of an ever-rising debt burden was broken. These ideas did not find support among many of the staff economists at the institutions, who found it difficult to turn away from their static calculations of financial support from assured sources, even though finance was no longer flowing from some of these sources. To me their concerns proved the point that unless we turned to the dynamic, but not necessarily guaranteed, support of private markets, the official community and governments would end up owning virtually all the debt of the troubled debtor countries. In the end, this would lead to a taxpayer-funded bailout of the countries. The Brady Plan, on the contrary, visualized no taxpayers' funds being deployed and instead depended on the power and imagination of private markets and investors to respond to new and attractive opportunities. There could be no guaranteed assurance that support would be forthcoming, which is why this moment was a watershed, dividing those who believed in the positive power of markets from those who preferred the certainty, however inadequate, of government actions.

At the spring meetings, with the support of the G7 countries, the necessary policy and procedural changes were agreed upon. The IDB, a willing supporter, joined in, helping to assure the supply of liquidity that would be needed. Negotiations between the banks and Mexico began almost immediately. The task of finding common agreement on the discount that would apply to Mexican debt proved to be difficult. Several meetings took place at the Treasury at which we also had to agree on the formula for setting the price for purchases by Mexico of thirty-year zero-coupon bonds. By late June or July the outlines of the deal between Mexico and the banks had been established. Other country negotiations followed: Brazil, Argentina, and Costa Rica, and parts of the Brady Plan approach were used in Chile as well as later in the Enterprise Initiative for Latin America.

There was controversy and criticism from serving members of Congress who either thought we had gone too far or not far enough. Few people in Washington in Congress, the administration (including, surprisingly, the CIA) and the media understood how the combination of Treasury collateral, the leverage in the value of long-term zero-coupon bonds, and the latent appetite in markets for both Brady Bonds and investment opportunities in the debtor countries fit together to resolve the debt crisis.

My view was that the Brady Plan might be hard to explain but easy to understand. The problem others thought would take a generation to solve and would probably require heavy government financial intervention with taxpayers' resources was gone in less than two years. In its place was a booming world market in Brady Bonds as the banks sold off their debtor-country exposures and a vast new flow of capital to the countries of Latin America, whose reforms were now generating growth. Perhaps the most moving moment for me in this remarkable accomplishment took place when President of Costa Rica Oscar Arias formally greeted President Bush at San Jose airport to launch Costa Rica's celebration of one hundred years of democracy. In his welcoming remarks, President Arias mentioned my name and the role I had played in restructuring Costa Rica's external debt. Reportedly, he said, "To you, Mr. President, one billion dollars is a small amount of money, but to us in Costa

Rica it is everything." I was not there to hear but I did not need to be. The moral of this story is that complicated financial problems can be solved by facing reality, pricing assets, and clearing the market. I have no doubt that with sufficient presence of mind in the U.S. Treasury from 2008 to 2010, the "truth serum" approach could have been applied to resolve the subprime mortgage crisis and move the United States back relatively quickly to a recovery in the housing market.

The speed and comprehensive nature of the collapse of the Soviet Union was a cataclysmic economic event for Russia. One of the most surprising developments in my first year at the Treasury in 1984 was the revelation that President Reagan clearly intended to bankrupt the Soviet Union by engaging them in an economic competition with the United States. When Secretary Regan explained this to me one afternoon in his office, I was struck by the simple clarity of such an ambitious proposition.

Several other policy priorities were also reduced to clear, single-dimensional propositions. One such example was President Reagan's tax cut proposals of 1982. When this legislation was stuck in Congress in the summer of 1982, President Reagan went on television and directly appealed to the American people to telephone their Congressional representatives, urging them to unblock the legislative impasse. Within minutes, chaos followed on the U.S. Congress switchboards. Another example was President Reagan's tax reform of 1986, which reduced the top U.S. income tax rate to 28 percent.

The Soviet equivalent was President Reagan's challenge to the Soviet Union in Berlin in 1987: "Mr. Gorbachev, tear down this wall." The Soviet economic model failed under the duress of competition with the United States. The penetration of information flows into the Soviet Union and Eastern Europe made the weakness of the Soviet economic model plainly visible for all to see. The emperor was starkly revealed without his clothes. Perhaps the most telling point was when Gorbachev removed Soviet troops from Eastern Germany in return for DM 8 billion from Germany, ostensibly to build military housing for the troops returning to Russia. Fortunately for the world, there was neither the will nor the resources to continue enforcing Soviet domination in Eastern Europe.

In the fall of 1991 came the moment in Treasury when the full magnitude of the Soviet predicament was brought into sharp focus. The G7 Finance Ministers convened in Bangkok in early October that year prior to the IMF–World Bank annual meeting. Soviet Finance Minister Grigory Yavlinsky asked to attend the meeting for the purpose of discussing the Soviet Union's current financial situation. To our great surprise Mr. Yavlinsky revealed that the Soviet Union would no longer be able to meet its financial obligations as of mid-November and would therefore have to default.

This was a stunning admission that left G7 ministers and central bank governors virtually speechless. Despite the disputes and tensions over the years with the West, the Soviet Union had always remained current on all debt obligations. Moreover, the assessment of the CIA in 1990–91 was was that the Soviet Union had some $25–27 billion in gold reserves. The gravity of the situation was immediately apparent, because in all G7 countries, ongoing official bilateral credits to the Soviet Union would cease to flow if the Soviets failed to make current payments of interest or principal. Such credit was vital for the financing of food and agricultural products, as well as for medicines and all manner of items essential to a nation no longer able to meet its own needs. With winter only two months away and rumours of impending shortages in the Soviet Union, one was immediately seized by the prospect of a complete internal breakdown in the economy and society of the Soviet Union.

The first priority was to regularize Soviet external debt so that the Soviets would be able to continue to access vital new official credits to finance basic needs through the upcoming winter. This would necessitate the Soviet Union acknowledging its inability to meet its obligations to the world at large by turning to the Paris Club to reschedule its outstanding debt. Once accomplished on a format or in a plan accepted by its creditors, the Soviet Union would not be cut off from Western credits. A frank admission of inability to pay by the Soviet finance minister to a private meeting of G7 ministers was vastly different, however, than a public admission and the humiliation of a world superpower unable to meet its most basic financial obligations.

It was agreed that the G7 deputies would convene immediately in Moscow to discuss with the Soviet government a plan for avoiding the full impact of this calamity. Obviously, the Soviet Union would be severely damaged, but perhaps by agreeing to a Paris Club debt restructuring the worst fallout could be contained.

In the weeks that followed I visited Moscow several times, once with the G7 deputies, once on my own, and once with Secretary Brady and Chairman Greenspan. It was autumn in Moscow, moving toward winter. The atmosphere was sombre in the extreme. Shop windows were empty and unwashed, there seemed to be few street lights in the city and a minimal flow of traffic with virtually none at night, and silent citizens standing in the streets with pathetic offerings of personal possessions for sale on blankets or tables before them. There was no effort to make sales, just silence, resignation, and sadness.

To my surprise, the G7 meeting turned into a kind of seminar, including the prime ministers and finance ministers of the Soviet Union and all fifteen republics. We met for four days in a large hall in the Oktyabrskaya Hotel around a vast round table. Ironically, this was the site in the past of high-level Communist Party meetings. Now we faced a financially inexperienced, deeply divided group of leaders of the central government and the republics, which all had a share in the debt.

The first day or two there was passionate confusion among our counterparts. The leaders of the republics claimed they had never seen the money borrowed by the central government and therefore had no obligation to bear some defined proportion of the debt. On the other hand, they clamoured for their fair share of Soviet assets, such as its embassies around the world and their share of certain supposed revenues, such as oil and gas revenues. Against this confusion, we had to explain that unless the Soviet Union acknowledged all its debt, confirmed its inability to pay, and subjected itself to a restructuring of its debt by the Paris Club of creditor nations (dominated by the G7 countries), it would not be able to access new official bilateral credits or draw down resources from the IMF under an agreed stabilization program. All this was new to the group gathered around the table at virtually all hours of those October days.

The purpose of the meeting from our standpoint was to establish central responsibility for Soviet debt and agree in principle on the necessity of approaching the Paris Club. From this standpoint, the objective seemed to be to bring the reality of the debt home to all the republics and force them to accept the principle that they were all responsible for the debt. It was also vital that everyone around the table would come to understand the serious implication for all of them of a default or interruption of payments on Soviet debt.

The vehicle for establishing this reality was the G7 demand that there should be a universally agreed memorandum of understanding stipulating that the Soviet Union and the republics were "jointly and severally" responsible for the external debt of the Soviet Union. Legally, this would mean that the central government and each of the governments of the republics were responsible for all the debt of the Soviet Union. This legal construction of joint and several liability was controversial and strongly resisted by Russia and the republics, each entity perceiving correctly that it would be fully responsible for the total body of the debt. In practice, however, the vital point for the G7 group was that Russia, the financial and political heart of the Soviet Union, would in the final analysis be responsible for all Soviet debt. Apart from the messy differences of opinion, the most sustained opposition to the joint and several liability principles was that according to the Soviet representatives, the concept of joint and and several liability simply did not exist under Soviet law. From our standpoint, agreement on this point would ensure that all future negotiation would be with the Soviet government or Russia and not with the turbulent republics.

During the course of our visit we met with Mr. Gorbachev to represent our views and to explain the absolute necessity of the Soviet Union agreeing to this legal format so that a credible and successful approach could be made promptly to the Paris Club. In the flow of the conversations, it was clear that Mr. Gorbachev was desperately seeking some other course to financial solvency that would see the Soviet Union through the winter and avoid the need to approach the Paris Club. He spoke of Soviet gold reserves being used to secure Soviet debt. Only later when Secretary Brady and Chairman Greenspan had visited Moscow was it revealed that Soviet gold stocks had been gravely depleted or possibly stolen during the 1980s.

The complexity and political difficulties that followed in the last desperate days of the Soviet Union extended beyond the Boris Yeltsin revolution and the final lowering of the Soviet flag at the end of December 1991. The G7 agreement on the outstanding official bilateral debt of the Soviet Union held up so that subsequent negotiations to sort out Soviet debt in the Paris Club were ultimately conducted with the Russian government. But what became strikingly clear to me was the total paralysis of the Soviet Union's state-planned and operated economy in the aftermath of the collapse of the Soviet Union. State heavy industries, whose operations were spread throughout the various republics, became virtually inoperable. Raw materials would be inserted into a long line of production where other elements were added in different republics, with the final product exiting in yet some other republic or in Russia. Gas and oil pipelines that crossed republic boundaries were also rendered virtually inoperable. It seemed impossible that this giant economy could ever have provided a lasting competitive threat to the United States. I vividly recall at a meeting with Russian economic officials in 1991 in Washington, when one senior official during a coffee break asking me in a conspirational tone, "Come now, tell me who in the U.S. government sets prices in America." The markets, I replied, but it was clear that either he did not believe me or could not absorb the concept.

As I made the transition from government back to investment banking in 1993, Russia under Yeltsin began to change. The most interesting evidence of Russia's new economic thinking was Yeltsin's voucher program. Whatever one may think about the wisdom of the voucher program idea or its many subsequent abuses, the program provided Russian citizens with their first experience of market-based decision making. In its simplest form, every adult

Russian was provided with a voucher with a set face value. The holder could exchange his voucher for shares in a privatized Russian enterprise, hold the voucher for another exchange decision in the future, or sell the voucher immediately or later for cash to some other owner, who would then hold the same options for its use. Many Russians, desperate for cash, sold their options into a budding market for cash. Others held on, and still others accumulated options and in some cases became rich through the process of exchange for shares. The main point, however, is that every recipient was presented with making his or her first market-based decision away from the omnipresent state.

The transformation of Russia continued throughout the 1990s, and the countries of Eastern Europe gradually embraced some form of market-based economies. Large-scale privatizations and entrepreneurial activity of all kinds spread across the entire region. No one could argue that the process was orderly or free from abuses and corruption. It did bring Russia and the countries of Eastern Europe into world markets for both finance and trade. There was no going back, and nearly twenty years later the evolution continues.

The end of the 1980s saw the peak in G7 economic policy cooperation. The global imbalances that plagued the world in the mid 1980s had all but disappeared. Japan was far more open as a financial market, and the "long distance runner" techniques used in the yen-dollar talks were picked up by the Office of the U.S. Trade Representative for its sectoral trade negotiations. The U.S. was enjoying solid growth and an improving fiscal outlook. Capital flows to developing countries, especially the former troubled debtors, jumped decisively in 1990–91 and continued to rise dramatically in future years.

Yet changes and new challenges developing in the world economy began to emerge as I was leaving Treasury in November 1992. These changes continued and carried through the global crisis of 2008, and fallout from them remains with us today. The weakening of G7 cooperation in 1991–92 continued as Europe became more and more preoccupied with its own unification efforts. The annual economic summits of the heads of government of G7 countries increasingly became politically driven media extravaganzas, where it was next to impossible to accomplish anything significant in the economic policy field. The invitation to include Russia in the summit in 1991 was rather bizarre, given the fact that its economy had collapsed and in any case was similar in size to that of Holland. By 1992, the last year of the Bush administration, the economic summit in Munich was powerless to accomplish anything significant for the United States beyond a measure of goodwill in Europe.

Europe's turn inward in the early 1990s forced the large European countries of the G7 to cede their traditional independence to the need to seek agreement with the smallest and least-influential members of the union on virtually every issue of significance. Gone was the quiet authority of the G7, which had dealt collectively with issues of critical importance to the functioning of the world economy. The EU bureaucracy now consistently sought to establish and expand its authority in European financial and economic affairs.

The politics of union seemed to drive everything with Europe. The Soviet threat was receding, thanks in large measure to the policies of Presidents Reagan and Bush in the 1980s and early 1990s. The unification of Germany was driven by the aging leaders of Europe, whose chief objective was to achieve the unity they believed would prevent the recurrence of future wars, rather than to ensure that Europe's newfound unity would work effectively in practice into the future. This applied to the economic terms on which the Germanys were united, the vision and structuring of Europe's single currency (finally launched in 1998), and the continued demand by Europe that it should be represented in international forums both by the EU and by the individual states of Europe, which were supposedly to submerge their individual sovereignty in the union. These preoccupations continue to influence current relations between the U.S. and Europe, as well as relations in the international institutions that no longer fairly or adequately represent the realities of today's global economy.

Large imbalances appeared once again in the world economy, but this time they were largely ignored by governments. Benign economic conditions continued through the 1990s. The dotcom break in 2000 pierced the stock market bubble, but imbalances and other signs of excess in the global economy continued to grow unaddressed by the G7. Regulators and market practitioners ignored the evidence of market excesses as global financial markets continued to expand and spread ever more widely around the world, as we discovered in the global fall out from the crash of 2008.

Many reasons are cited for the financial crisis of 2008–9, and most of them can be added to the list of causes. However, an important reason we went over the edge in 2008 was that for at least fifteen years there had been little attention and no serious effort by financial officials of the Clinton and Bush administrations in matters of international economic policy cooperation among the bigger nations to address global imbalances and rising market excesses. If these efforts had been carried out with energy and serious engagement, they would certainly have sounded warning alarms. In the end, we might not have avoided the calamity, which started in the United States; but without serious leadership in international economic affairs for some ten years before the crisis, the world was simply left to indulge itself in an extravaganza of liquidity, collapsing standards, and speculation. The U.S. Congress, the Treasury, the Federal Reserve, and the U.S. regulatory community failed to exercise leadership or prudent recognition of the rising tide of excesses, and of course bankers and miracle-spinning financial geniuses were there to shamelessly exploit the system, whether in Wall Street or out across the country in real estate.

Today, we have fallen even farther away from any real prospect of responsible leadership among governments in global finance. The G20, while symbolically important as a more realistic reflection of today's global economy, is not able to engage and to manage the global macroeconomic issues that face us today. The G20 may accomplish some results on the easier global issues that attract a popular following, but the presence of the G20 stands as an indictment of the international financial institutions we look to for leadership and guidance but which have not reformed themselves to reflect today's changing global economy. New power relationships in our world, such as the rise of emerging market countries such as China, India, Brazil, and Indonesia, will render international financial institutions increasingly irrelevant in matters of global economic and financial governance unless they are able to effect reforms that bring them into line with the world's new centers of growth and power.

The other seeds from the late 1980s and early 1990s that have survived to produce new growth in today's world are the rise of Eastern Europe, Europe's experiment with the formation and management of the euro, and the rise of emerging countries in Asia and Latin America. Taken together, these developments have already changed our world. The financial and economic crisis of 2008–9 has brought these forces into sharp relief as we seek to understand and adjust to our new world.

In the early 1990s President Bush reacted quickly to the breakup of the Soviet empire by immediately seeking to bind the countries of Eastern Europe to the West. Once again, economic initiatives were key in accomplishing this objective. The new European Bank for Reconstruction and Development was established in a matter of months, with a mandate that emphasized the importance of the market economy and private sector development in the countries of Eastern Europe. I know how important this initiative was to the president and to Secretary Brady because I led the U.S. delegation that negotiated the creation of the bank.

Equally important was the initiative to engage the countries of the G7 to negotiate a 50 percent reduction in Poland's official bilateral external debt. President Bush was the only head of government in the G7 willing to take the lead in this historic negotiation. I led the U.S. effort in this enterprise and can attest to the fact that when we began the U.S. supported a 55 percent reduction in Poland's official bilateral debt, when all other G7 countries advocated no debt forgiveness for Poland. In the end, we finished with a 50 percent reduction and signed the agreement in April 1991. Poland's economy recovered positive growth that September, and Poland has never looked back these past twenty years. Other initiatives were taken in Eastern Europe to quickly bind these countries to the West so they would not fall back in to the old communist sphere of influence. Contrast this with the complete failure of Europe these past ten years to bring Turkey, the world's largest secular Islamic republic, into Europe. This failure in vision and leadership may prove to be one of the West's most serious mistakes as we move into the twenty-first century. Likewise, Ukraine, which did not become an EU country and was not taken in to NATO, is slipping back into Russia's orbit, and the US and Europe appear unwilling to prevent it.

By the end of the early 1990s Europe was obsessed with the single currency. Like the unification of Germany, the single currency was driven by the vision of a united Europe that would never again fall into war. The introduction of the Exchange Rate Mechanism (ERM, or the "snake') was designed to bring European currencies into a narrower trading range as a preliminary step to moving to the single currency. What was often forgotten or ignored by officials involved at the time was that the ERM suffered a breakdown during the currency crisis of September 1992. Both the UK and Italy elected at that time to leave the ERM and its restrictive disciplines by opting out of the system. Both countries subsequently enjoyed years of stronger growth, rising exports, and job creation.

The lesson of the 1992 crisis for the future was that the euro would need some element of flexibility built into its operating rules or a far greater willingness to embrace a common fiscal regime for Europe than appeared to be acceptable at the time. An escape mechanism could perhaps have been incorporated into the euro or some financial support mechanism for countries facing a major crisis under the heavy discipline imposed by the euro. In both cases, the view in Europe was that any type of exit mechanism would encourage bad behavior that might lead to opportunistic departures. The creation of an emergency financing mechanism, on the other hand, to be accessed under certain extreme conditions and in accordance with preset criteria (a sort of IMF facility in the euro structure) was also rejected by the Europeans as a possible incentive for countries to avoid the euro's rigorous discipline. Instead, the eurozone countries adopted the "financial stability pact" under which countries that persistently ran fiscal deficits to GDP ratios in excess of 3 percent would be disciplined or even fined if they failed to restore their fiscal imbalances. Unfortunately, this attempt to build some institutionalized form of discipline into the system was violated almost immediately by Germany and France, undermining its credibility as a method for disciplining the other country members.

In the early days of the euro the disciplines that the euro imposed were a positive force for improved economic policies among aspiring member countries. This became known as the convergence process in which various countries, including Spain, Italy, Portugal, Ireland, and Greece brought down traditional inflation levels, interest rates, and fiscal deficits. These improvements, together with greater resort to debt available at substantially lower euro market rates, fueled growth in countries that had not continued to make the structural adjustments necessary to sustaining more efficient economies. When the crisis of 2008–9 hit Europe and the United States, the European countries that had enjoyed the early benefits of convergence and the continuing benefits of borrowing heavily at, for them, low interest rates found they had built up unsustainable indebtedness while failing utterly to embrace the structural reforms necessary for sustained growth and fiscal discipline.

The crisis in Greece in early 2010 was only the most dramatic example of unresolved structural problems for the euro. Unfortunately, the eurozone countries and the European Central Bank (ECB) initially failed to grasp the magnitude of the threat Greece posed to the credibility of the euro itself. As the crisis deepened financial markets responded by simply withdrawing from European risk in much the same panic-driven fashion that characterized markets at the height of the crisis in autumn 2008. Even then, the leading countries of Europe could not agree on a support plan for Greece. This spectacle of continuing disagreement had the effect of metastasizing the Greek crisis to the whole of southern Europe. Contagion became the primary preoccupation of global investors, who now focused on the structural weakness of the euro and whether the aging, low-growth welfare states of Europe could be financed over the longer term with their present levels of indebtedness.

8

Global Investment Banking

When President George H. W. Bush was defeated by William Jefferson Clinton in November 1992 there was no doubt about what I should do: leave Washington and return to international investment banking. I joined Credit Suisse First Boson (CSFB), and after a few months in New York I moved to London as CEO of CSFB Europe. Later I became chairman international of the firm.

I loved international investment banking as it was at this time. Success demanded extremely hard work, constant long-distance travel across time zones, the capacity to anticipate developments, and a good nose for when and how decisions would be made. I enjoyed the challenges and the cut and thrust of competition inherent in a business where transactional success carried significant rewards for the most successful firms and incentive compensation for those who excelled in the business.

I had the satisfaction of feeling that large-scale country and corporate transactions, especially privatizations and merger and acquisition deals, were changing the world, as indeed they were. Optimism about the next opportunity, regret for costly defeats, and the sweet feeling of winning a key strategic mandate were constant companions of the drive required to be successful.

Within Credit Suisse I observed that for any investment banking firm to succeed, it needed, in anthropological terms, both "hunters" and "skinners." Hunters engaged in the challenging effort to aquire business and the revenues associated with success; skinners prepared business brought in-house for execution in global markets. A senior colleague paid me a high compliment at one point when he said, "David was a great hunter, but also a consummate skinner." To me, it was a question of seeing money in the bank before any celebration, after a job well done on a transaction, with implications running well beyond the fees. This was how leading franchises in the business were built and retained over time. If you were an international investment banker, you had to be at the right place at the right time, and gain the confidence of the right people—not easy in a 24/7 world populated by aggressive competitors.

In the 1980s global financial markets had achieved a whole new dimension, especially foreign exchange markets. When I left Saudi Arabia at the end of 1983 for Washington, the market taking shape beneath the surface in the late 1970s and 1980s was now breaking out into an emerging global capital market. From its foundation to 1985 it was not complete. Russia, Eastern Europe, China, India, and Latin America were still for the most part on the outside.

The political implications of this breakout were yet to be recognized in the United States, but by 1985 evidence of change was growing. Two years of strong U.S. growth and the rapid spread of capital flows, supercharged by the revolution in information and communications technology, soon caught the attention of the political class. We were moving into a challenging new world. The signs of a global economy in transition included the deepening of the international debt crisis, which posed a threat to the stability of the world banking system in 1989, new levels of volatility in currency markets in the mid-1980s, and the accompanying rise in global imbalances in trade and capital account figures, which set new records month after month, were all signs of a global economy in transition. U.S. imports exploded, and large surpluses appeared in the economies of many of our trading partners. In 1985 attention in Congress shifted to protectionist initiatives. We saw the Plaza Accord and later the rise of the "Asian Tiger" economies (Korea, Hong Kong, Singapore, and Taiwan) and later still China, as its trade surplus with the United States blossomed. Congress legislated new duties for the Treasury, requiring the department to report to Congress on any country generating a large trade surplus with the United States and to determine whether such surpluses were the result of how they managed (or manipulated) their respective currencies. Suspicion of such actions required Treasury to engage in discussion, and if necessary negotiations, to encourage these surplus countries to permit the appreciation of their currencies.

By the mid-1990s one could say that the world capital market was now fully formed. The Soviet Union was gone, Russia was becoming a major player in foreign markets, and Eastern Europe was preoccupied with becoming a market economy doing business with the West. China was emerging from its shell, and Latin America, thanks to the global market in Brady Bonds and their derivatives, was attracting major new private capital flows. India had also begun the process of opening its economy and initiating domestic economic reforms.

In Latin America, Eastern Europe, Russia, and a number of emerging market countries the most widespread economic policy theme was the need for major structural reforms to promote stronger market-driven economies. The process of opening more to the world and dismantling regulatory structures that suppressed growth was gaining momentum. Among all the micro and macro policy reforms we had encouraged at Treasury in the 1980s was the privatization of large-scale government-owned enterprises that had been the vehicles of state intervention in the economy. Their dominance in what was normally the private economy in the United States and their inefficiencies were legion. A willingness to cede government control to private owners, private management, and boards peopled with private-sector directors were key litmus tests in determining how genuine and comprehensive was the commitment of any given country to credible economic reform. A country that simply wished to sell participation in a government-owned enterprise that it still controlled was in my view a country that wanted to raise money by selling a few bits of family jewelry without embracing the full magnitude of change implied by private ownership. Moreover, such minor-stake sales would create bodies of minority shareholders who could be easily victimized by the still state-owned firm of the future.

Genuine privatization, however, was gaining ground. This is where

I focused my attention in the investment banking business. Among the range of policy actions available to governments to restructure and reorient their economies, privatization of state enterprises could be advocated, structured, and marketed by private bankers. More stringent budget discipline or more open policies toward trade, foreign direct investment, and labor market reform were exclusively in the hands of governments and their legislatures. Privatization, on the other hand, required the assistance of outside expertise, knowledge of the markets, and the willingness to risk capital to execute such transactions.

Moreover, privatization, once accomplished, would bring with it benefits that would be difficult to reverse in the future. In fact, among the full range of policy reforms, privatization was clearly one of the most powerful engines for change. It sent a message both inside and outside a country that the government was embracing initiatives that would bring new management, new technologies, and fresh capital to a business that in most cases was inefficient and dependent on government subsidies. In short, privatization would help lift the economy and if successfully discharged would attract capital from inside and outside the country on a scale that government pronouncements welcoming new investment flows could not match.

From the standpoint of investment bankers, privatizations were seen as a prestigious and highly profitable business. They were usually large transactions that attracted widespread attention in the markets. Fees in the early years were good, and building a track record in the business carried with it the prospect of a top position for the bank in market league table credits, which in turn improved the firm's chances for additional equity capital market business.

But privatizations were not easy either to win or to execute. Nor was it a line of business that was widely supported in investment banks in North America, chiefly because the privatizations were not taking place in the already dominant private sector in the United States. Privatizations were largely offshore opportunities, admittedly with shares being sold into the United States, but the countries that engaged early in privatization were often seen as problem countries with dubious performance records in the past. The first big privatization opportunity I had after joining CSFB was Argentina's state-owned oil company, YPF. Until a year or so earlier, Argentina had been seen by the financial community as a "basket case" country. Who would want to buy shares in the country's largest state-owned company, a captive agency of the Argentine government?

Many privatizations were high-visibility transactions that seemed to enlarge the focus of world markets on the diversity of IPO investment opportunities. The privatization of Argentina's state-owned oil company, Yacimientos Petrolíferos Fiscales (YPF) was a classic illustration.

In July 1993 CSFB and Merrill Lynch successfully led a $3 billion IPO for Argentina's state owned oil company, YPF. The issue was listed on the NYSE and represented at that time the largest all-cash corporate IPO ever done on the NYSE. Two years earlier Argentina was seeking to exit its debt crisis status via the Brady Plan. A year before that Argentina was suffering hyperinflation after years of fiscal and monetary mismanagement, yet in July 1993 world investors accepted YPF as a leading international oil company based in a country that had brought inflation down to less than 1 percent and reestablished positive growth.

The history of YPF's privatization graphically reflected what was happening in global equity markets as they viewed the return of leading developing countries to financial and economic health. The government of President Menem in Argentina was intent on demonstrating to the world that it intended to truly privatize YPF, that is, to sell more than 50 percent of the company's shares to private investors.

In 1992 Finance Minister Domingo Cavallo, who had introduced radical monetary reform in Argentina in 1991, awarded CSFB the task of transforming YPF from a long-standing agency of the Argentine government to a corporation that would meet global standards for business organization, accountancy, and governance. This corporatization project required almost a year to complete. The aim was to transform YPF into a major corporation that would conform to the best international standards, ready to offer its shares to the international investment community. This assignment was largely carried out by CSFB before I joined the firm in November 1992.

In early 1993 the competition began for winning the mandate to lead-manage the subsequent IPO. The government's objective of selling majority control of YPF looked next to impossible to achieve due to the sheer size of YPF. The fully distributed value of YPF (the value achieved if all its stock were to be sold) was placed at $7.5 billion, so selling control of YPF would necessitate a stock sale in excess of $3.75 billion. No one in Wall Street believed that such a figure was remotely possible. In CSFB's New York–based sales and trading department I found the same remarkable lack of understanding of developments in Argentina that existed generally in the U.S. investment community. The assumption seemed to be that Argentina was still something of a "basket case." First indications from our people in New York were that floating a $1 billion stock offering for YPF was the most that world markets could absorb.

Meanwhile, Minister Cavallo explained that of all the bankers, I should understand how critical it was for Argentina to sell control of YPF to demonstrate to a skeptical world its intent and ability to truly privatize its largest corporation. I understood and renewed my efforts to educate my colleagues about the huge transformation underway in Argentina's economy. In Europe, we found a larger base of interest in Argentina and signaled that YPF might manage as much as $2 to $2.25 billion, a stretch perhaps, but conviction was growing that YPF could be a transformative transaction.

Still, we were a long way from the minimum of $3.8 billion it would take to privatize YPF in a single sale of stock. We searched for other sources of potential demand, which led us to focus on a financial situation unique to Argentina at that time. When visiting the Ministry of Finance in Buenos Aires, I saw that the building was often surrounded by elderly demonstrators carrying placards protesting against the government's treatment of their retirement benefits. I had not fully grasped the nature of their complaint, but the silent and orderly presence of hundreds of peaceful elderly people demonstrating around the building in Buenos Aires' main square touched a note of sympathy. Despite Argentina's radical monetary reform, which had brought inflation from astronomical levels to 1 percent in the space of a few months, the pensioners, known as *jubilados*, had not abandoned their campaign, which to the Menem administration might prove to be a negative feature in Argentina's otherwise improving image.

The pensioners' situation was tied to Argentina's past fiscal mismanagement. For a number of years pensioners had been issued government bonds in lieu of cash payments owed to them by the government. The bonds had maturities of some fifteen to sixteen years and carried a nominal interest rate, as I recall, of 8 percent. The interest, however, was cumulative, that is, it accumulated but was not paid during the first eight years of the life of the bond. Thus, pensioners were receiving no cash income for their retirement. All they were getting was older.

If a pensioner were desperate for cash, there was something of a secondary market for the bonds, but prices ranged around thirty cents on the dollar. The question we asked ourselves was, did the plight of the pensioners offer an opportunity for expanding the size of YPF's privatization issue?

Legal work and discussions with the Ministry of Finance moved forward quickly. If we could design some basis for exchanging the pensioners' bonds for shares in YPF we would perhaps achieve two important objectives at once: providing relief and opportunity to the pensioners and enlarging the sale of YPF shares to over 50 percent of the shares outstanding.

In the end we structured a voluntary exchange offer to pensioners under which they would be able to exchange their bonds, which earned no current return, for YPF shares bearing a cash dividend of approximately 4 percent. The ratio of exchange of bonds for shares was set at a level that gave their bonds a value of approximately seventy cents on the dollar. Announcement of the terms expected for this exchange immediately lifted the price of all such bonds to approximately seventy cents on the dollar, a vast improvement for any pensioner wishing to sell for cash. The prospect of obtaining and holding YPF shares earning a 4 percent dividend provided an additional incentive for pensioners to exchange their bonds for YPF shares.

The most serious drawback of the exchange proposal was that it would put into play in the market a volume of YPF shares nearly as large as the shares we believed could be offered for cash in the international market. The shares exchanged to pensioners would therefore represent a sizeable overhang in the market, which it was feared would put serious potential downward price pressure on the price of newly offered shares. Ultimately, this problem was addressed by placing a one year "lock up" on the shares provided to pensioners so that they could not be sold until a full year after the offering. Thus, the result was that the pensioners would receive value close to the nominal par value of their bonds, but this value could only be unlocked, and perhaps increased, depending on the stock's performance after a year's wait. This, we thought, would be acceptable to most pensioners, but those of us leading the YPF sale remained very concerned that the prospect of a wave of selling of YPF shares by pensioners a year into the future might depress the price performance of YPF shares over the near term. It might also adversely affect the initial pricing of the share offering and diminish the value of the proceeds gained by the government from the sale.

If the cash and exchange offering together were to accomplish the transfer of control of YPF to private ownership in a single marketing event, we needed to mount a substantial sales effort for both offerings. Cinema theaters were rented in Buenos Aires to explain the mechanics and benefits of the exchange offer and IPO to the large population of pensioners. Meanwhile, company representatives, officials from the Ministry of Finance, and the bankers conducted a full-scale global roadshow to market YPF's IPO and explain how the exchange offer in Argentina would accomplish the true privatization of YPF.

In the event, YPF's privatization drew widespread global interest. We sold $3 billion of YPF shares for cash in the IPO and exchanged another approximately $1.5 billion of shares for the pensioners' bonds, bringing the total sale of shares to approximately 54 percent of the company in a single combined offering. Remarkably, a company that had cost the budget of Argentina close to $500 million per year for years earned $750 million of profit in its first full year of operation, and paid taxes to the government of Argentina. Its workforce, many of whom were paid by YPF but reportedly had outside jobs elsewhere, was reduced from fifty-two thousand to twelve thousand. The stock price performed well in the first year, so that at the end of the lock up year, contrary to expectations, few pensioners sold their YPF stock. Those who did sell were made more than whole on the original value of their pensioner bonds. YPF had turned out to be a major success in both finance and political economy. Pensioners were no longer seen demonstrating around the Ministry of Finance, and Argentina had truly privatized its largest and most prestigious corporation.

More broadly, the YPF privatization demonstrated the capacity of markets to absorb high-quality investment opportunities on a global scale and to promote additional capital flows to Argentina for its continued development. The fact that Argentina failed many years later to maintain positive and credible economic policies does not change the fact that in the 1990s the nation successfully conducted significant reforms that achieved positive development for Argentina and its people. Global markets also became more engaged in providing cross-boarder capital flows that laid the basis for significant global growth and development.

Six years later, in 1999, YPF was acquired in an all-cash deal for $14 billion by Repsol of Spain, giving all shareholders of YPF a significant increase in the value of their original holdings. The crisis of 2008 in the United States and Europe did not alter this reality. YPF was but one transaction in the global movement toward privatization. Others were equally important in other parts of the world.

One such case of this global movement was the privatization of Italy's state oil company, ENI, in 1995. Here again was an example of a series of equity sales over a three-year period that privatized the company and provided significantly enhanced value to Italian and international shareholders, including the Italian government, which received large proceeds while enjoying a sharp rise in their remaining holding in ENI. The sale took place at an important moment in Italy's convergence to joining Europe's single currency and provided direction and momentum for Italy's improving position. CSFB was lead manager of all five tranches of the sale of ENI, beginning in 1995 and ultimately totaling some 65 percent of the company.

At the time, Italy was growing and had demonstrated both an improving fiscal situation and an important decline in inflation and interest rates as part of the preparatory process for joining the Euro. The culture in Italy at the time for ownership of equities was much less well established than the preference of most investors in Italy to invest in high-yielding short-term government paper. As interest rates came down, however, from traditional double-digit levels to the range of 5–6 percent, equity shares bearing a dividend yield of approximately 4 percent offered a relatively attractive investment, with significant potential for appreciation in Italy's premier oil company.

ENI's IPO offering was prepared over a period of months. The company's fully distributed presale value was placed at approximately $25 billion, and the plan was to launch an IPO for approximately 15 percent of ENI's shares. Demand for the issue was strong from outside Italy, but domestic interest, which was a high priority for the Italian treasury, was less robust. Interest in domestic equities in Italy was still developing, and we found that the marketing process in the large Italian banks was decidedly lacking in the kind of sales incentives that would accomplish widespread distribution of shares.

Over the next three years the follow-up sales of ENI shares were increasingly popular in a rising market for ENI. Far greater equity market participation emerged in Italy's domestic financial markets. After the sale of four tranches of ENI stock, producing some $25 billion of proceeds for the Italian treasury and bringing the government's ownership of ENI down to approximately 50 percent, the market value of the Italian government's remaining holding in ENI stood at only slightly less than the value of the whole company when the privatization process began in 1995. Once again, the point is the transformative power of privatization in a major Western European country. Equity markets in Italy continued to develop, and ENI distinguished itself as a leading international oil company with cross-border ownership firmly established in world markets.

The wave of privatizations continued through the decade and well into the new century. Countries privatized their public utilities, airlines, airports, and oil, gas and other natural resource companies. Dozens of telecom companies were sold to private buyers. Mexico privatized its railroads; China, its offshore oil exploration company; Hungary and Greece, their telecom companies. Brazil sold Petrobras, its giant state-owned oil company, and China privatized its main logistics company, its telecom companies, and several banks. Countries in Eastern Europe joined in, and Russia privatized numerous large state-owned enterprises.

Many of these transactions involved the sale of shares in the form of widely distributed public offerings, but as time passed growing numbers of deals were "trade" or "strategic" sales—that is, a direct private sale either to private investors or to another company in that line of business. Usually, these were smaller transactions. At one point, however, in the 1990s the flow of privatizations was estimated to have reached an annual value of approximately $100 billion.

Countries that engaged in privatizations were making an important policy declaration about their attitude toward private capital and future policy directions. Many countries liberalized their capital markets, lowered their corporate tax rates, opened their trade regimes, introduced pension fund reforms, and sometimes passed more flexible labor laws. In general, these countries were expressing a preference for stronger growth, and in due course many achieved it.

Global activity was by no means restricted to governments. Cross-border mergers and acquisitions exploded, and private companies sold shares in the international markets and listed their stock on foreign exchanges. These activities were often matched by the internationalization of production. Companies might assemble or partially assemble products in a given country, having sourced components manufactured in a wide variety of other countries. Their respective products might be sold in their home country or distrubuted widely around the world. Jobs were created in numerous locations, and local operations, wherever they were located, would probably be financed wholly or partially in local markets. Investment banking itself became a global business.

The same was true for investing, since global investment products were increasingly sold and traded globally. Much of this activity was being done in innovative ways that permitted broader, more global distribution and aftermarket trading. Investing and investment banking had become not only global, but effectively a 24/7 activity reaching well beyond the narrower national regulatory structures still commonly in place in world markets. A buyer of YPF's initial public offering in shares in 1993 naturally became a buyer of bank shares in Mexico, telecom shares in Greece, or bonds issue by German railways. As products became more sophisticated and global distribution expanded, so increased the appetite for risk and the margin for misjudgments or misunderstanding across national borders. But on balance, capital was more widely available and more easily deployable, and more financial products could be tailored to specific investor groups. On the other hand, when financial shocks occurred, as in 2008, the fallout was global, and markets that had been liberalized in previous decades immediately transmitted panic and pain to economic and financial players and stakeholders all over the world.

In this world transformation of markets, not all movement was forward, and not all developments were positive. The diversification of financial products and their increasingly broad global distribution offered opportunities for excessive risk taking, exploitation of investors in well-established developed markets and in newer markets unfamiliar with sophisticated investment products offered from outside or overseas. Negative political reactions to privatizations, external debt management deals, and the lack of transparency surrounding many investment products materialized up to and especially after 2008.

Large investment banking deals always have a significant element of political risk. This is because within a given government or country opinions are divided on the wisdom of any given transaction or the economic values that the government in power has determined to be appropriate. Not all deals go smoothly, and in some cases internal politics can generate a domestic crisis with long-term implications for a given country or for international markets.

Argentina is perhaps the best case illustration of how far-reaching adverse political reaction can become. In the 1990s Argentina was one of the leaders in South America in reforming its economy. A number of important privatizations were carried out in major areas of the economy, the most prominent being the sale of the oil company YPF to international investors in 1993. Even though Argentina experienced nearly a decade of strong growth and stability in the 1990s, the Menem administration's policies, which were strongly contested by opposition parties, weakened sharply toward the end of the decade.

In 2000 and 2001 Argentina experienced a major deterioration in its economy. Growth declined sharply, Argentina's domestic and foreign debt burden increasingly threatened its ability to maintain economic stability, restore sustained growth, and maintain the dollar-linked monetary system that had led to some ten years of stability. In spring 2001, Argentina's ability to continue to finance itself came into question. One policy option explored, and eventually implemented, was a comprehensive voluntary debt exchange proposed by Credit Suisse and JP Morgan aimed at restructuring Argentina's debt to give it the breathing space it required to reestablish its economic reform programs and to restart growth.

The "mega swap," as it became known, was a straightforward debt restructuring of virtually all of Argentina's debt. If successfully carried out, it would relieve Argentina of approximately $14 billion of near-term debt service requirements over the next eighteen months and also remove the need for Argentina to approach financial markets for new money for nearly two years. Of course, if Argentina failed to take advantage of this important near-term growth opportunity, it would face higher interest rates and even more burdensome financing requirements in the future. In May 2001, in the face of collapsing confidence in world markets, Argentina's government decided to carry out a mega swap and to accompany this with a renewed effort under its IMF program to introduce national fiscal reforms. In early June, markets enthusiastically embraced the mega swap, exchanging some $30 billion of Argentina's outstanding bonds for newly issued bonds with longer maturities.

In the months that followed the debt exchange, Argentina failed to accomplish its fiscal reforms, made the disastrous decision to reopen its tap into the domestic treasury market for new short-term funding, and challenged the IMF, resulting in a rupture of its IMF loan program. Minister of Economy Domingo Cavallo even intimated that he might welcome changes in Argentina's fixed dollar-peso exchange regime. By the end of 2001 Argentina was forced to default.

Argentina's default brought about a chaotic situation that destroyed President Fernando de la Rúa's government in late 2001, led to a series of interim governments, and eventually brought in the government of Néstor Kirchner in 2003. Within months, political forces opposed to de La Rúa sought to blame Argentina's previous president and his administration for the economic collapse. They also focused attention on the banks, both foreign and Argentine, that had managed the mega swap transaction. As a leading figure in that banking group and in light of my high-profile involvement in previous rescues of Argentina during my years at the U.S. Treasury, I was singled out among the private bankers for special attention by the media and by the new government.

Soon thereafter, in early 2002, the political rhetoric turned more serious. The populist party Alternative for a Republic of Equals (ARI) joined forces with a public prosecutor to pursue an investigation of the mega swap, focusing on the former government officials and the bankers who led it. The prosecutor originally sought to bring charges of fraud against the former government officials. The court of appeals overturned these charges, however, because the evidence surrounding the execution of the transaction and the consensus opinion of two panels of experts appointed by the court could not support the charges. After more than five years of investigation, the prosecutor had not been able to produce any evidence of fraud, bribery, or illegality in the processes leading up to the exchange or in the exchange itself. The mega swap had been carried out in full compliance with the laws of Argentina and with no irregularities regarding the award, transaction fees, or selling practices engaged in by the syndicate of banks. Pure and simple, the mega swap was a standard bond swap transaction, although of record-breaking size.

I cooperated with the investigation by providing two lengthy statements explaining the mega swap operation in detail and answering questions posed by the acting magistrate judge overseeing the investigation. Nevertheless, the prosecutor continued to demand that I come to Argentina to give testimony on the mega swap. The prosecutor continued to portray me as the key banker in developing the mega swap strategy with Minister of Economy Domingo Cavallo. This of course was untrue. Many other bankers were involved, and Minister Cavallo was not serving in the government until late March 2001, long after the mega swap proposal was put forward.

After the initial fraud charges were overturned, the prosecutor renewed his campaign against former Minister Cavallo and his deputy, Daniel Marx, as well as me among the private bankers. The prosecutor changed the basis for his investigation to charges of "incompatible negotiations," a vague charge specific only to Argentina and one not recognized by most democratic countries. The court indicted Minister Cavallo and Minister Marx on these charges. The charges against Marx were later dismissed due to an acquittal in a another case with similar allegations. I was not indicted by the court. The prosecutor, however, continued to pursue his investigation of me. In August 2009, more than eight years after the mega swap, the court summoned me to Argentina to give testimony. I offered to cooperate by providing my testimony in the United States under the terms of the U.S.–Argentina Mutual Legal Assistance Treaty (MLAT). The Argentine court agreed and filed a request in late 2010 for this proceeding with the U.S. Department of Justice.

While this request was proceeding through U.S. channels, the acting magistrate judge issued a surprising and brazen order demanding that the United States take my testimony within "a non-extendable" period of forty-five days. The order threatened an international arrest warrant for me if the United States did not comply. The Argentine court of appeals—apparently recognizing the irrationality of the magistrate's demand, overturned the magistrate's order.

This was followed by a similarly abrupt order in June 2012. After requesting a status update from the United States, but before waiting for a response, the magistrate cancelled the MLAT request and again ordered that I appear in Argentina to provide testimony under threat of an international arrest warrant if I did not appear. When I did not appear, due to previously scheduled medical treatment of which I had informed the court, the magistrate issued an international arrest warrant on August 30, 2012. Curiously, the acting magistrate's change of course in the summer of 2012 occurred only after receiving a letter from members of the Argentine congress urging him to move forward quickly "under pain of declaring [the magistrate] liable should the cases lapse." A month after issuing the warrant, the magistrate appeared before the Argentine senate for a confirmation hearing for a permanent appointment as a federal judge.

Argentina sent the arrest warrant to INTERPOL, disseminated it to all INTERPOL member countries through INTERPOL's systems, and sought INTERPOL's assistance in issuing a Red Notice, an international notice for my arrest and extradition. INTERPOL immediately recalled the dissemination of this warrant while it considered the request for a Red Notice. In October 2013, INTERPOL denied the request for a Red Notice and took the further step of prohibiting any use of INTERPOL's systems in connection with Argentina's request for my arrest.

Throughout this entire period, now some twelve years, Argentina continued to make demands for my testimony and threaten me with arrest. I was not charged with any crime in Argentina. I was sought for apprehension simply because they wanted me to appear in person to give testimony the substance of which I had already provided twice in writing and had expressed a willingness to provide in the United States pursuant to the bilateral treaty. As time went on, I was concerned, and so were many others, about the risk of appearing in Argentina because of the unpredictable and unjust legal process I had experienced in this case. The Argentine government's outrageous attempts to intimidate me and to disrupt my ability to pursue my international investment banking career (not to mention threats while I served for five years as U.S. Ambassador to India) was nothing short of bizarre. The Kirchner government, fully aware of this harassment, took no action to stop it and, in fact supported the pursuit by transmitting requests to the United States and INTERPOL. This long-running campaign to obtain my testimony recently prompted the United States government to express its concern to the Argentine government about the length of this investigation and the means used by the Argentine government. Nevertheless, Argentina's harassment continues to this day, demonstrating how political risk can trump any semblance of the rule of law in some countries.

Over these twelve years, the government of Argentina has expropriated YPF from Repsol, its Spanish owner; deported some of Repsol's Spanish employees at YPF; and refused for several years to negotiate or even discuss expropriation compensation to Repsol. In addition, Argentina has defied global markets with regard to honoring its own agreements to meet its international debt obligations and rescheduled its debt with international bondholders twice in the intervening years. As a result, Argentina does not have access to international capital markets today.

9

Writing a New History with India

There are times when one has to be completely honest with oneself. How often have we heard some public figure over-dramatize a new appointment or opportunity with the words, "Everything I have done and experienced in my life up to now has prepared me for this moment." Outbursts like this have always struck me as excessive and probably inaccurate. The truth, however, is that when I became U.S. ambassador to India in January 2004, that very thought took shape in my own consciousness. Fortunately, I made no statement except to Jeannie, who had herself come to the same conclusion. In fact, she went further, saying "You must write a book about your unique life, and I already have the title: 'Packing for India.'"

No doubt India was poised to emerge as a great nation. When I was approached in the summer of 2003 about serving as U.S. ambassador to India, I was sure of India's rise. The surprise turned out to be that it happened so quickly and dramatically in the succeeding years. President George W. Bush's appraisal was right on the mark: one-sixth of humanity, over one billion people, living peacefully in a successful democracy. This has to be important for the United States.

Secretary Colin Powell called on a Saturday afternoon in June 2003 to ask on behalf of President Bush if I would be willing to serve as U.S. ambassador to India. I had been outside vacuuming the car when Jeannie rushed out, shouting, "Turn off the vacuum, the Secretary of State is calling!" Jeannie listened with alarm to my side of the conversation:

"I have never thought of being an ambassador before, in fact I've never wanted to be an ambassador."

"You know, Colin, that I do not have an ambassadorial personality. I am the less-flexible Treasury type of person, as you know from our past dealings."

"If I were to be an ambassador the only countries that I would be interested in are India and China."

Luckily for me, as Colin put it, it was India the president had in mind, and he wanted an answer by the following Tuesday morning. Apparently, the president wanted someone with extensive government and business experience, because he believed this was what was needed now in India.

Following the call, Jeannie and I sat at the kitchen table and within the hour had made the easiest big decision in our twenty-five years together. We had both visited India in the 1990s on business and as tourists. We called it the country of kaleidoscopic diversity—color, action, confusion, pathos, politeness, convictions, and huge aspirations. India was so much more than a large, exotic land. Indian culture had occupied the same space of the subcontinent for five thousand years. It had been conquered and ruled by many different rulers, but it had captured its rulers and co-opted them into its own ethos, remaining today a country uniquely representative of its cultural and religious roots.

To me, the modern miracle of India was that in its first fifty years as an independent nation it had overcome the tragedies of partition and massively destructive communal violence after independence to become a lively, secular, multicultural, multireligious, multiracial, multiethnic, multicaste, multilingual, multiregional democracy. India was diversity personified, but its governance was a settled matter under a comprehensive, much-amended constitution. In a world in which the United States professed to teach democracy to many nations with only minimal success, in just sixty years India established itself as a great functioning democracy . In fact, democracy for India was the means by which it had created itself, governed itself, and become a great nation.

Relations between the United States and India in those first fifty years were a very up and down affair. There was affection and admiration between the two democracies but little in the way of sustained common interests. India ran a planned economy modeled on the Soviet Union, which was also India's chief supplier of weapons. India's economy was characterized by extensive government intervention, high protective tariffs, prohibitions against foreign direct investment, and a smothering bureaucracy inherited along with the English language from British colonial government. This model, essentially an import substitution economy with heavy government intervention, constrained India's growth during its first forty years of independent nationhood. India's growth remained mainly 2–4 percent, never exceeding 5 percent for any sustained period, while the population exploded from about three hundred million at the time of independence to over one billion after the turn of the century. India's agricultural sector, which occupies the great majority of India's population, seldom grew beyond 2.5 percent per year. Burdened with a rising population and low growth, India generated massive poverty and most of the ills that go with it.

Among the poorest developing nations, India nominated itself as the leader of the developing world, head of the movement of ostensibly nonaligned states. No wonder that in the 1980s at Treasury I found that India took a contrary position to virtually all international economic and financial policies of the United States, particularly including in the International Monetary Fund and the World Bank, which remained through the period one of India's only large sources of external capital. The same pattern of opposition to the United States characterized India's positions in the United Nations.

Two major developments in the early 1990s brought fundamental change to India and began a process that started moving India's interests closer to those of the United States. One was the tearing down of the Berlin Wall and the collapse of the Soviet empire. The second was the near-bankruptcy of India in 1991 that marked the beginning of India's reform process and gradual opening to the global economy. Suddenly, the Soviet economic model had collapsed, not only in the Soviet Union but across the whole of Eastern Europe. Just as abruptly, India virtually ran out of foreign exchange and was on the brink of economic disaster. This was when Prime Minister Manmohan Singh, then acting as India's finance minister, instituted India's emerging economic reform program, which gradually pulled India back from the brink. The implications of the Soviet collapse took more time to filter through India's intelligentsia, but within two to three years India realized that it was in its interests to seek stronger relations with the world's now-sole superpower.

It is important to understand the unique nature of the economic reform process in India. Throughout the 1990s India was governed by a series of multiparty coalition governments. Therefore, it is fair to say that since 1991 the vast majority of Indian political parties have been part of a government coalition that at one time or another engaged in advancing the process of economic reform. Indian politics can be colorful and divisive, but achieving broad consensus on economic transformation has been a priority in the political process. Thus, while reform in India and its movement toward opening to the global economy has been frustratingly slow (compared, say, with China), reforms once established have stayed in place. Despite changing governments there has not been backward movement or major reversals of reforms already put in place. This, it seems, is a tribute to India's consensual approach to change as it put in place during the 1990s the foundations that later would promote stronger growth. Of course, the outside world sees India as slow and disorganized, both accurate assessments to some extent, but what is not so visible is the steady movement forward without major political blowups. India conducts reforms gradually, under the political radar. Rarely are matters brought to a truly divisive confrontation that results in retaliatory backward movement or a collapse of the coalition government.

As the decade of the 1990s advanced U.S.–India relations improved and attention was given to modestly reducing the role of government in India's economy. India's version of privatization, known in India rather strictly as "disinvestment," visualized the sell down of government positions in state-owned enterprises but nowhere near levels that might threaten government control. At one point in the mid 1990s, for example, Credit Suisse First Boston, my investment banking firm, and Goldman Sachs won the mandate to lead-manage a share offering (disinvestment) to the public of 10–15 percent of the Indian Oil Corporation. Under subsequent coalition governments, the stock offering never went forward.

Two exceptions to state control emerged in the 1990s, however, that over time would have a profound effect on India's transformation. One was liberalization in the telecommunications sector, including new startup opportunities and privatization of government entities. The second was the unimpeded rise of India's information technology sector, which was to show the way forward for an industry outside the grip of government ownership or the excessive reach of government bureaucracy.

There was also growing evidence of progress, both on the political and economic fronts, in relations with the United States. My assessment of the reform process in India at that time was that despite its slow and uneven progress, the reform impulse was genuine and enjoyed significant political support. India had accepted that it could no longer afford its respectable socialist, slow-growing, import-substitution economic model.

Once again, two major events intervened near the end of the nineties to set back India's progress and its improving relations with the United States. The first was the Asian financial crisis of 1997 and the second was India's decision in 1998 to test a nuclear weapon in direct contravention of the Nuclear Non-Proliferation Treaty of 1974, which India had never signed. The currency crisis that washed across Asia in 1997 was a short and destructive wakeup call to the global financial community, but India, thanks to its tightly regulated financial markets and its capital and exchange controls, was for the most part protected from the turbulence of international markets. Liberalization of India's financial markets as a part of its further opening to the global economy was now on the back burner and would remain so for years to come.

The nuclear test of 1998 was also a costly setback to India's global opening aspirations. India developed its modest nuclear capacity for energy and nuclear weapons to defend against its two nuclear-armed neighbors, Pakistan and China, but for this India was ostracized worldwide and punished for its strategic nuclear program.

The United States and most other members of the nuclear suppliers' group of nations, signatories to the 1974 treaty, imposed sanctions on India that disrupted India's economy. The Clinton administration, which had seemed friendly to India's overtures for closer relations, suddenly became the key disruptive influence to India's economy and its sense of military security. The fact that India was not a signatory of the 1974 treaty and had developed its nuclear capacity without inward or outward proliferation counted for nothing. India's isolation from nuclear commerce was deepened and fortified, while modest military equipment purchases were disrupted with painful and deeply resented implications for India's perceived military security.

U.S. sanctions lasted fewer than four years before they were lifted by President Bush after the 9/11 attacks. Still, the negative fallout from sanctions on U.S.–India relations has been long lasting and even today is still only gradually being overcome by U.S. defense suppliers.

Shortly after the lifting of U.S. sanctions Pakistani terrorists attacked India's parliament in a blatant and destructive effort to undermine Indian democracy and political stability. Suddenly the world at large was focused on the terrifying reality of two mortal enemies, sharing a border, armed with nuclear weapons, and inexperienced in nuclear diplomacy, locked in a high stakes confrontation. The politicians and global investors who might have seen India as a nation with prospects were severely rattled, even after the zenith of potential nuclear confrontation had passed. The subcontinent was now seen as a more dangerous place; at the same time, the near-miss nuclear experience seemed to have had a sobering effect on the rhetoric of both nations. By 2003, economic growth had picked up in both countries. This is how things stood at the opening of 2003, the year I use to date the emergence of India's modern high-growth economy. In December 2003 the Senate confirmed my appointment as ambassador, and I was in New Delhi in early 2004.

Jeannie and I arrived from London in the middle of the night and were taken directly to Roosevelt House, the official residence and our new home in India for the next five years. The full staff of eleven and the residence manager greeted us with a brief candlelit Hindu ritual of welcome. Delicious Roosevelt House soup was served, and as we waited for our bags to arrive from the airport, we could see out into the deep, softly lit garden and pool area. The night was deliciously cool with a pungent haze of fog from the settling coolness and the smoke of fires in the sleeping dwellings and encampments of road workers and police strung along the roads of Delhi.

It was Sunday, so we had a day to rest and prepare for the first business day at the embassy. Winter mornings in Delhi are invariably hazy or even shrouded in heavy fog. When we arose, soft, filtered sunlight filled the garden of large, exotic trees, some covered in bright orange blooms, and a wide variety of brightly colored flowers. But what struck us first that day in the garden, and every day for the next five years, were the brilliant green parakeets and other birds that formed what we came to call the "magic kingdom."

Stepping directly into a major diplomatic post is not easy, especially for a political appointee who had never before been in an embassy, except as a visitor. My arrival had been anticipated for months, in both the country and the Embassy community. When we arrived, the U.S. mission in India numbered more than two thousand employees, of which approximately six hundred were American citizens, with the balance being Indian nationals, many of whom were loyal and longstanding employees. In our years in India, the mission became the largest civilian mission in the American system and also the most diverse in its representation of U.S. government departments and agencies. A number of U.S. embassies have large groups attached to them, such as the U.S. Agency for International Development (AID) contingent in Cairo, but in India the diversity of representation reflected the broad interface between India and the United States, which touched virtually every field of human activity one could imagine.

Roosevelt House stood in its own garden next to the main chancery, both buildings designed by the American architect Edward Durrell Stone in the early 1950s and now categorized as preserved buildings by the United States. The full compound covered forty acres, three city blocks, and included a chancery annex where the large visa operation was housed, garden-type housing units, a recreation center, medical clinic, the marine barracks, a baseball field complete with lights, support buildings, and the American School of some fifteen hundred students and teachers. Delhi city streets surrounded the compound and cut through in two difference places, one separating the school and causing a significant security challenge, and the other separating the Marine barracks from the chancery and exposing the annex, where visa applicants waited in long lines.

In the State Department training for new ambassadors and their spouses, which takes place in Washington for two weeks, one is constantly reminded that your first duty as ambassador is the security of the embassy and all its staff at all times and under all circumstances. This is no empty challenge. The marine detachment (ours was eleven at full complement) is there to protect the embassy from intrusion and to secure the communications facilities and interior of the embassy from attack. The setback of buildings from the surrounding streets, as well as the walls and gates giving access to the embassy, have to be protected and kept under constant surveillance for signs of possible attack. One needs only to read the daily intelligence traffic to know that it is not an empty threat that America faces around the world.

The inspector general of the State Department had informed me before leaving Washington of the serious morale problem that existed in the U.S. mission in India. This had apparently arisen from a combination of factors stretching back over the years of disrupted relations as well as from the management approach of my predecessor. Deputy Chief of Mission Robert Blake had been sent to Delhi pending my arrival to begin to address the local situation. Bob was a competent and respected Foreign Service officer who by the end of 2003 had improved the situation, but with no sitting ambassador present morale remained a significant problem when we arrived.

The job challenge for an ambassador in the American system is very much a team challenge for the ambassador and his or her spouse. An American mission is a family community that responds to a leadership approach that is based on the recognition and practice of family values. The sense of family, though different from one family to the next, is an important binding force for workers and dependents working for the United States in distant places, often under difficult circumstances.

Therefore, Jeannie and I began day one at the Embassy meeting people, one by one, in their place of work. We did not hold a large townhall meeting, but instead greeted and shook hands with virtually every employee in the embassy, first in Delhi, then in Mumbai, Chennai, and Kolkata. We made this our priority of the first two weeks, and it worked well with both American and Indian employees.

One of the chief benefits from this process was that it gave me the opportunity to meet a large group of friendly, able, interesting people and to gain an early understanding of how diverse and far reaching our contacts and working relations were with the Indian community.

To understand the magnitude of the transformation in U.S.–India relations that followed over the next five years, it is essential to recapture the cross-currents and sensitivities in play between the two countries at the beginning of 2004. The 9/11 attack in New York had deeply shocked India, and many Indians and Indian Americans had been killed. There had been an immediate outpouring of sympathy for the United States, but more than two years later, there was a mixture of alarm and opposition to the U.S. response in Iraq. India, after all, had a Muslim population of nearly 150 million, some two thirds of whom were Sunni Muslims. Four months after 9/11 India suffered a bloody attack on its parliament building in New Delhi, the symbolic and operational heart of Indian democracy. The U.S. had, of course, declared itself outraged by the attack and expressed its deepest sympathies with the people of India. From India's point of view however, the attack, carried out by Pakistani terrorists against India's parliament, went unpunished by the U.S. in its relations with Pakistan. When the State Department issued booming statements that all terrorism anywhere in the world was equally unacceptable, where was the evidence of that conviction in America's continuing close relations with the perpetrators of India's own 9/11? No wonder that even at senior levels of society, Indians believed that America, despite its strong words, had a double standard when it came to terrorism in India, especially terrorism spawned from America's friend and ally to the northwest.

Meanwhile, the lingering resentments from the 1998–2001 sanctions, the sense of injustice caused by thirty years' isolation from the world of civil nuclear commerce, the denial of full access to sophisticated space and defense technologies, and India's rising concerns about America's entry into Iraq and its presence in Afghanistan complicated relations. Finally, among India's intelligentsia, media leaders, academics, think tank communities, foreign service personnel, and many retired bureaucrats, there remained a legacy of mistrust and suspicion of the United States reaching back to the U.S. support of Pakistan in the Indo-Pakistani War of 1971.

India, I discovered, was not alone in having such lingering suspicions and resentments. They were also present in the U.S. State Department and Foreign Service as well as in the U.S. defense establishment and the CIA. In fact, while going through my brief period of orientation at the State Department in Washington, I was told I faced a very tough job in India and that I would no doubt have trouble recruiting Foreign Service officers to serve there. Two years later I had fifteen to twenty keen applicants for any senior embassy or consulate position opening in India. So much for lingering suspicions and resentments!

My first three to four months in India made a deep and lasting impression on me and set the basis for my approach to India over the next five years. Our widespread visits throughout the U.S. mission also gave us the opportunity of meeting Indians around the country. This permitted us to begin gathering a wider sense of Indians' attitudes away from embedded views of the political community in New Delhi. As midwestern Americans who understood the limits to how Washington represents the people spread across America, we assumed, correctly as it turned out, that the same was to some extent true in India.

Many of the people we met had children or relatives in America or had visited America themselves. We found that the United States was popular, admired, and respected. This did not mean that everyone agreed with our policies or supported what we were doing in the world. It did mean, however, that they admired what I called the ethos of America, our basic values, the clear sense that America was a land of opportunity, where a person's prospects were not constrained by the multitude of limitations and complexities of Indian society. Many of the people we met had relatives, offspring, or acquaintances who had made these opportunities a reality. We were also seen as a generous nation and high expectations were held for our willingness and capacity to stand up for the right things in the world. Most saw America's involvement in Iraq as a mistake. The removal of Saddam Hussein was considered a positive result, but perhaps at too high a cost. Many thought our support for Pakistan was unconditional and therefore viewed as a sign of America's traditional naiveté and a barrier to the establishment of a relationship of full trust between our governments. Yet despite the traumatic events since 9/11 in the United States, it was clear that India's large Muslim population was not radicalized. Islamic opposition to the United States had simply not taken root in India. India's Muslims it seemed were Indians first and Muslims second.

The three key conclusions I drew from these early experiences in India were, first, that an enormous reservoir of goodwill existed toward the United States among the great majority of citizens of India. Americans enjoyed dynamic and friendly relationships with Indians that were separate from and in my opinion more important at that moment than our official bilateral relationship.

The second conclusion was that Indians' attitudes toward Pakistan were not at all uniform. Whereas the common view of the State Department in Washington was that Indo-Pak issues dominated all aspects of our relationship, this was not the case on the ground in India, even in Delhi. To be more precise, I found as I moved around India and became acquainted with younger people in Delhi considerable variation in the strength of views about Pakistan. In the south of India I did not feel Pakistan mattered very much to people. The young were not particularly interested in Pakistan; they were much more engaged with issues to do with education and opportunities to get ahead. India's young parliamentarians were also much less engaged on Pakistan issues than were their elders. Their focus was on India's future, its rise in the world, and the opportunities for modernizing India's position in the global economy. The high tech and business communities likewise had other priorities. In the final analysis, it was the "mandarin" community in Delhi that felt the strongest and seemed to obsess the most about Pakistan. This included India's think-tank community and many of its academic leaders and media people. Pakistan was also a dominant issue among the Muslim communities of the north (an important voting block in state elections) and also especially among India's older generation and their descendents who had suffered through partition and its aftermath.

The third conclusion was perhaps the most important. The wide range of subject matter and issues that came forward to me, together with the variety of people and programs in the Embassy, impressed upon me the far-reaching diversity of America's growing interface with India. The U.S. mission in India was on its way to becoming the largest civil mission in the system, but also the most diverse in terms of departmental and agency representation on the ground in New Delhi. In addition, India was now second only to Mexico in the issue of visas to the United States, and it was far and away number one in the world in the issue of H-1B foreign worker visas.

For me, all of this underlined that the future of U.S.–India relations would be driven more by our civil societies, private sectors, and person- to-person relations than by the official bilateral core of the relationship. The range of engagement was truly comprehensive, touching virtually every area of human endeavor. In addition to the highest priority areas of political and economic relations, the United States was engaged in science; health care and disease control (through the Center for Disease Control in Atlanta); agriculture; space; education; transportation; civil aviation; U.S. AID; all branches of the military; defense sales; human trafficking; religious freedom; public diplomacy; FBI and legal affairs; intelligence; counter terrorism; and commercial services, for which there were seven branch offices.

These many areas of engagement promised to generate a steady flow of government, NGO, and private-sector visits. As ambassador, and given the kind of broad-based relationship I could see developing between the United States and India, I decided to give attention to every type of program interface with India that was present in the mission community. This would not only build morale in the mission, it would also recognize the particular areas that I saw building in our relations. In short, I decided that I needed to approach the ambassador's job as a chief executive officer managing about twenty divisions instead of simply a traditional ambassador focusing on the high-level aspects of bilateral diplomatic relations. In the end I was able to do both. In fact, the ambassador role and the hands-on CEO approach were mutually reinforcing throughout my five years in India and account for the success I feel I achieved there.

In early 2004 the BJP government was nearing the end of its five-year term. Elections had to be held by May, and the BJP believed itself well placed to win the general election comfortably. The Indian economy had reached growth levels of approximately 8 percent in recent quarterly reports, and the BJP adopted the campaign slogan for the election of "India shining".

An Indian general election is a major democratic event by any standard. India's approximately 650 million registered voters turn out in force on specified dates during a roughly five-week period of voting in sequentially designated areas of the country. All voting in India is electronic. The results are stored until the designated day for the announcement of results—in this case May 15, 2004. Exit polling is not permitted by India's formidable election commission.

In the lead-up to the election the pundits, media, and the mandarin community in Delhi were strongly of the opinion that the BJP would win the election without difficulty. In fact, the retiring BJP government had pledged that it would lift the foreign equity ownership cap in the insurance industry from 26 percent to 49 percent in the first twenty-one days of its new government. But it was not to be. The BJP was defeated despite India's stunning growth record, and the Congress Party, long out of government, was given the opportunity of forming a new coalition government.

It was hard to say who was more surprised. The BJP had not expected to lose, and the Congress had not expected to win. The next few weeks produced high drama. Mrs. Sonia Gandhi, the leader of the Congress Party and the natural choice in India's parliamentary system to become prime minister and form a new coalition government, withdrew from the invitation issued by the president of India. There was strong opposition to her becoming prime minister because she was foreign born and had entered elective politics only as the widow of Rajiv Gandhi, who was assassinated in 1991. Nevertheless, Mrs. Gandhi was and remains the leader of the Congress Party. Her withdrawal was seen as a great act of selflessness, which in Indian politics virtually sanctified Mrs. Gandhi. She proposed Manmohan Singh as prime minister, and the Congress set about the complex task of forming a coalition government. This required the support of India's leftist parties, the Communists of West Bengal and the state of Kerala. In the end, the Communists supported the formation of the government but declined to take responsible cabinet positions in the new government, thus preserving their freedom to oppose specific policy initiatives and to withdraw their support from the government at any time.

In the next weeks the consecration of the new United Progressive Alliance coalition required the negotiation of a common minimum policy agreement binding the coalition partners together and setting the broad policies for the new government. The diversity of the parties made this a difficult and time-consuming task. The leftist parties that were essential to the formation of a government but which had elected not to serve as responsible ministers in that government were particularly difficult negotiating partners. Certainly, they would not sanction a provision in the common minimum policy agreement asserting the importance of a "strategic partnership" with the United States. We could therefore only wait through the weeks of negotiation, and then, when the common minimum policy document was finalized, we waited through the many days required to hand out ministerial posts among the coalition partners. For many weeks there was no clear signal as to whether the new Congress-led government would move forward with the U.S. strategic relationship or return to the policies of Congress's past.

Prime Minister Singh was not one of the large beasts of Indian politics. He was considered a technocrat but also as an honest politician who led India's opening reform efforts in 1991, a challenge of extreme difficulty he had met with intelligence and authority. It was said that he did not have his own political constituency but enjoyed the full personal trust of Mrs. Gandhi. It was perhaps this last consideration that set Manmohan Singh apart. He brought a gracious and sturdy patience to the sensitive complexities of establishing a new government in India. Beyond the formation of the coalition and the assignment of ministerial portfolios, Prime Minister Singh was burdened with the outspoken criticisms of the opposition, waiting in the wings for the coalition process to collapse, that he was not prime ministerial material, that he was a mere functionary of Sonia Gandhi, and that inevitably he would be neither capable nor empowered to run the whole government of India.

Prime Minister Singh survived these attacks and many more like them over the next five years. As time passed, these challenges were shown to be well wide of the mark. Prime Minister Singh consistently demonstrated patience and respect in dealing with colleagues, caution regarding inflammatory political issues and capability— all integral in dealing with this unique format for parliamentary government—all while being a prime minister separate from the leader of the governing party, who held no official position in government. These became the distinguishing features of leadership by Prime Minister Singh.

There was, therefore, no grand announcement that India would continue its strategic partnership efforts with the United States. Instead, there was an informal message, quietly given and without detailed definition. By September it was clear that the relationship with the U.S. was on track, tentatively perhaps, and without the benefit of formal public confirmation. With plenty of other issues to occupy the new coalition government and the Indian media, formal recognition of renewed U.S.–India relations could only be counterproductive.

Prior to the general election the effort to build a closer strategic relationship between the United States and India was already under way. Relations with India's BJP government in early 2004 were good. An initiative that had been given the awkward name of Next Steps Strategic Partnership (NSSP) was launched at the beginning of 2004. Its purpose was to bring together elements of the two bureaucracies to identify and if possible to eliminate regulatory and administrative barriers that prevented India and America from working more closely together. The target of this collaboration was the debris left over from sanctions that discouraged or prevented the expansion of trade relations in sensitive fields such as high-tech exports, defense or space-related products, and missile defense technologies. We expected that significant progress could be achieved in these and other areas without having to make changes in U.S. legislation. The initiative was aimed at deepening political relations with India and improving prospects for India's recently launched peace initiatives with Pakistan. Prime Minister Vajpayee was seen by the United States in a very favorable ligh, and his national security advisor, Mr. Brajesh Mishra, was seen as the chief visionary both for the peace initiative and the effort to strengthen U.S. relations.

NSSP, despite its cumbersome name, marked an important step in the new beginning. Although it operated chiefly at the technical level and in the end bridged two different governments in India over the space of little more than a year, its progress was both immediate and measurable. Approximately twenty-six percentof high-tech U.S. exports in 2003 required burdensome export licensing procedures left over in many cases from the 1998 sanctions. A year later exports requiring licensing of this type were reduced to only 1 percent of the total. Raytheon, a major American defense contractor, concluded a small but important radar contract with the Indian Ministry of Defense, and confidential briefings were started between our two governments on missile defense technology. Efforts were also made to improve our interface with India in the defense sales field generally.

On the other hand, NSSP revealed the magnitude of the challenge we faced in overcoming the past. Before leaving Washington I had been alerted to the extreme sensitivity of Indo-Pak issues, as they were termed in the State Department. Once in India I began to make my own appraisal of Indo-Pak relations. I had learned long ago that standardized, prepackaged philosophies seldom hold up on the ground.

It was not a question of Pakistan being unimportant to the United States. Obviously, it was very important, and there were clearly matters of great sensitivity in Indo-Pak relations. Nevertheless, it was clear to me Pakistan was not the dominant issue: India did not need to see every issue through the prism of its relationship with Pakistan. I believed that we should work to dehyphenate Indo-Pak and make clear to the Indian government and to the Indian public that the United States perceived its relationship with India as a free-standing bilateral relationship and was supportive of India's vision of becoming a world power. Our relationship with Pakistan was also a free-standing relationship with an important ally, but the vision was regional, not global in scope.

Initially, this evolving approach had limited traction. Rumors that Congress would consider selling new or upgraded F-16s to Pakistan was front-page headline news in India. The terrorism double standard and the United State's apparent unwillingness to exercise credible conditions on its aid to Pakistan in order to force a reduction in its hostility to India continued to be major complaints in Delhi.

There was a particularly graphic example of these sensitivities in March 2004 when Secretary of State Colin Powell visited New Delhi. India had announced its general election to be concluded in May of that year. The secretary's visit was warmly welcomed, and Secretary Powell did an outstanding job of conveying the warmth and support of the United States for India. He was due to visit Pakistan following India and was pointedly asked by the Indians not to say or do anything in Pakistan that would upset the ongoing election process in India. The next day in Pakistan, the secretary announced that the United States would give major non-NATO ally status to Pakistan, giving Pakistan easier access to certain types of military equipment.

A firestorm of rage swept through Delhi in the next few days. The concession granted to Pakistan was not particularly significant, and we at the embassy, with Secretary Powell's approval, immediately acknowledged that the secretary's announcement had been an inadvertent error and would not in practice pose any significant disadvantage to India. But the damage had been done, and the outrage was something to behold.

Yet within the first few months of India's new government becoming operational, an overture was made to me that provided an important opening for future relations. One evening in November a senior official asked to see me informally at the residence. Over a cup of tea on the veranda he explained that India wished to expand its business relations with the United States, but that within the Indian government it was felt that important U.S. companies did not show the top-level interest or commitment that India expected. He cited as an example the Boeing Company's approach to Air India's current interest in the tender for sixty-eight wide-body airliners as a part of India's plan to transform its airline industry. India and the United States, after years of fruitless dialogue, had agreed after brief negotiations in 2003 to establish the world's most liberal bilateral open skies agreement. In late 2003 India had agreed to buy forty-three single-aisle Airbus aircraft after a contentious tender competition between Airbus and Boeing, in which Boeing believed it had not been treated fairly. Boeing raised its case with the secretary of state in late 2003 and asked the U.S. government to intercede on its behalf with the government of India. Secretary Powell had declined to make an approach to the Indians, and I likewise had advised Boeing's representatives in India against taking steps in court to try to force Indian Airlines, India's domestic carrier, to rebid the contract. Boeing's representatives claimed that the company could have improved its price by approximately 20 percent but were not given the opportunity to do so. My advice, based on extensive experience with similar situations, was to refrain from starting a fight they were unlikely to win. The best strategy would have been to present their most competitive price the first time around and be prepared to improve marginally if that were required to win the business.

In any case, the Air India purchase would be for large, long-distance aircraft that could perform nonstop service between India and the United States. India perceived that it was losing its most important market, the United States, to other airlines flying routes through Singapore, Dubai, and Frankfurt, and to recover that market under the new U.S.–India open skies agreement it would need a fleet of the most competitive long-distance aircraft. The value of such a transaction would be approximately $9 billion.

Hence, when my visitor mentioned Boeing as an example of the kind of U.S. company India would like to develop a relationship with, it is not hard to imagine how alert I became. Essentially, the point the Indian official made was that Boeing did not project a broad vision for India from the top leadership of the company. Its representatives were lower-level local sales representatives whose sole preoccupation was to market airplanes to Air India, neglecting the fact that Boeing was a major American corporation manufacturing a wide range of products applicable to India's future for air travel and defense. As a businessman, the official felt certain I would understand the point he was trying to make, and indeed his message was clearly understood.

A few days later I telephoned Harry Stonecipher, CEO of the Boeing, in Chicago. The tender deadline for the sixty-eight aircraft was set for December 24, and it was now late November. When Mr. Stonecipher took the call I explained the approach I had received and suggested that he should make a visit to India in the next two weeks to meet with India's top political leadership. His agenda should be to project Boeing's vision for India above and beyond the forthcoming tender. He should be as broad as possible in product terms and emphasize what Boeing could bring to India as a business committed to India's own development. I explained that I had on my desk a letter from the secretary of state to the prime minister advocating on behalf of Boeing, which I would feel much more comfortable sending forward if I knew Mr. Stonecipher would visit India's top leaders in the next two weeks. Mr. Stonecipher came to India, paid visits to its leading ministers, including the prime minister (all meetings I attended), and successfully projected Boeing's broad vision for India. The following year Boeing won the order for sixty-eight new airplanes and went on over the next three years to sell some $25 billion of aircraft to India. Later still, its defense business made important breakthroughs as the entire scale of its commitment to India changed.

The year 2005 marked the beginning of our great breakthrough with India. President Bush had won his second term. Condoleezza Rice was our new secretary of state, and she was succeeded in the White House as national security advisor by her number two, Stephen Hadley. As far as I was concerned, this was in every way a winning team. In the president's first term, his national security assessment had singled out India as a top foreign policy priority for the United States. The NSSP negotiation, which marked the first step toward a new strategic partnership, had made good progress.

Secretary of Defense Donald Rumsfeld stopped in New Delhi in early December 2004 on a tour through the area that also included Pakistan. This was an important visit because it provided the secretary his first opportunity to assess India's new coalition government. There is nothing like face-to-face contact to see and feel India's dynamism. The visit helped repair the hurt feelings and lingering suspicions of the major non-NATO ally fiasco the previous March. This was also the first high-level defense visit since India had announced that it planned to refurbish its air force with the purchase of 126 multi-role fighter aircraft. I appealed to Secretary Rumsfeld to reconsider the Defense Department's irritating decision not to display any high-end fighter aircraft at India's second biannual Bangalore Air Show. Happily, within a month after his visit, Secretary Rumsfeld authorized the presence of two U.S. F15 fighters, which stole the show in Bangalore.

Secretary Rice's first visit to India was set for March 2005. The thoughtful preparation of this visit and the secretary's deft presentation of a new initiative for India caught the Indian government by surprise. With the NSSP process nearing completion, the visit was defined by the need for a new, ambitious initiative with India.

In a surprisingly visionary statement, President Bush declared that the United States was prepared to support India's vision of becoming a great economic power. India's annual growth had surged to near 9 percent, which, if sustained over a period of years, would raise India to be one of the world's top three economies and at the highest levels of economic power.

In my public speeches and private conversations with Indian officials, I set out what India needed to become a great economic power. If India were to sustain growth in the range of 9–10 percent consistently over the next ten to twenty years it would achieve its global vision and substantially alleviate its vast poverty. There existed, however, three major constraints that India would have to overcome to reach its destination. The country would have to build world-class infrastructure across the full range of its economy, diversify its energy base to enhance its capacity for growth, reduce its dependence on imported oil and domestic coal, and transform its rural economy, home to some seven hundred million people, to raise growth levels substantially in its agricultural sector. Each of these broad constraints were, of course, comprised of many macro- and microeconomic and social themes, but I believed that grouping the constraints into broad challenges would render India's task more manageable and easier to portray in political terms.

For the United States to become a credible strategic partner for India, we would need to make a vital and concrete contribution in one of the three broad areas of constraint. Obviously, U.S. companies could and would be investors in India's infrastructure projects, but we would be one of many in a complex field that requires private-sector commitments of long duration. The United States had already played an important part in India's "green revolution" in its agricultural sector, but transforming India's rural economy was a challenge far exceeding just agriculture. Dozens of other challenges relating to this vast enterprise were well beyond the reach of the United States.

This left the diversification of India's energy base, where it might be said that the United States held the "magic key." This key was civilian nuclear energy, a field of high priority in India but one in which India had been isolated from the world for more than thirty years by its unwillingness to sign the 1974 nuclear nonproliferation treaty and by its nuclear tests. The sanctions imposed by the United States against India as a result of its 1998 nuclear test had increased India's isolation from the world. This meant that India was limited in its ability to scale up its industry by its inability to attract investment and technology from outside the country, and also by its lack of any sizeable uranium supplies within India, which had handicapped but not prevented India from developing its own limited civil nuclear capacity. In 2005 nuclear power generated approximately 2.5 percent of India's total supply of electricity. India might be hampered in its efforts to expand its civil nuclear industry, but it was not rendered powerless to gradually expand its domestic production. India had also developed its own strategic nuclear weapons as a deterrent against both Pakistan and China. India's nuclear capabilities were accomplished without inward or outward proliferation, and so in spirit India had complied with many of the rules of the 1974 treaty without being a signatory. Signing the treaty would have prevented India from developing its own nuclear weapons and required it to give up its existing weapons if it had elected to sign the treaty after 1998. Given the tensions with its two neighbors, Pakistan and China, both nuclear powers, this was out of the question.

India's exclusion from the world's nuclear nonproliferation regime meant that India's limited but growing civil nuclear facilities were not covered by International Atomic Energy Agency (IAEA) safeguards that applied to other signators of the treaty. Thus, if the United States were to make an exception for India in U.S. nuclear nonproliferation policy, India would be in a position to significantly diversify its energy base away from heavy dependence on foreign oil and dirty domestic coal supplies. The growth needed for India to achieve its goals of economic development and a rising economic status in the world at large would require a huge increase in electric power over the next twenty years. If coal were its chief resource for electric power, India would become one of the world's great economic powers and also the biggest polluter of the environment.

An expression by the United States of its willingness to consider altering its nuclear nonproliferation policy would be a radical departure from U.S. nuclear policies of the previous fifty years, something not remotely expected in India from the approaching visit of Secretary Rice. Condoleezza Rice was in every way a figure who appealed to Indians. She was self made, accomplished in several fields, elegant, optimistic, charming, incisive, and highly intelligent. She received a warm welcome, including from the U.S. mission, where she made a special effort to meet embassy staff and their families in Roosevelt House garden.

Instead of the usual get-acquainted visit that reviewed existing policies without breaking new ground, Secretary Rice had prepared carefully for this visit. She understood that if the United States were to genuinely convince India of its intention to help it achieve a place among the leading world powers, we would require a concrete, forward-looking agenda. Moreover, she understood that our agenda needed to be visionary, optimistic, and play to India's own unique sense of destiny.

Secretary Rice's proposal that we should consider working together to address India's isolation from the world of civil nuclear technology so that India could diversify its energy base over time and expand the scale of its civil nuclear industry took the Indians completely by surprise. Secretary Rice issued an invitation for discussions on behalf of the president, not a finished proposal. This invitation, which created a vision for a future achievable only with the sponsorship of the United States, utterly disarmed the Indians of their habitual doubts and suspicions. Indeed, two days after Secretary Rice had left India one had the impression that the implications of this surprising proposal were only just beginning to sink in. We had clearly changed the tenor of relations, and try as the Indians might to retain their usual detachment there was a genuine and unmistakable enthusiasm that they could not suppress.

Preparations began for Prime Minister Singh's July 2005 state visit to Washington. Both India and the United States began to reflect on how such a nuclear initiative might be carried out. On India's side there would have to be a willingness to separate its civil nuclear activities from its strategic nuclear defense program. This was no easy matter, since civil and strategic nuclear development in India was one and the same. Also, although India had a clean record of nonproliferation, it did not follow the established regime of international safeguards on nuclear facilities or conform to the standards within the group of forty-five member states making up the Nuclear Suppliers Group. India was not open to IAEA inspections or potentially intrusive U.S. demands for compliance in highly technical areas of civil nuclear activities.

The president understood and accepted that there was no possibility of India giving up its nuclear weapons and signing the nuclear nonproliferation treaty of 1974 in order to gain better access to civil nuclear technology. India had developed its own nuclear weapons and modest civil nuclear industry itself. Its nuclear science community occupied a special place of respect and financial support within the Indian government. Accommodating this mandate would, we believed, require a change in U.S. law, which would call into question the sanctity of the world's nuclear nonproliferation architecture. These possibilities raised deep problems for the United States, which had sponsored, developed, and defended that architecture since the 1950s. The U.S. bureaucracy and the staff of relevant members of Congress had spent their entire careers building, perfecting, and enforcing the world's nuclear nonproliferation regime.

Still, the discussion between the U.S. and India proceeded. I was blessed with certain members of my staff who were knowledgeable on nuclear subjects, and from them I was able to glean a valuable education. We had discussed the civil nuclear area before the secretary's visit to India as a means to help meet India's energy requirements, but once the subject was opened for serious consideration the potential complexity for resolving major political and legal problems became evident. Nevertheless, we engaged with the Indians to determine whether any such vision could realistically be framed for the state visit to Washington of the prime minister in July.

As we worked, a new political dimension took shape in India. Indian intellectuals, some retired foreign policy officials, the large population of New Delhi think tankers, and the leftists in the political arena began to raise the sinister possibility that the new U.S.–

India civil nuclear initiative was a plot by the United States to entice India into an arrangement that would cripple or remove India's strategic nuclear capability. This was the "back door" through which the United States would subvert India's strategic nuclear weapons program. They argued that the American strategic partnership proposal was designed to bind India helplessly to the United States. This theme gradually took hold in some quarters in India and later became a serious threat to the entire enterprise.

But first we had to reach a preliminary agreement that would permitt the long and complicated negotiation that must follow to move forward. Not surprisingly, the turning point came at the state visit by Prime Minister Singh to Washington on July 18. After weeks of discussion and negotiation we had reached an impasse around midnight the night before the beginning of the state visit. The two sides left the meeting resigned to failure. At six the following morning, the Indians called to propose one last effort. Two hours later the final issue was resolved, and work began on a brief vision statement to be issued by President Bush and Prime Minister Singh announcing that the United States and India would move ahead with the negotiation of an agreement that would open the world of civil nuclear commerce to India. Final preparation of an agreed text was still in progress as the two leaders stood before the assembled media in the White House East Wing.

Reaction was mixed. The vision statement was read with much enthusiasm in India, but to many in the U.S. media, Congress, and the U.S. bureaucracy the statement raised more questions than it answered. Chief among them was, why had the United States taken such a radical step into a field that for many observers was fraught with complexities, poorly understood by politicians and the public, and possibly dangerous for global security? The questions and arguments that had surfaced in India after the visit of Secretary Rice were now raised in the United States. It would be many months before the vision outlined in the joint statement would be tested between the two countries and placed for a vote before the U.S. Congress.

However, before we could make a serious beginning we had to clear another hurdle. Following a world wide diplomatic effort by the United States in August and September 2005, a vote took place in the IAEA in which for the first time India voted with the United States and others to refer Iran to the United Nations Security Council for consideration of a resolution on sanctions.

The IAEA vote was a major foreign policy decision for India. Its relations with Iran went back over thousands of years. The Mughal invasions of the fifteenth and sixteenth centuries had come from Persia and had left a pervasive influence on India's life and culture, including India's nearly 150 million Muslims. India invariably exercised extreme care in its dealings with Iran. On Iranian nuclear matters India's position had been that Iran, having signed the nonproliferation treaty (India had not), should honor its obligations under the treaty. India also indicated that it did not favor Iran developing nuclear weapons. These general expressions had never resulted in India actually taking positions against Iran in international forums. On the contrary, India was distinctly soft on Iran.

One could understand why—Iran was important in India's politics. Apart from historic and cultural links, India's large Muslim population was deeply sensitive to issues that appeared to disadvantage Iran or pushed the government of India to take steps unfriendly to Iran. A large portion of India's Muslim population was Shiite, with sizeable concentrations in northern India, where despite still being a minority they could exercise very considerable electoral influence. It was common to hear people declare that India had a relationship with Iran going back five thousand years, whereas India's relations with the United States were only a few years old. Others, while acknowledging the long-standing relationship, felt that little in the way of concrete benefits had come from Iran. Additionally, at the time of the campaign for an Iranian sanctions vote, a grand energy project was taking shape on India's northern horizon. This was the Iran-Pakistan-India gas pipeline proposal, which visualized massive supplies of Iranian gas being piped across Afghanistan to Pakistan and India. Despite the obvious practical and political difficulties of such a venture, there was no doubt that the vision had strong political appeal. Pakistan would require new sources of gas within a few years to feed its domestic utility industry, while

India was looking for ways to reduce its dependence on imported oil. Beyond the diversification of India's energy base, there was the dream by some of a vital cooperative venture that would bring the principal countries more closely together.

Opposition to this project carried significant political costs in Indian politics, and not just in the Muslim community. Alternatively, supporters of the pipeline enjoyed a costless political boost unlikely ever to be put to the test of geographic and operational practicality. Inconveniently, however, U.S. legislation in the form of the Libya and Iran Sanctions Act of 1996 required the United States to impose sanctions on any investment project that provided significant assistance to Iran in the development of its natural resources. This legislation, which had never been employed, was used in India as an example of the arrogant extraterritorial reach of U.S. law into the domestic affairs of other sovereign nations. On the other hand, some members of Congress argued that the law might need to be applied to any such pipeline if India were to become too cozy with Iran, needlessly creating resentment in India and a distraction from the U.S. effort on sanctions. The IAEA vote to refer Iran's case to the Security Council brought these matters into the foreground in both countries. TheUnited States was considering a historic change in its nuclear nonproliferation policy that would provide India with a unique global position in the field of civil nuclear commerce, while permitting de facto recognition to India's nuclear weapons. The pipeline initiative, which appeared to favor Iran in the energy field and might very well violate existing U.S. legislation, was bound to be resented in Congress. Failure by India to stand with the United States on an issue as sensitive as Iranian sanctions would draw attention to the pipeline and clearly undermine support for India's civil nuclear initiatives, both in the administration and in Congress. "Playing footsie" with Iran at this point in time was simply unacceptable to many members of Congress, no matter how many centuries of friendship India had shared with Iran.

Critical and threatening comments from members of Congress, together with reminders that under U.S. law Indian companies could face sanctions if they were to advance the gas pipeline with Iran, were held up in India by opposition politicians and even members of the coalition government as unacceptable interference in Indian domestic affairs. This, they argued, is what a strategic relationship with the United States would lead to. The civil nuclear agreement was portrayed as nothing less than the thin end of a U.S. wedge that would subvert India and lead to a "backdoor attack" by the United States on India's strategic weapon's program.

The task of navigating these complex and emotional issues without provoking a rupture in relations fell to me. It was vital to strive for clarity on these matters with the Indian government so that the risks, which could not be controlled by the administration, would not overwhelm the basic interests on both sides. However, as frequently is the case with parliamentary governments, there is a tendency to forget or refuse to recognize the realities of the U.S. form of government. The power of the executive in the United States is limited in its ability to direct or discipline the Congress. An administration might favor a particular policy initiative but find that Congressional opposition makes it impossible to realize. Hence, some Indians might well believe that an administration that has agreed on a certain policy direction with India would subvert that policy by secretly encouraging opposition in Congress or using its influence to make Congress its stalking horse for the negotiation of concessions or simply to interfere in India's domestic affairs. There was virtually no limit to the range of interpretations and allegations of bad faith applied to the United States in India's media, its think tanks, and in the parliament. Leftist parties, in particular, seized on the most extreme arguments to attempt to derail both the civil nuclear negotiation and the growing strategic relationship with the United States.

In the Foreign Ministry and the prime minister's office relations remained polite and essentially constructive, but one could not say relations were comfortable and happy. In my many meetings with Foreign Secretary Shyam Saran I tried simply to explain in the clearest terms the risks India would be running if it were to abstain or to vote against sanctions on Iran. Reports of arm twistings portrayed in the press were unfair. The underlying realities for India may have been unpalatable at the time, but it was essential that they understand and believe the downside they would face going forward on the civil nuclear initiative if India were unwilling at this critical point in time to stand up for sanctions on Iran. Once that message was firmly and convincingly conveyed to the Indian government, it was my view that they were likely to make the right decision; but, more important, it had to be their decision and their decision alone. This strategy was adopted by Secretary Rice and in turn by President Bush when he met Prime Minister Manmahon Singh at the UN meetings in New York in September 2005. Whatever the twists and turns of Indian politics, the prime minister could not have been under any illusions about the importance of the test India faced in the UN vote.

In September India voted for sanctions on Iran for the first time and thereby strengthened its credibility on nuclear affairs with both the administration and Congress. This was not an easy decision for India. I came away more convinced than ever of India's serious intentions to stay the course on civil nuclear commitments and to continue building a strategic partnership with the United States.

A second initiative launched by President Bush and Prime Minister Singh at India's State visit in 2005 has survived from one administration to the next. This is the CEO Forum, which brings together ten CEOs from each country to form a business council to determine and seek to resolve the five or six most serious barriers to expanding economic relations between the United States and India.

I had decided to run a mission in India that was open to and supportive of U.S. business. Many American companies were already represented in India, but the rules and regulations that governed foreign direct investment made entry and operation difficult. Some companies, such as General Electric, had large and successful investments in India, but other companies were engaged in disputes with joint venture partners or faced political resistance to growing their businesses.

India's lack of a comprehensive infrastructure was a major deterrent to investment and development. Without intellectual property protection, clear ground rules for the settlement of disputes, and transparency and fairness in dealings with state governments and the bureaucracy in general, foreign direct investment was constrained. My idea of a CEO Forum involved more than simply bringing businessmen together. I had seen other such business groups in Saudi Arabia, Europe, and China and in every case the fact that the forum or commission was run by governments rendered them largely ineffective over time. The level of corporate participation tended to decline because governments had little feel for the kinds of commercial and political challenges faced by businesses, challenges often designed or imposed by the governments themselves.

I therefore sought to form a group open only to CEOs responsible for leading the entire company, the final arbiters of global strategy and allocation and deployment of the company's global capital. I stood firm on the principle that we accept no substitutes for attendance at meetings, no matter how august that replacement person's corporate title might be. A chairman drawn from each country was responsible for running the forum. Ministerial-level government officials were invited to take part in meetings, but government bureaucracy should not manage the meetings or the process leading up to the meetings. Finally, American participants were chosen selectively and invited to join by the American ambassador, instead of issuing an open invitation to companies at large. Preparations and secretariat functions were carried out by the private-sector leaders, not by U.S. or Indian officials. In this way the meetings encouraged free, frank, and off-the-record exchanges of views. I believed that if we achieved these objectives, neither businessmen nor government ministers would feel constrained or feel exposed by the group's deliberations.

After a good deal of irritating wrangling with our own government officials and lawyers in Washington, we were able to achieve virtually all our objectives, avoiding the bureaucratization of the forum. The kickoff meeting at the White House in July 2005 brought the twenty invited members together to become acquainted and to see the serious attention given to the forum by the two heads of government. William Harrison, CEO of JP Morgan Chase, and Ratan

Tata, chairman of the Tata Group in India, were the first chairmen of the group. Afterward, the forum convened approximately every nine months. Three senior cabinet ministers from each side attended each meeting and engaged in the kind of informal dialogue that captured the attention of the CEOS and made it possible to air sensitive business issues between the United States and India. No compromising reports appeared in the press. CEOS on both sides were able to get better acquainted which advanced relations more effectively than formal dialogue.

The U.S–India Civil Nuclear Initiative launched in July 2005 at Prime Minister Manmohan Singh's state visit to Washington was a complex and controversial undertaking that would require years of focused effort, patience, and faith. By the end of 2005 it was clear to me that we had embarked on a historic enterprise whose magnitude and intricacy constantly seemed to unfold before us. In autumn when visiting Washington I called on a number of members of Congress whose support was needed for the expected legislative process. I was discouraged to find that the most common reaction to my visit was, "Why on earth have you done this?" To those with knowledge of the nuclear nonproliferation regime the United States had championed for over fifty years it seemed inconceivable that the administration should be willing to give de facto recognition to India's nuclear weapons and at the same time provide India full access to the world of civil nuclear commerce. After all, apart from the Big 5 nuclear powers, all other signatories of the 1974 treaty had agreed to deny themselves nuclear weapons in order to have full access to civil nuclear technology and commerce.

Those views were fueled by Washington's nuclear nonproliferation "establishment," whether in congressional staff, the executive departments, or in the think tank community. These people had both passion and extensive in-depth knowledge of nuclear materials, weapons, technologies, and the history and intricacies of nuclear diplomacy. To many of them President Bush's civil nuclear vision for India was a dangerous misadventure.

We faced a formidable challenge to explain and justify to Congress the president's proposed change to the world's nuclear non-proliferation architecture. The task of gaining support in the U.S. government and among the Nuclear Suppliers Group of nations was divided into two stages. The first was to lay out the case for India to be brought into the world's nuclear nonproliferation regime. India was clearly a rising nation whose population represented approximately one-sixth of humanity. It had its own homegrown community of nuclear scientists who had developed both a modest civil nuclear industry and sophisticated nuclear weapons. India had not engaged in nuclear proliferation activities and was acknowledged to have observed the standards of the 1974 Nuclear Non-Proliferation treaty, despite being isolated for some thirty years for its failure to sign the treaty. Nor had India, the world's largest democracy, shown itself to be militarily aggressive beyond its borders. China and Pakistan, India's two nuclear-armed neighbors, both of whom fought a war with India in the past fifty years, were still regarded as major threats to India's security. There was no realistic prospect that India would give up its nuclear weapons capability to gain access to the world of civil nuclear commerce, especially since doing so would require India to accept IAEA nuclear safeguards on its domestic nuclear industry. Finally, India had a clear need to enhance and diversify its energy base. Over time India would clearly become one of the world's leading economies. If it were to depend entirely on its national supplies of coal to generate the power it would need for development, India would as also become the world's largest polluter.

In the face of these realities, our conclusion was that keeping India isolated from the world was both unrealistic and a threat to the world's present nonproliferation regime. If isolated, India's nuclear industry would develop its growing body of reactors without being covered by IAEA safeguards. Better to have India's future civil nuclear reactors covered by international safeguards than to leave all of India's nuclear facilities entirely outside the system. India had already demonstrated that its strategic nuclear program had been kept to a scale sufficient for deterrence purposes as opposed to being a growing arsenal for foreign aggression. In future, India's nuclear science community would clearly be able to make an important contribution in global nuclear affairs, which today in its isolation was beyond reach.

In the face of these arguments, we posed the following question: If you acknowledge that India is a major nation of rising world importance, and you don't like this plan, what is your proposal for dealing constructively with India? The response to this question was usually silence or, sometimes, to keep India outside the system because the risks and costs of entry were just too high.

The second step was to educate Congress on the procedures and specific conditions required of India in order to be granted the exception that would incorporate them into the world's nuclear nonproliferation regime. The first requirement would be that India negotiate a credible arrangement to separate its civil nuclear industry from its strategic nuclear program. This needed to be framed into a formal separation agreement between the United States and India that Congress could approve as part of the process to amend the Atomic Energy Act of 1954. The separation agreement would specify, among other things, that Indian reactors already built and operating, as well as those to be built in the future, would be covered by international nuclear safeguards to be negotiated and implemented between India and the IAEA.

Because India's nuclear industry had been developed by its scientific community as a single united industry, separating the civil and strategic elements of the industry was both complex and very costly. The division within the industry had to be verifiable, as would the application of nuclear nonproliferation safeguards. The application of safeguards also had to follow nuclear fuel and spent fuels to safeguard against potential leakage from the civil to the strategic side of the industry.

Once the separation agreement was completed the next step was to approach Congress for an amendment to the Atomic Energy Act. This change would permit the United States to conduct civil nuclear commerce with India, provided that certain other actions were completed. The first of these was the U.S.–India Section 123 Agreement, which would be a bilateral agreement providing for the implementation of U.S.–India nuclear cooperation. In addition, following the completion of the 123 Agreement, India and the International Atomic Energy Agency (IAEA) in Vienna would negotiate a freestanding bilateral safeguards agreement that would set the arrangements for the introduction of safeguards into India's civil nuclear industry. Finally, the forty-five nations of the Nuclear Suppliers Group needed to agree by full consensus to recognize and accept the exception granted to India by the change in U.S. law. Bear in mind that many of these countries had denied themselves nuclear weapons in order to access civil nuclear technologies. India, on the other hand, who had never signed the 1974 Treaty would gain access to civil nuclear commerce without giving up its nuclear weapons. Thus, the amendment of the Atomic Energy Act of 1954 would represent only the beginning of a process which, if completed in full, would allow the U.S. to ratify the agreement permitting India full access to the world of civil nuclear commerce.

Setting out these rigorous and lengthy steps, which required many months of vigorous negotiation and in the later stages very considerable international diplomacy, brought a measure of comfort to many of those who were skeptical of the President's civil nuclear vision for India. Yet most participants and observers did not believe an agreement could be accomplished. A number of times, often for long periods, the vision seemed to be impossible to achieve. The detractors were then out in force in India, America, and the international community at large.

Altogether, the negotiation process for the U.S.–India civil nuclear initiative required nearly four years. It was a constant and continuous part of my life as ambassador, since most of the ongoing discussion and much of the negotiation took place in New Delhi. President Bush visited India in March 2006, Congress had its first votes on the amendment of the Atomic Energy Act of 1954 in July and December 2006, and we negotiated the U.S.–India 123 Agreement for most of 2007. Not until the middle of 2008, when many thought the opportunity to complete the agreement had been lost, did we move toward the conclusion.

Meanwhile, in the period from 2005 to 2008 it would have been a mistake to place too much weight on the U.S.–India civil nuclear initiative, because for most of that period it was doubtful that the agreement could be successfully completed. Past efforts to negotiate similar agreements with Japan and China had taken up to ten years and did not involve the magnitude of policy and legal changes that the Indian deal required. In India, one had to face the reality that the left parties in the coalition government were deeply hostile to the initiative. Media commentators and think tank pundits were suspicious of U.S. motives. The debate went on, rising in intensity at each small step forward. For me it was vital that this standoff not dominate our relations. There was too much to do, too many challenges, and too much dynamism in our growing relationship to let civil nuclear power issues interfere.

The rich diversity in U.S.–India relations became more apparent with each passing month. Visitors streamed in from the United States: Congressional delegations, officials from virtually all the major departments and agencies of the U.S. government, business leaders, presidents and trustees of American universities, philanthropists, artists, and entertainers. The flow of Indians to America also multiplied dramatically as more business leaders and their employees visited the United States. India's student population in America rose to seventy-five thousand and on to ninety-four thousand, the largest foreign-student community in the United States by a substantial margin. Government officials traveled to Washington frequently, and many Indian families chose America for their holiday travel. Visas processed by the U.S. mission climbed to a peak in excess of eight hundred thousand per year, second in the U.S. system only to Mexico, with whom we had a common border and long-standing economic relations. India was also the world's leading user of H-1B employment visas.

India was getting broader and more frequent coverage in the U.S. and international press. Tourism began booming as millions discovered "Incredible India." The stage was set for a program to educate Americans about rising India. It seemed to Jeannie and me that the world was coming to India. At the embassy and Roosevelt House we met with countless delegations and visitors of all kinds and gave personal briefings to hundreds of visitors. I discovered that in the more than sixty congressional delegations I met with over five years, the vast majority of members of Congress, even those who had served multiple terms, had never visited India before. Most visitors were struck by India's dynamism and by its potential as a serious friend and partner of the United States. As time passed and the list of influential visitors grew larger, I realized that a campaign for a better understanding of India in the United States would be critical to winning support for the U.S.–India civil nuclear initiative, not to mention support for foreign direct investment and institutional investment flows, defense sales, and cooperation in education, science, and technology. As 2005 turned to 2006 there seemed to be no limit to the opportunity to expand and deepen U.S.–India relations.

The other purpose in cultivating support was to maintain the flow of funds for U.S. AID's widespread and effective social and economic programs. I was a long-time skeptic of U.S. AID, which remained a formidable bureaucracy. However, I found that in India AID programs in the fields of agriculture, power, water, women's rights, and health to be effective and valuable, especially from social and economic returns on the relatively small amounts invested. I also found AID's people in India to be of high quality and committed to their projects.

AID's projects were effective because they addressed innovative necessities in India's economy. AID promoted and provided minimal financial support to, for example, a project to to provide a farming community with insulated, antitheft electric power lines (a large amount of electricity in India is stolen directly from power lines), and financial support for the purchase of modern water pumps. With insulated power lines, a constant supply of electricity was assured so that the water pumps could be turned on and off as needed, instead of being left on day and night in case electricity became available. Throughout rural India, in areas where free electricity was promised by politicians, electricity was available only from time to time. In the rural AID scheme I visited near Delhi, the steady supply of electricity had to be paid for by the farmers, who also financed their own new pumps. Contrary to the common belief that people would not pay for electricity, these farmers paid 99 percent of their billings for the certainty of electric power and the ability to control their watering of crops. Beyond the improvements offered to the farmers for watering crops, their village was also electrified. When I visited in midafternoon, the women of the village were gathered in a classroom learning to read and write. Before the new electric program the afternoon hours of daylight would have been used for household chores. Now these were done in the evening under electric lighting so they could go to class in the afternoon. Electric bills in the village were paid 99 percent of the time. This obviously important demonstration project showed that electric power could be commercialized at the village level and rendered economically and socially effective. Instead of embracing this successful model, large parts of India's agricultural sector remain steeped in poverty and illiteracy, waiting for free power that never comes.

I regarded programs of this type as outstanding investments that gave the AID staff a place at the table for planning and financing such projects, often conceived by AID itself. India was a country "on the feed" for such ideas, and yet the State Department chose this moment to cut funding drastically on all projects apart from health care projects mandated by Congress. The AID budget fell from $150 million to approximately $80 million in two years. Large numbers of irreplaceable AID employees were terminated just as they were in demand as never before for projects in which minimal financial outlays could be leveraged by the rising interest of a population of entrepreneurs.

I lobbied members of Congress to understand that the State Department's rationale for cutting funds for AID projects in India based on the fact that India's economy was growing at 9 percent made no sense because the growth level was confined mainly to urban areas, and India's seven hundred million rural inhabitants remained desperately poor. I also highlighted the potential for promoting important structural changes in India's economy.

My colleagues and I were successful to some extent in reversing a modest amount of funding. For my success, however, I was reprimanded in writing by the seventh floor of the department for appearing to be working counter to the purposes of AID's senior management. The quality of leadership at AID in Washington was abysmal and out of touch with their people in the field. They promised to consult their field officers and promptly failed to do so. We found active support among many members of Congress, and by 2011, two years after I had left India, AID budget levels in India were restored. It was depressing, however, to find that senior State Department officials in the Bush administration were ignorant about how growth and structural economic reforms are accomplished on the ground and why they are so important in a country thirsting for progress.

Other policy areas were equally challenging. I found it was necessary to engage ministers directly, bringing with me key staff members responsible for any particularly difficult policy area, to ensure the access we needed at lower levels of the bureaucracy to carry our business forward. This meant, for example, raising the sensitive issue of India's poor record on human trafficking and child labor directly with the minister of home affairs. It meant seeing the minister of health on the campaign to eradicate polio in India and talking to the agricultural minister about U.S. wheat sales and barriers against importing U.S. almonds and other agricultural products. It also meant working with the agricultural minister to allow Indian mangoes into the United States after twenty-five years of futile effort. The defense minister was essential to building confidence in the United States as a supplier of military equipment and weapons following the damaging fallout from U.S. sanctions in 1998. The minster of aviation was key to negotiating and implementing the U.S.–India open skies agreement and the sale of U.S. commercial aircraft to India. The minister of human resources, effectively the minister of education, and the foreign secretary were vital to resolving problems we experienced with the Fulbright Program in India. These followed equally important challenges with the ministries of foreign affairs, science and technology, finance, the Reserve Bank of India, and India's space program, where once again the damage wrought by the 1998 sanctions had to be repaired.

In any case, there was no substitute for a direct personal visit by a U.S. ambassador well informed on the relevant policy issue and ready to follow up with the full resources of the U.S. mission. Nor was there any better tonic for raising morale and commitment among the embassy staff than to be supported by the ambassador and launched at the ministerial level into the Indian government bureaucracy.

I thought I was doing an important job for my country and that I was also an important person in India. A sense of pride and accomplishment was with me every day. Then I learned true humility and profound admiration for the courage, dignity, and humanity of another person. This person was my wife, Jeannie Mulford, Madame Ambassador, the keeper of Roosevelt House and the love of my life.

In April 2005, during a visit with family in Phoenix, Arizona, Jeannie was discovered to have breast cancer. A young woman of picture-perfect lifetime good health was struck by the most dreaded and most frightening disease we could imagine. We remained in the United States and took immediate steps to confront the disease. At Memorial Sloan Kettering in New York Jeannie decided to take aggressive action, despite the cancer not being in an advanced stage, electing to undergo a double mastectomy and breast reconstruction, followed by chemotherapy and Herceptin treatments. We consulted the cancer surgeon and the plastic surgeon who together would carry out the surgeries over the coming months. They were joined by Jeannie's oncologist, and surgery was set for May 19.

We did our best to prepare. Jeannie's two sisters came to New York; Jeannie and I took an apartment and made the decision that we would stay the course in India. After the surgery, I would return to New Delhi, Jeannie's sisters would share staying in New York with Jeannie, and I would return regularly to visit during the chemotherapy treatments. Over the next nine months, Jeannie's sisters, Kathleen in Arizona, and Randee in Colorado, made the incredible and loving commitment to never leave Jeannie alone in New York. They became her guardian angels.

It was not long before the doctors and nurses at Memorial Sloan Kettering knew they had a very special patient: always smiling, unafraid, never a harsh or unkind word, courage and faith beyond imagining. When the surgery was over, Jeannie recovered quickly, and we discovered a maker of wigs for theater and film in Greenwich Village who would take Jeannie's long blond hair and fashion it into a shoulder-length wig. The day Jeannie's long hair was to be cut, the day before the chemo treatments were to begin, it was agreed I would leave for Delhi, as she set off to the hair salon for her first significant haircut since the age of eight. When she saw the result, she broke into laugher while her sister burst into tears, and from the photo I received she did indeed look chic and beautiful.

Twenty-four hours later, when I was back in New Delhi, I received a phone call from Jeannie, who said the chemotherapy had not gone forward. Instead, the cardiology doctors had focused on a heart anomaly Jeannie had had from birth that was thought to be basically benign. The cardiologist, however, believed that chemotherapy could put a strain on Jeannie's heart anomaly that could impose a significant risk to her life. It was recommended that Jeannie proceed immediately to the Cleveland Clinic to see a prominent surgeon specializing in heart anomalies.

A day or two later we were on a conference phone call with the surgeons at the Cleveland Clinic, weighing and discussing the results of tests Jeannie had undergone. The decision was that Jeannie would need to undergo immediate open-heart surgery to correct the anomaly. The date was set for June 28, the day after my birthday, which Jeannie insisted celebrating at an Italian restaurant in Cleveland the night before her surgery.

All the doctors had agreed that there was no time to lose in completing the heart surgery some forty days after the breast cancer surgery, so that chemotherapy could be started by a date in August within ninety days of the original surgery. We stayed together in Cleveland for two weeks, and once again doctors and nurses there saw a kind, calm, and fearless woman face a second great surgical intrusion in the space of a month. A few days later Jeannie was walking fourteen-minute miles with me in the cool July Fourth weather along Lake Erie.

We left Cleveland for Washington DC on July 14. Four days later, Jeannie attended the full day of events at the White House for the state visit of Prime Minister Manmohan Singh. That evening she was seated at President Bush's table for the state dinner, looking stunning in a long, high cut gown with her short, chic hair style. She gave no hint of pain or fatigue and neither asked for nor received special treatment of any kind.

I knew that night, as I had known for two months, that Jeannie was and is the most extraordinarily brave and composed woman I will ever know. She stood through that day and evening for me, for our president and first lady, and for our nation—truly a lady from the great heartland of America.

Chemotherapy began in August and would not finish until mid-January 2006. Jeannie's sisters had never left her alone in New York. I came back from India as often as I could, and together we faced the transformative effects of chemotherapy. We went together to the chemo treatment center, where again it was clear to me that Jeannie's steady kindness and good humor had made her everyone's favorite patient. In August a serious infection required surgical removal of one of her breast inserts. Chemotherapy treatments continued through the fall and lasted to January 18, Jeannie's birthday and also the beginning of the Herceptin treatments, which were to last for a full year. These she vowed to complete in India, where she was determined she would return prior to the state visit of President and Mrs. Bush at the end of February.

My job was to find a hospital in New Delhi that could safely administer Herceptin, a relatively new cancer drug. Jeannie's job was to find and transport a supply of Herceptin, refrigerated and stable, all the way to India. Jeannie came to New Delhi in mid-February, nonstop through London, carrying the Herceptin, and ready to begin the preparations for the state visit. A few days later, the ambassador, with his eight-member armed security detail, accompanied Madame Ambassador to the Ganga Ram hospital for her treatment, the arrival witnessed by hundreds of Indians gathered around the hospital for outpatient treatment services.

Jeannie carried her supply of Herceptin with her from the embassy clinic for mixing and application at the hospital. A private room was arranged, with a doctor and nurse in attendance. The treatment session was less than perfect the first time, but Jeannie's patience and the respect and kindness she always showed to those around her brought forth the effort to get the treatment process just right.

Everyone was glad to see Jeannie back at post. In part this was because it was by then understood that unlike most previous ambassadors' wives, Jeannie had no personal agenda removed from the mission, no private business interest, no social set she maintained in Delhi. Jeannie was entirely devoted to the mission community and the task of leading and managing Roosevelt House. It had been a lonely place for me and the staff without her for ten months, but now "Jeannie Madame," was back and we would soon be visited by President and Mrs. Bush.

President George W. Bush and First Lady Laura Bush made their state visit to India for three days, beginning February 28, 2006. Advance planning had begun in late 2005 and picked up in intensity in the opening months of 2006. Planning and working with the White House staff, the State Department, and the Secret Service, as well as with all their counterparts in India is a challenge of the first order for any ambassador. In the case of India the challenge rises to perhaps new levels of complexity and sensitivity. State visits by American presidents receive intense scrutiny from all elements of government and from India's large and extremely active media. Precedents from previous presidential visits are dug up and carefully analyzed and India's complex bureaucracy engages across the board, giving, as I discovered, an American presidential visit that subtle mix of top priority attention with defensive efforts not to create or feed "American exceptionalism."

The sheer magnitude of the U.S. advance team and subsequent official delegation surrounding the president was overwhelming. The presidential party took over the entire Sheraton Hotel in New Delhi, two dozen vehicles and limousines were brought into India, together with helicopters and back-up aircraft positioned at key points around the nation in the event that a rapid or otherwise unusual exit by the president was required. All motor routes expected to be used by the president during his visit were given a close inspection by a helicopter manned by American military a day or two before the visit. Each of these activities conducted in the sovereign state of India needed to be negotiated and approved down to the last detail.

There were moments of entertainment and frustration in the preparation process. When the U.S. Secret Service personnel impressed upon the Indians their sensitivity to the prospect of large crowds gathering, the Indians turned the faces of the U.S. agents pale with the observation that getting a crowd of one million together in India could be accomplished almost anywhere in a few minutes. On the other hand, selecting an interesting location for President Bush's main speech in India and obtaining permission for using such a site was a sensitive and frustrating affair up to the very day of the speech. I was intent that the president not speak in a hotel ballroom or other closed site. He should speak out of doors at a site easily recognizable on television as India. We choose a park encompassing a view of the ruins of an ancient Mughal palace. Still standing, as a backdrop, were the ancient walls and Indian-style turrets and rows of fulsome palms lining an avenue running back to the outer wall and forming the vision before which the president would stand at a single lectern. To the side were views of a Hindu temple, and in the foreground an ancient Mosque. This place called Purana Qila was perfect for the vision we wished to convey.

The Foreign Ministry took the position that we could not be permitted to use a national treasure like Purana Qila without setting an uncomfortable precedent for other head-of-state visits. Eventually, it was determined that we could apply to the Indian Department of Antiquities for permission to use Purana Qila, provided the event was organized and sponsored by India's two leading business associations, the Confederation of Indian Industry (cii) and the Federation of Indian Commerce and Industry (fici). When it came to issuing invitations to the selected crowd of some five hundred people, the two Indian federations took the view that only the American ambassador could send out invitations in the name of the United States of America. When the Foreign Office learned that I had designed and sent out the invitations there was a mighty explosion, with accusations of bad faith on our part and the threat that the event would have to be cancelled, now just two days before the specified date. Explanations that it was the Indian federations who declined to send out the invitations, deferring instead to the American ambassador, were brushed aside. Several hours later, cooler heads prevailed, and it was explained to me that the Foreign Office would now send out a duplicate batch of invitations that would render my batch inoperable, because an ID number would be printed in one corner without which the invitee would not be permitted through security at this climactic event. I agreed to this new procedure without difficulty, but at a meeting with Foreign Office officials shortly before the event I could not resist reminding them to be sure to bring the right invitation with the correct number so as not to be excluded at the gate. This raised a constrained laugh. The event itself was a major success.

The other event that proved sensitive to arrange for the president in India was his request for a meeting with Indian religious leaders. Despite India's diversity of religions, the president, as a leader with strong convictions of faith, knew that India is a country of widespread religious belief. When President Bush visited China he attended a Christian church service, which caused some modest controversy in China. It was recognized that in India, where a number of major and minor religions are represented, attending a religious service was out of the question. Instead, I proposed that I would bring together a group, if necessary at the embassy, that would be comprised simply of influential religious leaders from the various communities. The proposal was met by strong resistance from the Indian Foreign Office on the grounds that such a meeting would be sensitive for them to arrange, and in any case the main religions of India—Hinduism, Islam, Buddhism, Sikhism, Christianity, and Jainism—generally do not have a single head figure who would widely be seen as the correct and legitimate leader of that faith. Any attempt by the Indian government to bring together such a group would entail endless bickering and possibly strong emotional outbursts. Instead, I proposed that I would bring together a group at the embassy if necessary that would be comprised simply of influential religious leaders from the various communities. This the government could not prevent, nor did they try to block such an initiative when they understood that we at the embassy would take the responsibility and would avoid attempting to select the supreme head of one or other of the groups in India.

When the meeting was held it was successful beyond my expectations and I believe beyond those of President Bush. Eight individuals were invited to meet the president: two Hindu leaders; two Muslim leaders (one Sunni and the other Shiite); a Protestant; a Roman Catholic; one Sikh; and one Buddhist. The tables for the meeting were arranged in a U shape with the president, Secretary of State Rice, and me seated across the top of the U and the religious leaders down each side.

When the religious leaders had been introduced and seated, most of them clutching notes or texts from which to speak, the president preempted any comments from their side by speaking first. He spoke without notes and in a highly personal vein about the importance of his faith in giving him the strength to carry the burden of the presidency. The frank and unguarded passion with which President Bush spoke took the group by surprise, rendering their prepared statements to rather passionless commentary. The president listened patiently and there followed a brief informal discussion. What I recall in particular from that gathering was the concluding remarks of several leaders to the effect that no previous head of a state of any country had ever sought them out for a meeting of this kind and how unique and much appreciated was this gesture by President Bush. In my mind's eye I would have been willing to wager that before the meeting, each leader would have ranked as highly improbable any meeting of this nature with President Bush. No such meeting had occurred before with a foreign head of state, and it was generally understood that the schedule for President Bush's visit would be crowded with meetings and events. When the gathering took place, they were shocked by his candor and faith and deeply moved by the consideration he had given them.

The president's official bilateral meetings with the prime minister and other senior ministers at Hyderabad House were in all respects friendly and constructive. The purpose of these meetings, which at times were formal gatherings and somewhat stilted, was to highlight the broad interface of engagement between the United States and India. In the run-up to the visit we had nearly completed negotiations with the Indian government on India's nuclear separation agreement, which would divide India's civil nuclear industry from its strategic weapons program. Several key issues remained to be resolved, the most difficult of which was the need to meet India's demands for assurances or guarantees from the United States concerning supplies of nuclear fuel to India over the medium to long term. The United States was unwilling and unable under U.S. law to guarantee future supplies to India under all prevailing circumstances. If India were to violate, in the opinion of the United States, future nuclear safeguards applied to India, U.S. cooperation with India would cease immediately. India's fear was that in such circumstances the United States would use its global influence to once again isolate India from fuel supplies, even if the rest of the world had not reached the same judgment as the United States. At Hyderabad House on a sunny and pleasant day the president approved the final draft language, which would be inscribed in the separation agreement and in subsequent agreements to implement U.S.–India civil nuclear cooperation.

At the press conference in the garden of Hyderabad House, the prime minister led off with the announcement that U.S.–India agricultural cooperation, which had powered India's "green revolution" in the 1960s and '70s, was to be restored, with a focus on new technologies. The civil nuclear initiative received intense interest from the media in India and from overseas. By putting cooperation in agriculture first on the press conference agenda, at the request of the prime minister, we had avoided making the civil nuclear initiative the dominant theme and possibly causing division within the coalition. The overall impression following the meetings was that the outcome reflected wide and diverse cooperation between our two countries.

The president's small, informal meeting with Sonia Gandhi, leader of the Congress Party and in effect India's most influential leader, was warm and on policy issues extremely positive. This had not always been the case over the many years of contact between the United States and the Gandhi family.

On the final day of the visit, President and Mrs. Bush flew to Hyderabad for the day. Jeannie and I accompanied them on Air Force One and Marine One for the whole day, and as during the entire visit, the president and first lady could not have been more friendly and gracious to their Indian hosts and to us. We had selected Hyderabad for the one-day visit away from New Delhi because it is a major city in the south of India in one of India's largest and most populous states, Andhra Pradesh. Hyderabad has developed a diverse and rapidly growing economy (especially agriculture, IT, and pharmaceuticals). Its population is 41 percent Muslim (although Andhra Pradesh is only 13 percent Muslim, which is the national average for India), and Hyderabad is home to India's most prestigious modern business school. That evening the president announced that the United States would open a full-service consulate in Hyderabad, the fourth such consulate in India and the first full-service consulate established by the United States in more than twenty years. This project had been developed over a number of months and involved the sensitive decision of selecting Hyderabad over Bangalore as the location of the new consulate. The thousands of citizens of the city selected who applied for U.S. visas would no longer need to travel to Chennai in Tamil Nadu to make their application.

In the morning the president visited one of India's premier agricultural universities, including a walk through the fields and conversations with the agricultural workers, and in the afternoon he had a highly active two-hour seminar with successful entrepreneurs under the age of thirty-five in the courtyard of the business school. These outings gave the president an opportunity to gauge the dynamism of India, away from the capital, and to meet with India's youthful population of aspiring entrepreneurs.

Finally, there was the style and elegance of the visit. The president's speech at Purana Qila was a masterpiece of atmosphere and presentation. In the soft cool of the evening, and with the effective lighting on the palm tree avenue, the ancient walls behind the President, the Hindu temple and the sixteenth-century mosque, the elite and discriminating audience was deeply and visibly impressed by the president's uplifting speech, his forceful delivery, and the genuinely friendly demeanor that he so effectively conveyed.

In a single paragraph President Bush perfectly captured the essence of the relationship he and his administration had created with India:

"For many years the United States and India were kept apart by the rivalries that divided the world. That's changed. Our two great democracies are now united by opportunities that can lift our people and by threats that bring down all our progress. The United States and India, separated by half the globe, are closer than ever before, and the partnership between our free nations has the power to transform the world."

Likewise, the state dinner set that evening in the Mughal gardens behind the Imperial Palace, now known as Rashtrapati Bhavan. This vast and elegant building, designed by English architect Edward Lutyens in the 1920s in the great imperial style of India, provided the setting for a spectacular gathering of elegantly dressed Indian glitterati, India's music and fireworks. It was of course after dark, but the lights that played on the surrounding flowers and flows of water exactly rendered the atmosphere of mystery and romance that lies at the heart of India.

When it came time to see the presidential party off, the president told Jeannie and me that of all the places they had traveled, India was the country they had most wanted to visit and that this had been the best of all their visits. What came through to us and remains with us today from the president's meeting with embassy staff in the garden of Roosevelt House to the state dinner at the Rashtrapati Bhavan was the down-to-earth, genuine kindness and goodwill of the president and first lady toward every person and situation they encountered in India.

The next phase in the follow-up from the president's state visit to India was the campaign to move forward with the civil nuclear initiative. With India's separation agreement now concluded, we turned to the next and most difficult challenge: the need to amend the U.S. Atomic Energy Act of 1954 to permit India to enter into civil nuclear commerce with the United States. This involved not only a careful review of the separation agreement by both houses of Congress but also a legislative strategy on the part of the administration that would permit a united front to be presented to Congress. There had always been opposition within the executive branch and among staff of both parties on the Hill toward any concessionary change toward India in the global nuclear nonproliferation architecture. Despite the formally declared policy of the Bush administration, we knew we would face internal opposition and acts of resistance in the legislative process.

Congress would support the necessary change in U.S. law only if it were satisfied that the separation agreement we had negotiated with India would effectively separate India's strategic nuclear weapons from its present and future capacity to develop and operate a program of civil nuclear commerce, subject to the application of international nuclear safeguards. The separation agreement would have to be viewed as water-tight by Congress and later by the IAEA and all forty-five members of the Nuclear Suppliers Group.

Draft legislation and the plan for approaching Congress developed over the next three months. The first and most important legislative issue to resolve was whether the proposed legislation that would amend the Act would be India specific or criteria based. The former approach would make only one exception from the global regime by isolating and naming India. The criteria-based approach would lay out the criteria to be met by any country in the future that might seek to be given an exception without requiring a specific change in U.S. law for that country. I was appalled by the second option because it was the utterly unique nature of India's nuclear history, its track record of nonproliferation, and the fact that it was the world's largest democracy that to me made India the only case for exception in the world, both now and in the future. There were arguments on both sides of the issue, but in general officials in the administration favored the single named exception approach. The other approach would lead to unfortunate possibilities for slippage in the future as other countries with support among groups in Congress or the executive sought to extend India's special and well-deserved advantage to themselves. In the end, the legislation named India as the only country in the law to be provided with a special status.

This, of course, made India's case easier to sell in the Congress, because India stood on its own. There need not be speculation about any other country being given special treatment by virtue of a future bureaucratic decision that a country had somehow met the terms of a body of specified criteria. For any other country to be granted an exception under which it could have a strategic nuclear weapons program, engage freely in civil nuclear commerce with the world, and not be required to sign the 1974 Nuclear Non-Proliferation Treaty, the Congress would have to pass a new law. Surely this was better protection for America and the world than leaving such a matter to the decision of a future administration, or worse to a future secretary of state without requiring the formal consent of Congress.

The wording of the legislation also proved to be controversial when brought to bear against the existing wording in the Atomic Energy Act concerning prohibitions against nuclear leakage or proliferation. Legislation in the House was submitted in May; hearings were held but floor action was delayed. Finally, in July, as the congressional summer recess approached, the legislation was voted out of the committee and went to the floor for the vote. This took place on July 26, 2006, and the legislation was carried by 359 votes to 68 votes, a most remarkable triumph by any measure. Members had given India a stunning bipartisan majority, recognizing India's critical importance in the world, its special priority for the United States, and the faith America had in India's capacity to contribute positively to the evolution of the world's nuclear nonproliferation architecture. I was proud of the unity achieved in our House of Representatives, its far-sighted capacity for leadership and the fact that we had successfully transformed early skepticism into an understanding of India's importance to the United States and the world at large.

The House vote was only the first step, however. We still faced the challenge in the Senate, where conditions for passage would be much more unpredictable and our time clock would be that much more advanced. There were also the forthcoming midterm congressional elections that would dominate the agenda after the summer recess and carry us through November. President Bush's declining approval ratings and the bitter partisan atmosphere promised for the elections seemed to blight prospects for a statesmanlike focus on the case that had to be made to move the U.S.–India civil nuclear initiative forward to the next stage. The Senate's version of the bill was similar to the bill passed by the House in July, but Senate procedures posed a far greater risk of destructive amendments being introduced from the floor, or other amendments that might be well intended but would be unacceptable to India.

The climax of the midterm Congressional election campaign in September–October 2006 saw the full force of partisan politics break onto the scene. Any chance of Senate action on the House bill or anything resembling it before the election proved nonexistent. Indeed, we could hardly imagine any basis on which Republicans and Democrats could find common ground to consider and debate a foreign policy issue as sensitive as altering the world's nuclear nonproliferation architecture to accommodate India in a world of rising concerns about North Korea, Iran, and Iraq. Even if the legislation could theoretically be raised after the election in a "lame duck" session, there would hardly be time for hearings and a vote before the end of the 109th Congress in January 2007. Time was slipping away, and we had not even begun to think about how a 123 Agreement could be negotiated were we to succeed in overcoming the Senate legislative hurdle.

Thanks to the skill of the State Department's legislative affairs people, the active support of the White House, and the leadership of National Security Advisor Steve Hadley and Undersecretary of State Nick Burns, the legislation was brought forward in the December session that followed the midterm election. In the course of floor debate eight potentially damaging "killer amendments" were proposed and defeated. Significantly, several of these amendments were supported by then-Senators Obama of Illinois and Clinton of

New York. When the amendments were defeated and the dust settled, both senators then joined the eighty-two other senators who voted in favor of the Indian civil nuclear initiative. From the distance of New Delhi, and without personal contact with either of the senators, it was impossible to know whether their motivation was to derail the nuclear deal with India or simply to deny President Bush what, if ultimately successful, would turn out to be an important part of his foreign policy legacy. Whatever one's final judgment, the Indians were aware at the time and remain aware today of the reluctant, last-minute support that both these important Democratic Party leaders recorded for the cornerstone initiative of the U.S.–India strategic partnership. It is not surprising to me today that the warmth in relations between the United States and India from 2003 to 2009 has cooled significantly under the Obama administration.

Thus, as the year 2006 drew to a close, Congress had amended the Atomic Energy Act of 1954 to permit India to become the sole exception in the world's nuclear nonproliferation regime: namely, to be acknowledged de facto to be a state with nuclear weapons (as opposed to a nuclear weapons state) that would be permitted full access to the world of civil nuclear commerce without signing the 1974 Nuclear Non-Proliferation treaty or giving up its nuclear weapons. By the action of Congress, we were authorized to move forward with India to negotiate the 123 Agreement that would set out the bilateral arrangement between the U.S. and India that would govern our nuclear cooperation. This agreement, if it could be achieved, would also serve as the basis for approaching the IAEA for approval of India's nuclear nonproliferation safeguards and for the comprehensive consensus that would have to be achieved with all forty-five members of the Nuclear Suppliers Group (all signatories of the 1974 treaty). Finally, Congress would have to approve the 123 Agreement and all the other arrangements before its legislative action could come into full force.

The Senate vote on the civil nuclear initiative marked the turning point in the U.S.–India civil nuclear initiative. This was the moment when the opponents in the administration knew that they would have to cooperate in the effort to complete the agreement or be forced into open opposition. Until now, they had had the luxury of hiding behind the prospect that Congress would reject the change in law or place it on long-term hold. Instead, the impressive post-election bipartisan majority that materialized in the Senate meant that we would move on immediately to the next phase of negotiation with India of the formidable 123 Agreement.

10

Going the Distance

The American ambassador enjoys a very special position in India that brings with it almost unlimited opportunities to make a real impact on day-to-day relations between the two countries. The combination in one position of ambassador plenipotentiary and chief executive officer of the United States in India comes to mind again. One is almost never alone, never beyond the reach of colleagues, of most government officials, or the multitude of Indians who accord to the American ambassador the most remarkable respect and admiration. This is not a personal matter for which one can or should take credit, but truly a phenomenon inherent in the office and in Indian society. America is deeply respected and greatly admired in India, and its ambassadors are seen, rightly or wrongly, as important people who are the personal representative of the president of the United States. It is a sobering reality and takes some getting used to. It is also humbling and sometimes deeply and unforgettably moving. As time passed, I became more aware of the importance of living up to these expectations and trying to use the respect and goodwill inherent in my position to maximize the impact I could make on the overall U.S.–India relationship. There seemed no end to the daily opportunities for progress.

I grew to love India, or I should say Jeannie and I grew to love India together—the great human kaleidoscope, the place of perpetual activity, color, movement, pathos, chaos, beauty and reverence for the Creator, the gods of all things and the exotic mysteries of life. India's seasons were part of its charm, even the blinding heat of the days that would soften in the evening or the chill and fogs of winter. Then there were the perfect days—so many sunny, comfortable days—and India's diverse and exotic wildlife and plants, trees, and flowers, and especially the birds. And also the music, so often bringing peace, and the dancing, whether classical or passionately traditional, was also a part of daily life in India.

We traveled widely in virtually every region and found the people invariably kind, considerate, and polite. At times, I hardly knew how to respond to the respect shown to us, the representatives of America. At country hotels or rest stops, I would often be asked to review the local guard, drawn up in lines, armed with old rifles and commanded by energetic officers shouting out the command to present arms. Or there would be people at airports, relatives or friends of the airport manager, who had requests usually associated with visa aspirations. On one occasion at Udaipur airport a young woman dancer in full costume, who was a member of a traditionalist dance troupe invited to perform at Carnegie Hall in New York, asked that I intervene at the embassy to change the date of her visa interview appointment because it conflicted with the date set for her computer science final. She presented photos of herself dancing with live fire lanterns balanced on her head.

Jeannie and I developed the humorous phrase between us that "In India it's all about visas." In fact, by late 2006 the visa process as conducted by the U.S. mission in India had become a significant problem with negative fallout for our image in India. Ambassadors are admonished by the State Department to stay out of the visa business, which as a general rule is sound. For an ambassador to intervene personally in the visa process on behalf of an individual is frowned upon, and I was told, illegal. In India, however, the huge demand for visas to the United States had generated serious problems we needed to address.

By the summer of 2006 the backlog for the visa applications, each of which required a face-to-face interview with a U.S. consular officer, had reached the point where applicants faced a wait of 187 days to be interviewed. For Indian citizens needing to go to the United States for business meetings, weddings, funerals, or school this was an impossible situation, and in many cases it was deeply resented. Despite an express program for certain designated businesses and an effort to move students to the front of the line, the continuing pressure was such that applicants were calling the embassy, including the ambassador, for preferential treatment or paying visa agents with whom the embassy had formal working relationships for earlier-priority interview appointments. In fact, the visa agents were buying blocks of visa appointments and selling them to desperate applicants who could not wait six months for an interview. It was easy to see the scope for abuse or influence in the management of the interview appointments process.

The consular department, however, faced genuine problems that weighed heavily on their people, many of whom were young, first-assignment Foreign Service officers. When one considered that the mission through the embassy in New Delhi and its consulates in Kolkata, Mumbai, and Chennai was processing some eight hundred thousand visa appointments per year, simple math conveys the burden that these officers were carrying. On every business day some thirty-five hundred visa applications had to be processed, each requiring a brief face-to-face interview conducted through the bulletproof glass of a cubicle manufactured and imported from the United States. The pressure on young officers conducting in some cases over a hundred interviews per day after reviewing each applicant's online application was clearly very challenging, especially when it is understood that it was the responsibility of the young officer to accept or reject each application and to affix his or her signature on the bottom line reflecting that decision. This requirement alone tended to encourage a risk-adverse attitude, especially among young, inexperienced officers, with the result that rejection rates could often run quite high.

As the delays for processing visas grew longer I became more uncomfortable with a program that seemed to function in isolation from the rest of the mission and was both defensive and protective of its apparent prerogatives. Admittedly, visa fraud and security legitimately impact the consular department's mandate, but it seemed unreasonable to me that the visa backlog should have built up so dramatically and that reducing it to more reasonable waiting times should be beyond our capabilities.

I therefore took an interest in this specialized field, which few ambassadors pay any more than fleeting attention to, and even then usually on an individual case basis. To me, the issue of visas to the United States was a service business. We charged each applicant an upfront fee of $130 to apply, which was not refundable whether the applicant obtained a visa or not. America is an open society, and so long as our security is protected and we are satisfied the applicant does not intend to remain illegally in the United States, we should welcome visitors without imposing excessive bureaucratic constraints on legitimate visitors. Making all applicants wait 187 days to have the interview and receive the final decision seemed to me to fly in the face of our claim that America is an open society.

I began to watch the visa operation—for example, how many windows were open and in use how much of the time? Could we get additional help from Washington in the form of temporary officers? Could we enlist assistance from other qualified officers in different departments in the mission to pitch in and help the consular people? And finally, could we break the systemic practice among agents to hoard and subsequently sell blocks of visa appointments?

In September I convened an offsite meeting in Jaipur for all senior leaders and consular officers in the Mission. The idea was to recognize the serious challenge we faced and to expose and discuss solutions to these problems. We also needed to show our young officers that we were concerned about the burdens they were working under and their need to be exposed to other types of work in the mission in order to avoid a condition popularly referred to as "visa burnout." Above all, we needed to make a mission-wide commitment to removing the visa backlog and maintaining the waiting period in future at some more reasonable level. I was surprised by the level of support this initiative received. People clearly felt unhappy and defensive about the position we had put ourselves in with the Indian public. We concluded the offsite with a mission-wide commitment to defeat the visa backlog and named the enterprise the "visa blitz."

Through a combination of measures, extra support from the State Department in Washington, assistance from competent officers from other areas in the mission, and the discovery that by putting out more aggressively a significantly larger number of visa appointments, we broke the back of the visa backlog. This breakthrough was because visa application appointments were usually arranged by applicants through a visa agency. The long backlog of visa appointments had resulted in agents booking blocks of appointments running into the future, which they apparently could sell at a markup to visa applicants desperate for an earlier appointment than the 187-day wait generated by the embassy system. Once we expanded and accelerated our own appointment schedule, we found that "no shows" for appointments rose sharply, thus showing that the system was being gamed and immediately shortening the backlog.

Within three months, the wait for a visa application was down to six days throughout India. In the balance of my time as ambassador the waiting period only rarely exceeded fourteen days. I received a weekly report and graph of the visa application situation, which if deterioration occurred we immediately discussed among colleagues to determine the causes of any change in the visa backlog.

The response from the Indian public was perhaps the most satisfying aspect of the campaign. Positive messages flowed into the mission, and in thanking my colleagues I pointed out that money couldn't buy positive publicity like this for America. The State Department also responded by sending out messages to other missions in the world saying "if they can do this in India, why can't you?"

There was another rewarding experience of quite a different kind that brought unexpected results still present in India today. After the president's visit Jeannie returned to New York for additional surgery. When she came back to New Delhi she was invited to speak at the New Delhi Women's Press club with two other prominent Indian ladies who had not spoken earlier about their cancer. Until then we had not considered Jeannie's battle against cancer as anything other than our personal affair. At the Women's Press Club that day in a room filled with TV cameras and press, Jeannie opened a whole new and very surprising world.

By all accounts afterward, Jeannie's deeply personal and emotional remarks "literally took the oxygen out of the room." That such remarks should be given in the Press Club by the wife of the American ambassador in such a simple and direct manner amazed the gathered crowd. We soon understood the reason. Cancer, and breast cancer in particular, is virtually a taboo subject in India for public conversation. Women in India with symptoms of the disease feared to reveal it, either because health problems of other members of the family were given priority by most mothers or because women feared to be ostracized by friends or their extended families.

The nature of marriage in India, especially dowry marriages in rural India, made women particularly vulnerable to adverse health developments that make them a liability to the family. Worse still is talk of families rejecting a woman with breast cancer as a person afflicted in this life with the sins of previous lives.

Whatever the reasons, the outcome was, as we discovered, that women in India do not take preventative steps to detect breast cancer early, and when afflicted with physical signs of cancer they seek to avoid revealing their malady. The result is that stage four breast cancer is all too common with very high death rates, which in turn strikes fear into the general population, contributing further to the veil of secrecy surrounding this potent disease. An important contributor to this shameful situation, where men in particular can be either insensitive or hostile to women's afflictions, is the shortage of equipment and clinical facilities for mammogram checkups and other cancer-related services throughout India.

Shortly after the Press Club event, Jeannie was invited to be interviewed on NDTV's *60 Minutes* program. In a ten-minute segment, with quiet, elegant composure, Jeannie spoke to an audience estimated at forty million people spread across India. Here again was the wife of the American ambassador speaking openly and with quiet confidence on this very personal and sensitive subject. Afterward, Jeannie received personal handwritten letters from women in the remotest parts of India, thanking her and blessing her for speaking out on their afflictions. She was invited to be the keynote speaker opening several medical conferences on cancer. She was asked to repeat her testimonial as a breast cancer survivor to the audiences of doctors and technicians, and at each gathering I watched this beautiful, composed woman describe the seven surgeries and chemotherapy treatments she had endured and her plea for greater efforts for social transparency and early detection throughout India. Whenever she spoke there was perfect silence. Doctors and technicians learned that she was not afraid, that she practiced a constant optimism in all phases of the treatments, that she took aggressive measures by choice to combat the disease, that she had no medical advice to give beyond focusing women on self examination and early preventative measures, and finally that if by speaking she could help one woman in India to successfully defeat breast cancer her prayers would be answered. Afterward, she was surrounded by doctors and technicians telling her she had given the most important speech of any medical conference.

Among the doctors present at the First Annual Asian Breast Cancer conference was Jeannie's surgeon from Memorial Sloan Kettering in New York, Dr. Hiram Cody, and an Indian doctor, Dr. Rajeev Ram, of Hyderabad. Jeannie was invited to commemorate the opening in Hyderabad of Dr. Ram's digital mammography center, the first in southern India. She was also asked to open a large pop music concert at Hyderabad's new convention center. I will never forget Jeannie bathed in moving strobe lights, giving her personal testimonial to thousands of young people before the music was permitted to begin.

Lastly, in February 2008, Jeannie was asked to lead the first-ever breast cancer Walk for Life in New Delhi, organized by CanSupport, an Indian NGO headed by Hermala Gupta. Prime Minister Manmohan Singh's wife, Mrs. Gursharan Kaur, and Jeannie launched this event together on a chilly sunny morning, accompanied by some five thousand walkers dressed in white and yellow T-shirts. Since then, Jeannie and Mrs. Kaur have kicked off seven consecutive "Walks for Life" in New Delhi, each with a growing number of participants who make the four-kilometer early-morning walk.

This was the surprising and uplifting outcome from Jeannie's struggle with breast cancer. We have both been marked by the wondrous and unexpected consequences of her personal experience and by the fortuitous circumstances that placed her in India at that time, as the wife of the American ambassador, performing a personal gesture of courage, faith, and humility before the countless millions of friendly people in India.

Perhaps the broadest challenge with implications for India's social and economic progress over the next decade centers on education. Part of the case for India sustaining high growth over the next thirty years rests on its claim to have the largest young population (55 percent of Indians are under the age of twenty-four) among all the major countries of the world. Moreover, India's young people have high aspirations, are desperately keen to obtain an education, are comfortable with technology, and in general are fluent in English. Thus, while China, Russia, Japan, Europe, and even the United States will suffer in the near future from declining populations of young people, India will have the largest, most productive and youngest work force in the world just at the right time to propel India's economy forward. This optimistic projection assumes that India successfully educates this bulge of young workers and provides them with jobs and adequate health care. Otherwise, an aspiring body of frustrated young people might prove to be a political liability.

The reality in India today is that India's primary and secondary education systems are sadly lacking in both scale and quality. It is true that education is a top priority for families and that India's elite schools and universities produce large numbers of brilliant students who we see in America in large numbers. But tens of millions of young people are left behind in the Indian education system, and the government's present policies, although improving the situation somewhat, lack the scale and commitment necessary to accomplish the education of this young generation, which will be entering India's workforce in the next few years.

While serving as ambassador I received more than sixty visiting American university presidents, provosts, chancellors, deans, and delegations of boards of trustees who came to India to explore accessing India's giant education market. A group of progressive ministers in the government advocated greater change and the opening of India to foreign universities, which at present are not permitted to enter India on a fully accredited basis to offer their degree programs in-country to Indian students. Although education is a state subject under India's constitution, the federal government plays an overriding role in India's national education policy. The minister of human resources, who was in charge of education at the federal level, successfully resisted the reform efforts by younger ministers during the full term of my service with the result that only now, under the new Congress-led government, is India beginning to consider legislation to open India to foreign direct investment in education. Unless India opens more fully to the outside world and expands its own existing education system it seems doubtful that it can scale up quickly enough to educate millions more of its young people.

My relations with India's minister of human resources were generally unproductive. Minister Arjun Singh was an important but aging political figure who was also a cultural nationalist who strongly opposed entry to India by foreign educational institutions. He also seemed to be opposed to the U.S.–India Fulbright Scholarship program set up by treaty between the U.S. and India in 1951 under the leadership of Senator William Fulbright.

India's Fulbright program had been a major success story over many years. Between the two countries there were thousands of Fulbright alumni, and the program continued to enjoy the prestigious reputation it enjoyed in other parts of the world. Yet major problems appeared under the then-current government. These were of two kinds: one was inordinate delays in obtaining the necessary visas for American Fulbrighters coming into India; the other was the fact that some 12 percent of the study programs of foreign Fulbright scholars were denied without explanation. As ambassador, I began receiving letters of complaint from Fulbright participants and in some cases from their families. These complained of delays that greatly inconvenienced Fulbrighters who had resigned from positions, given up appointments or scholarships, or had otherwise put themselves in circumstances inconvenient to them and their families to accept a Fulbright grant in India. I discovered that of the approximately one hundred students and faculty awarded Fulbright scholarships in 2007 more than three-quarters had waited up to a year for a visa and some longer. Others had had their study projects rejected without explanation or appeal. One group of English language teachers had already waited for visas beyond the term of absence agreed with their home school, as well as beyond the portion of the Indian school year during which they were supposed to teach.

When I looked more fully into the problem I was struck by the casual injustice of the system in India. At the embassy we issued visas to Indian Fulbright students going to America in a single afternoon and did not examine or question their study project in the United States. When I reviewed the American study projects the Indians had rejected I could see no justification for such sensitivity and the blatant interference with academic freedom. Contrary to the agreed-on timetable that was to govern the program—awards in April and visas to be processed by June—our people were waiting up to nine months for visas and in some cases longer. My staff, who were charged with pressing the Indians to act more quickly, were forced to shuttle between the Ministry of Human Resources and the Ministry of Home Affairs to discover where the delays were being generated. In the process, I discovered that both the students and my staff were not being treated with the respect and goodwill one would assume should apply to a jointly agreed academic program between two major democracies. Finally, I discovered (as most anyone in the State Department already knew) that since 1951 the United States had itself paid for the entire U.S.–India Fulbright Program, whereas in virtually all other countries with a Fulbright Program the host country contributed up to half of the funds required to operate the program.

After months of effort with the Foreign Ministry as well as with the two ministries charged with running the program, it was clear that without firmer action we would not clear the visa backlog and resolve the interference by the Indians with the content of the study programs. I also found a distinct lack of willingness in our own State Department to push the Indians more aggressively.

We had reached a point where determined action was required. Such action brought forward by the ambassador might succeed in resolving the problem, or it might seriously strain relations between the two countries at the expense of the ambassador's reputation. I had reached the point, however, where I felt it was intolerable that American Fulbrighters should be so blatantly discriminated against, that we should seem to accept interference with the academic freedoms implied in the Fulbright Program, and that we should continue to pay all of the program's costs, as we had these past fifty-two years, in a country clearly able to afford some financial contribution. Indeed, if the Indians continued to enjoy a free ride on Fulbright there was every reason to believe they would make little effort toward reforms.

I decided to take several steps that I hoped would restore the prestige of the Fulbright Program and lead to its expansion as a premier vehicle for education and better understanding between India and America. I began by writing a letter in early 2008 to the newly selected Fulbright scholars, saying in effect, congratulations for being awarded a Fulbright, but please be aware that this could be bad for your health. The letter went on to explain the problems we had been having with the Indian program, so that no new Fulbrighter would be unaware of the potential inconvenience they might face.

The next step was to call on the foreign secretary, Mr. Shankar Menon, who was invariability friendly and had himself made a significant effort to clear up the process problems with the ministries of Human Resources and Home Affairs. The Foreign Ministry's efforts, though welcome, had been only marginally effective. Mr. Menon was very supportive of the Fulbright Program and understood its importance to India over the past half century. But entrenched bureaucracy is difficult to overcome anywhere and especially perhaps in India. I showed Mr. Menon the letter I had sent, which he found rather shocking, and proposed that in the next months we should work together to achieve the following objectives. The first was to remove the visa backlog and to stop the practice in India of rejecting the study programs of Fulbright scholars. The second was to amend the original Fulbright Program agreement to provide for India to expand the program by paying half of the finances each year. And, finally, that we should amend the agreement to permit private-sector parties to contribute to the program. If we could not achieve the first two objectives, I indicated that my inclination would be to suspend the program until its problems could be fixed.

This meeting marked the turning point for transforming the Fulbright Program into a true U.S.–India partnership. Thanks to the intervention of Mr Menon, the visa backlog began to shrink, study programs stopped being rejected out of hand, and we began the dialogue that would result in India agreeing to finance half the program by matching the amount contributed annually by the United States. They also agreed to permit private solicitations of resources. The outcome was a doubling of the Fulbright Program from approximately 130 grants (covering both Indians going to the United States and Americans coming to India) to close to 300. In the future, if private resources could be enlisted I saw no reason why the program could not in due course grow to a thousand scholars each year.

The Fulbright Board in India was reconstituted to incorporate higher quality, more enthusiastic people who were willing to consider greater diversification of the study content of the program. I successfully advocated for the program to move away from too heavy a focus on literature and culture to include technology and agricultural science.

When Mr. Menon and I signed the amended agreement in 2008 at a small luncheon at Hyderabad House I could not have been more pleased. The experience with Fulbright perfectly reflected the dynamic of the U.S.–India relationship and the mix of official bilateral and private civil society interests. It is this aspect of our relations that causes me to believe so firmly in the future our two nations will share.

Two other experiences intervened in my last two years that left an indelible mark on Jeannie and me. The first was our visit to His Holiness the Dali Lama in Dharamsala. He is a most remarkable individual, and Dharamsala is a unique replica of Tibet. The United States has supported the Tibetan community in exile for many years, especially by funding and supporting various kinds of schools for orphans and other children left by parents who brought them over the mountains from Tibet to leave them in freedom at Dharamsala. The extraordinary presence of His Holiness pervaded the entire Buddhist community in Dharhamsala and not surprisingly accompanies His Holiness wherever he goes in the world.

Our other experience came with the responsibility the U.S. ambassador to India has for the Kingdom of Bhutan. Formal relations between the United States and Bhutan have never been established, but the U.S. embassy in New Delhi is responsible for U.S. visa services and other matters for Bhutanese citizens, and the ambassador is required to visit Bhutan periodically. This proved to be a pleasant and stimulating responsibility. King Jigme Singye (abdicated 2006) of Bhutan, who had been on the throne since 1972, when he was seventeen years old, was a man of extraordinary vision. Over some twenty years he gradually introduced elements of democratic governance into Bhutan, culminating in 2008 in his abdication and the introduction of a constitutional monarchy with his son, Jigme Khesar Namgyel, crowned as the first constitutional monarch of Bhutan. In light of my earlier interests in constitutional engineering in Northern Rhodesia and the holding of elections, I was fascinated and impressed by the wisdom and administration King Jigme Singye developed to accomplish this impressive change. Jeannie and I attended the memorable and colorful coronation in Bhutan of King Jigme Khesar Namgyel in December 2006.

In early 2007 the United States began an intensive engagement with India on the negotiation of the U.S.–India Section 123 Agreement which, when completed, would govern bilateral arrangements between the United States and India for civil nuclear cooperation. This would be a true test of the resolve of both sides to determine whether a workable 123 Agreement could actually be hammered out in a fashion acceptable to both sides, to the world at large, and ultimately to the U.S. Congress. The U.S. negotiation process in Washington was led by Undersecretary of State for Political Affairs Nick Burns. Responsibility was shared with National Security Advisor Stephen Hadley and his assistant John Rood, a man with knowledge and experience in the field of nuclear policy. In the State Department the chief expert among the negotiators was Director of the Office of Nuclear Energy, Safety and Security Richard Stratford, who had negotiated previous 123 Agreements for the United States. Although skeptical of success, Dick Stratford was a complete professional, a man of deep experience, loyal dedication to the agreed-on agenda of the U.S. government, and realistic in his approach to a complex and politically sensitive process.

Most of our meetings took place in India with three key figures in the Indian government. First, Shyam Saran, former foreign secretary and now the prime minister's representative for the express purpose of this negotiation; National Security Advisor M. K. Narayanan, often referred to as the keeper of the equities of the Gandhi family; and finally, Foreign Secretary Shankar Menon, who was the former Indian ambassador to China and Pakistan.

Progress was slow, partly because the education process concerning the comprehensive reach of the 123 Agreement took time to be digested by the Indians, but also because a key element on the India side, namely India's powerful and privileged nuclear science community, was not regularly present at our meetings, not in any case at its most senior level. In fact, as negotiations proceeded during the first six months of 2007, it seemed to me that India's nuclear science community had lost its initial enthusiasm for the deal. There was no doubt that rising leftist opposition was making itself felt in the nuclear community and in the cabinet coalition. In addition, a community that had enjoyed the particular favor and respect (not to mention funding and other privileges) of Indian governments over some thirty years began perhaps to recognize that it would be subject to new constraints and far greater demands for transparency than in the past.

By March 2007 we had reached a point where further progress seemed doubtful. A distinct paralysis had set in regarding the more difficult issues, especially concerning India's demand for ironclad fuel assurances, minimal control over international use and allocation of fuel and technology between the civil and strategic sides of the industry, and finally the degree of intrusion into India's nuclear affairs by outside players such as the IAEA, the Nuclear Suppliers Group, and the United States. The Indians also sought to give the widest and most flexible interpretation to the amended language of the Atomic Energy Act to permit them the greatest latitude possible in the provisions of the 123 Agreement. For weeks on end we waited in vain for the Indian side to put its bottom-line demands on the table. Instead, there seemed to be endless sparing when it seemed to us that India's leadership should force its nuclear scientific community and bureaucrats to face up to the fundamental political decisions that would have to be made if India was to see its grand project through to completion. Several highly touted meetings in Washington fared no better, and we began to wonder who in India was really in charge of the nuclear initiative.

Meanwhile, we also engaged in our first discussions about how the enterprise would be advanced to the IAEA and the Nuclear Suppliers Group once we had completed the 123 Agreement. These exchanges highlighted very deep differences on the degree of responsibility to be borne by each party in the next phase. The board of governors of the IAEA met several times a year, but not all country members of the Nuclear Suppliers Group were represented on the IAEA board. In addition, the 123 Agreement, when completed, was not itself subject to the formal approval of the IAEA Board. Instead, the IAEA-India bilateral Nuclear Safeguards Agreement would require the formal approval of the board, and, so far as we could tell, the Indians had not yet seriously engaged the IAEA in this negotiation. It seemed that perhaps India was assuming it could get by in the IAEA with a relatively simple pro forma safeguards agreement pushed through the board by the United States. Our view, on the other hand, was that the IAEA Nuclear Safeguards Agreement was a bilateral matter between the IAEA and India to be voted upon ultimately under the standard procedures of the board.

The second issue divided us even further: how India was to win the support of the Nuclear Suppliers Group for the transformation of its status from nuclear outcast to full civil nuclear participant in the world's nuclear nonproliferation regime,. The Nuclear Suppliers Group met in plenary session at most only twice a year. The United States had made an explanatory presentation to the group, but we clearly looked to India to follow up with its own campaign to sell the plan for civil nuclear development as well as the credibility of its plans to comply with the principles and practices of nuclear nonproliferation. As the months passed we urged India to make its case before one of the Nuclear Suppliers Group plenary meetings to begin to build the support that would be needed when the 123 Agreement and the IAEA-India safeguards agreement were placed before the group for formal consideration.

No doubt the process for achieving a full consensus supporting India in a group that functioned only by consensus as opposed to majority vote was extremely challenging. Our view was that it was vital for India to lay this groundwork at the few plenary sessions that would present themselves over the next eighteen months. India's view was that it was the responsibility of the United States to achieve the needed consensus on India's behalf. Only the United States could bring the necessary influence to bear on all the member nations to move them to a full consensus. India's efforts, they feared, would be divisive, and in any case India lacked the power to force recalcitrant members to come to the table with positive attitudes. The result was that as plenary opportunities passed, we waited for India and they waited for us while members of the group enjoyed the comfort of almost complete withdrawal.

The climax of the 123 negotiation came in July at a meeting in Washington. The outstanding points that remained unresolved were few in number. Bringing the Indian side to the table for final resolution of these issues had taken months of talks that failed to move toward resolution. One began to wonder whether it was the chairman of India's nuclear power authority who held the power of final decision or the prime minister. The coalition itself was divided, with the leftist parties holding a position of inflexible hostility toward the entire enterprise. Finally, we succeeded in getting all the senior negotiators from both sides in the same room on the seventh floor of the State Department, with Chairman of the Atomic Energy Commission of India Anil Kakodkar ensconced in a nearby hotel room, positioned for private consultations with the Indian team. I was present at the table with grave misgivings about the once-removed status of Anil Kakodkar, who apparently would have to sanction final concessions by India.

India sought to strengthen in its favor the provisions referring to the supply of nuclear fuel to India under all circumstances and conditions that might prevail in the future. The language governing this subject had been agreed on with President Bush at the time of the completion of India's nuclear separation agreement the previous year. The gist of India's concern was that if, in the future, the United States imposed sanctions or otherwise terminated nuclear cooperation with India, the United States also might attempt to block the provision of fuel for India even while India's agreement with the Nuclear Suppliers Group and the IAEA remained in place.

In order to soften India's fears we had agreed to assist India in creating a nuclear fuel stockpiling facility which if rationally managed by India would overcome any U.S. supply problem. For example, if India stockpiled fuel not from the United States and used U.S.–origin fuel for current operations, the threat of a U.S. disruption, which we believed in any case not to be a relevant threat in world uranium markets, would be overcome. The functioning of the world's heavily private uranium markets in our view removed the threat to India of the United States exercising control over the world market. But India, which apparently had weak faith in the dependability of markets and in its own ability to manage a stockpile operation, remained fearful of U.S. influence and their vulnerability to political criticism in India. In the end, we refused to soften the original presidential language to give India the comfort it was seeking.

India's other major demand was that it should be granted the right by the United States to establish a facility for reprocessing nuclear fuel. While we were willing to consider the matter in principle in the future, India sought the granting of this right upfront in the 123

Agreement. This proved to be a deeply contentious issue. The Indians refused to budge. In the end, President Bush agreed to make the concession in the form of agreement by the United States to immediately grant India the right to establish a nuclear fuel reprocessing facility, subject to some carefully crafted language which in effect required a further negotiation with the United States within a set time period and in accordance with certain agreed procedures and conditions.

By the last days of July the 123 Agreement text was completed. Formal parliamentary approval of the agreement was not required in India, but the government was anxious to have the issue fully aired in the form of a parliamentary debate during the monsoon session of parliament in August and September. Only then would the government move ahead to the next phase of completing its negotiation of India's bilateral nuclear safeguards agreement with the IAEA. We were now only eighteen months away from the end of the Bush administration.

The monsoon parliament erupted in chaos when the motion was made to introduce debate on the U.S.–India 123 Agreement. Day after day, whenever an attempt was made to introduce debate, order could not be established to permit debate. India's media was vociferous and divided on the merits of the deal reached with the United States. India's BJP opposition, which had initially introduced the idea of civil nuclear cooperation prior to 2004, now refused to recognize that its own aspirations had been achieved and even exceeded. They refused to accept the written facts of the case as presented in the agreement and demagogued all the old shibboleths of a U.S. conspiracy with the Indian government to rob India of its nuclear independence and to subjugate India's foreign policy to U.S. control. Leftist parties exceeded even these extreme accusations and stated that if the government of India took any steps toward advancing the process to the IAEA or the Nuclear Suppliers Group they would immediately withdraw their support of the UPA government and call for a vote of confidence that surely was likely to bring the government down. Other groups made the case that even though a parliamentary vote was not required to "ratify" the

123 Agreement, the nuclear initiative was so unique in India's history that a debate and vote of confidence to reflect the sense of parliament should be mandatory.

By early September we faced a complete standoff, and India's political process regarding the agreement was frozen in place. As I tried to engage India's senior officials, pointing out the timetable constraints we and they would face in completing the entire process, I was met with empty assurances of a rapid move forward to the IAEA. To the argument that agreement had already been reached between us on the 123 text and that India must advance to the next stage, there was only a nodding caution and reminders of the complexities of Indian domestic politics. September turned to October with no sign of movement and no real engagement with the United States on when any action would be taken.

Finally, on October 12, the opening day of the Hindustan Times annual world forum event, Mrs. Sonia Gandhi and Prime Minister Manmohan Singh announced that maintaining the coalition government for its full term through May 2009 would take priority over completing India's civil nuclear agreement with the United States. I was stunned by this remarkable statement and simply unable to comprehend the rationale for turning away from what the Indians themselves had characterized as the most important diplomatic initiative of the past sixty years. There was sharp anger in the State Department and White House, together with the usual charges of incompetence, untrustworthiness, and plain double dealing by the Indian government, a staple of the past fifty years of behavior between the two great democracies.

This preemptive action was a heavy blow after two and a half years of dedicated effort on an initiative that I knew to be of vital importance to the Indian government. One could understand the UPA's fear of a withdrawal of leftist party support from the coalition, and one could equally recognize the Congress Party leadership placing a high priority on successfully managing a coalition government for the full five years of parliament. What I found less easy to justify was the fact that this government had negotiated and agreed on the text of the 123 Agreement after the U.S. Congress had agreed to amend the Atomic Energy Act of 1954 for the first time since its original passage, and only then had they balked. I also thought direction from the Congress Party leadership to the nuclear science community to comply with what the leadership had set as India's future nuclear policy was more than overdue. We heard reports of complicit actions between the nuclear science leadership group and the leftist parties to delay the agreement, which to me seemed as incredible as it was unacceptable. Who was really in charge of India, I wondered, as the prime minister and the Indian cabinet had decided long before to move ahead with the 123 Agreement.

Yet I had lived and worked for many years among difficult people and in politically sensitive situations requiring supreme patience and iron discipline against the temptation to become outraged and to engage in satisfying but essentially unproductive public statements. Besides, I knew from experience that an outspoken stance could result in further backward movement. I firmly believed that the nuclear deal was a fundamental interest of India, that the leaders genuinely wanted to do the deal, and that given the complexities of Indian politics, the best strategy was to wait, say virtually nothing, and be prepared for any break. It was no different from my early football experience: if you were sitting on the bench, your first duty to yourself and your team was to be ready at any moment to enter the game and to score the first time you touch the ball. It had worked for me in the past, and I was sure there would at least be one chance at some point, and if the chance came it could not be missed.

Once the government acknowledged that its top priority was the preservation of the UPA coalition through the full term of its authority (May 2009), it had in reality made itself hostage to the leftist parties in the coalition and even to divisions within Congress and among its more loyal coalition partners. The weakened position of the government's leadership therefore extended well beyond the question of India's civil nuclear initiative with the United States. The next eight months would gradually reveal the weakened ability of the Congress leadership in India's government to lead, and to fall to a level of impotence across the whole policy spectrum. Rising subsidies, giveaway programs to rural India, and the inability to cope with a sharp rise in inflation in food and energy prices had by May 2008 reduced the government of Prime Minister Singh to what I characterized at the time as feeble impotence. With the next general election only a year away, one would have given no chance for this government to be reelected. Its single claim to credibility was the fact that the Congress Party would have managed a coalition government for the full five-year term, but that accomplishment would come at the expense of nearly two years of paralysis, with no significant policy achievement and an economy in decline. In June 2008 the government was forced to cave in on its policy of preserving ceilings on energy prices and to concede that inflation would peak at approximately 14 percent over the coming months. There was a public outcry on both fronts, and the government fell into the habit of blaming these setbacks on a poor monsoon in 2007 and world energy price rises in 2008.

On the all important questions of the 123 Agreement negotiation I adopted a policy of quiet patience, first to understand the full magnitude of the government's dilemma and second not to insert the United States directly into India's troubled political scene. From our standpoint it looked as if the prime minister's pronouncement of October 2007 would result in a fatal blow to the timetable to see the deal through to completion during the Bush administration. The common wisdom was that there were too many complex steps still to be achieved before final approval could be gained from the U.S. Congress, which would have its own timetable constraints. Once the administration ended, the view in Washington was that even though Congress had amended the 1954 Atomic Energy Act, the nuclear initiative would have to begin all over again in a new Congress and administration where its prospects looked distinctly less bright. We would be back to square one.

At first the idea persisted in India that somehow the impending timetable issues could be overcome, apparently by the magical powers of the United States in the IAEA and the Nuclear Suppliers Group, as well as by the U.S. administration's powers to manipulate the Congress. Once again, India's facile assumptions that global realities could be overcome at some final moment by the importance of the U.S. and India conducting some kind of lightning strike persuaded the Indian bureaucracy not to worry. I was told that the government wanted the agreement to succeed and would find a way to work around its political limitations. The reality was, however, that on the U.S. side the shrinking timetable and the complexities of Congressional action would overwhelm us. Meanwhile, the main point in India was not to politicize the situation, a significant challenge in a country of constant political turmoil with a hyperactive media.

For a period of nine months I made no aggressive remarks in public, rose to none of the bait offered by the media or India's active think tank community. Instead, I expressed our understanding and respect for India's political process and our willingness to let the political process work itself through. On two occasions I added simply that we were aware of and concerned about the passage of time and its effect on the deal timetable, with no further elaboration on the dozens of questions which inevitably followed.

Privately, with Indian officials and with senior ministers, including the prime minister, I was more specific about the rising importance of our timetable constraints. Foreign Minister Pranab Mukherjee, an extremely able and politically astute leader on many fronts in the Indian government, was charged with chairing a committee in the Indian government on the question of moving civil nuclear forward in a fashion that could be supported by the coalition, and especially by the leftist parties. This, of course, was next to impossible, because the leftist parties had not been able to prevent the negotiation of either the separation agreement or the U.S.–India 123 Agreement, and as a result, their only chance of blocking progress was to oppose any movement by the government to begin negotiations with the IAEA on India's nuclear safeguards agreement. This, the left argued, represented the first and critical step in making the 123 Agreement operational. Were the government to take such a step, the leftist parties would withdraw their support from the government and call for a confidence motion in parliament, which would surely bring the government down. Thus, Foreign Minister Mukherjee was conducting a negotiation formed on the basis of how many subtle steps could be debated on the head of a very sharp pin without imperiling the survival of the government. As time passed and the government became more enfeebled on a number of different fronts, one could sense that the leftist parties had less to lose by withdrawing support from the coalition and possibly something to be gained by disassociating themselves from a government that was both less effective and more unpopular.

As the weeks following October 12 turned into months of waiting and watching for the smallest signs of progress, I developed a vigil mentality, waiting on the sidelines for the chance to enter the game, take the ball, and score. I had to be ready, to visualize every possibility, however dull the waiting might be, and to avoid at all costs any sense of hopelessness. Every day I was turning over our problem in my mind. Meanwhile, Nick Burns left the State Department in May 2008, and I sensed that others in Washington had given up and accepted what seemed to be inevitable failure.

June 2008 was the low point in the popularity of Prime Minister Singh's government. A dramatic rise in inflation, especially in food prices impacting India's multitudes and in the price of petrol at the pump, fuelled the government's widespread unpopularity. Looming food shortages and price inflation even persuaded India to prohibit exports of essential foodstuffs, such as rice, to poor countries in Africa and elsewhere. India, the traditional leader of the Third World and who had so often lectured the West about the morals of assistance, turned inward to brace itself against the possibility of another failed monsoon.

We were approaching the annual economic summit of the heads of state and governments set for early July in Tokyo. Prime Minister Singh was to meet bilaterally with President Bush. The meeting looked like the very last chance in an already failing nuclear initiative. In the second half of June I asked to see Prime Minister Singh to make it clear to him that whatever he might be hearing from the bureaucracy we were at the last possible moment for any hope of completing the U.S.–India Civil Nuclear Agreement.

In the constant process of turning over the problem of our impasse on the civil nuclear agreement, I had developed a line of argument for action by India that I thought might be appealing to Indian thought processes. If India were to advance now to the IAEA and then to the Nuclear Suppliers Group and finally lodge these accomplishments before the U.S. Congress in its last session, India might well achieve two highly significant results. By gaining the approvals of the IAEA and the Nuclear Suppliers Group, both of which would be supported by the United States, the burden for further action would shift directly onto Congress and the administration. Even if the congressional time table and the rules laid down for processing final approval made the task impossible to complete, India would be in a position to argue that it had done its part to fulfill its commitments to the Bush administration.

The second element of this approach was to consider what India's position might be if the exception granted to India by U.S. law to access civil nuclear technology from outside India were to be formally recognized and accepted by both the IAEA and the Nuclear Suppliers Group. These actions would have been proposed and supported by the United States. The U.S. Atomic Energy Act of 1954 was already amended with commanding bipartisan majorities in Congress. The change in U.S. law, of course, would not have been activated by final congressional approval of the actions taken by the IAEA and the Nuclear Suppliers Group. One had to wonder, however, whether actions taken by recognized international bodies of sovereign nations, including the United States, might not remain valid for those countries who decided to honor these decisions in their dealings with India. If India, having accomplished these approvals, moved ahead and submitted its completed actions to Congress by early September 2008, and Congress failed to act before January 20, 2009, the status of India's position in the world of civil nuclear commerce after that date might be open to widely different interpretations. Even if such an outcome could be forestalled, would the U.S.–India Civil Nuclear Agreement really be dead in the eyes of a new administration in 2009, especially with all other conditions with other nations already met? I did not believe a new administration would be able under these circumstances to hold the position that the nuclear deal had died on January 20, 2009. There had been ample time for consideration of the agreement (nearly four years) in the United States, a change in law supported by overwhelming bipartisan majorities in Congress, and approvals in the IAEA and Nuclear Suppliers Group, supported in each case by the United States as to their compliance with the intent of Congress and the Bush administration. Finally, if India did choose to go ahead with other countries who had approved the agreements, the U.S. nuclear industry would be left out in the cold while the French, Germans, and Russians secured the crucial opening round of contracts.

My point to the prime minister when we met and discussed these issues in late June was that moving ahead immediately to obtain IAEA and Nuclear Suppliers Group approvals and afterward to place the matter before the U.S. Congress in September held far more hope for India than simply remaining inactive. If these actions brought about a confidence vote in parliament by the leftist parties and the government won, India would no longer be held hostage to the threat of the leftist parties, and it would be in a position to put pressure on Congress and the U.S. administration. By proceeding in this fashion, India would have honored its commitment to the United States to complete all steps and submit the result to Congress for approval. The pressure on Congress and the administration would be very significant in the closing months of an administration hoping to burnish its legacy. Congress had its rules, but the congressional leadership also knew how to alter its rules from time to time. India had everything to gain by going forward, provided that the government could survive calling the bluff of their communist coalition members. If the final deal could be placed before Congress with all other approvals accomplished by the opening of the session after Labor Day in early September, it would not be India's fault if the agreement were not finally ratified before January 2009.

The prime minister listened intently. I had purposely arranged to meet with him alone so I could speak freely in hopes of planting a seed I might not want to openly acknowledge. He expressed his extreme regret over having to go to Tokyo and meet with his friend,

President Bush, with nothing to offer for the remarkable efforts of the United States over the past three years. I knew, however, that he had taken in the logic of my proposal without acknowledging its somewhat Machiavellian twist so far as the U.S. might be concerned.

Some two weeks later, while seated in my office, a news flash came over the wires that Prime Minister Manmohan Singh on his flight to the Tokyo summit had announced to traveling reporters that India would commence immediately to move the nuclear deal forward to the IAEA in the form of its application for the board to vote its approval of the IAEA–India Nuclear Safeguards Agreement. This, everyone agreed, was the first step to operationalizing the civil nuclear agreement. I will remember this moment as one of the most courageous decisions in my experience by a prime minister for the future of his country. I knew then that we would make the final run for ratification by this administration, and my heart could not have risen with more excitement in my breast.

Back on earth, the leftist parties immediately signaled their withdrawal of support for the coalition government, provoking the prospect of an immediate parliamentary vote of confidence that would test the ability of the coalition and the civil nuclear agreement to survive. The confidence vote was set for the third week of July, and the first media judgments were that the government could not survive.

For the next two weeks the chief activity of the media was to count and recount potential votes on a daily basis. Sometimes the government lost by twelve to fifteen votes. Other times it lost by fewer than five votes. Then, in the waning days there were rumors of the government gaining the support of one of their severest critics, Amarh Sing and his handful of twenty-three votes in the lower house. Rumors were that his party would not join the coalition government, but on this important test it would support the policy of the government. In the end, Prime Minister Singh won the confidence vote by a comfortable margin, but not before some highly dramatic theater in parliament during the debate preceding the vote. One member marched into the chamber with a large suitcase in hand, which he opened on the speaker's rostrum to spill millions of rupees across the table and onto the floor. This, he said, was the cash he had been offered to change his vote to support the government. He raised his arms shouting that he would have none of it. The government brushed the theater aside and immediately began its efforts to advance to the IAEA and Nuclear Suppliers Group. Once again we were engaged with India in a common purpose whose urgency with the summer break looming in Europe could hardly be over estimated.

Bureaucrats in Europe and those based in Europe from other countries invariably shut up shop in the month of August. We needed an IAEA board meeting vote and we estimated at least two plenary sessions of the forty-five member Nuclear Suppliers Group—all before early September. It was common practice not to hold an IAEA board meeting in August, and plenary meetings of the Nuclear Suppliers Group normally took place approximately nine months apart. We also faced the problem that the Suppliers Group would refuse to meet until the IAEA had completed its work.

So, Vienna became the target for meetings in the languid days of summer. One could imagine delegates being dragged back from holidays for business that many were not in any case keen to process. The U.S. Congress would reconvene on September 8, so we had five weeks for a process we had imagined would require many months. We also had a U.S. Congress whose last session running up to the presidential election in early November was rumored to be shrinking so members could be home campaigning by early October.

Our first break came in early August when the IAEA agreed to hold a board vote on India's Nuclear Safeguards Agreement. Work had already been done on safeguards by India, and since the draft agreement followed the many other precedents the IAEA had established with other countries, the agreement was acted on relatively quickly. This brought the focus of attention onto the Nuclear Suppliers Group, which had a diverse membership of both large and small countries.

Consensus was reached that there should be a meeting set in Vienna for August 20–23, where the first full discussion would take place with a view to reconvening in early September after governments had the opportunity of home office consultations, which for most countries meant that top political leaders would have to make the final decision to support or oppose India.

I attended the Vienna meeting, which was a much larger, more formal affair than I had imagined. Its plenary gathering numbered more than two hundred, with delegates spread at desks across a wide but rather shallow hall. The chairman presided at a small desk that was not raised onto a rostrum and did not provide space for lieutenants flanking him on either side. Statements were brief; there were a large number of contributions, and the debate that followed was neither especially active or substantive in nature.

I suspected it was largely a behind-the-scenes affair, with most participants there to gather information and impressions for their subsequent deliberations back home. One event that greatly surprised and troubled me was a briefing we had scheduled for the Indian team led by Shyam Saran and Shankar Menon. The briefing was held in the luxurious plenary hall of the IAEA. The Indian team led off with summary remarks before opening the floor to questions and discussion. To my surprise not a single delegate raised a question. I concluded that either the periodic briefings over the past two years had effectively answered all outstanding questions or that minds were already made up and delegates did not wish to show their hands. I began to wonder exactly how a consensus by the suppliers group, which had never had a seriously divisive issue to decide, would be formed, and, more to the point, expressed. There was to be no formal vote. What would happen if a country simply abstained from reaching its view on the India issue? Would a consensus be based only on those present at a future meeting, or must it include every country expressing its decision in some forum at a particular moment in time?

What was clear from the Vienna meeting was that several smaller countries with socialist governments and strong environmental communities were not supportive of the agreements. I also noticed that delegates were almost exclusively drawn from the nuclear nonproliferation or defense offices of the various foreign ministries. These officials, like their counterparts in Washington, were highly specialized and generally unenthusiastic about any change in the global nuclear nonproliferation architecture. The broader issues we had advanced with members of Congress in the United States when preparing for the vote to change the Atomic Energy Act were simply not discussed by our team or by delegates in general.

An exception was at a dinner hosted by the U.S. Ambassador to the IAEA in Vienna, where a small group of delegates engaged in the kind of broad based discussion we had been hearing in Washington for nearly two years. Afterward, the Swiss delegate, whose country reportedly was against authorizing the deal, conceded to me that he had learned more in one evening than in the past forty years. He was from the Swiss Foreign Office's section dealing with nuclear nonproliferation, which was where I imagined he had been for most of the past forty years.

When I returned to Delhi from Vienna it was clear that six countries were likely to hold out against India: Austria, Sweden, Denmark, Holland, Ireland, and New Zealand. China was also a holdout, although for different reasons, and they had not at this point formally declared their position. Before leaving Vienna I met with Austria's foreign secretary, who, like others, had not been exposed to the broader range of arguments for bringing India into the global system. Clearly, what was missing in many of these countries was a broader political awareness of the importance of finding a basis for India to participate in the world's nuclear nonproliferation regime. Austria, for example, prided itself on having no nuclear reactors in its country, but as everyone knew, Austria imported large amounts of electricity generated from nuclear reactors in neighboring countries. There was no understanding of India's situation, its energy needs for its growing economy, and the environmental damage that would flow from India, as with China, from supporting its high growth in the decades ahead almost entirely from power based on exploiting coal. India would surely continue to thrive and in doing so could well become the world's largest polluter, unless it succeeded in the coming years to build and operate a world-class civil nuclear industry large enough to support its future growth. This point was generally accepted in the Delhi diplomatic community but not by several of the smaller countries that would need to support India in the Nuclear Suppliers Group consensus.

Back in New Delhi I saw the urgency of engaging politically with these possible "holdout" countries. Before going to Vienna I had invited the ambassadors of the Nuclear Suppliers Group countries to my residence for a briefing. This had been appreciated on the ground in New Delhi but had accomplished little more than to provide an information flow back to foreign offices, which in many cases were already in summer break mode.

I felt I had to engage the ambassadors of the countries that were likely holdouts in a way that would provoke them into raising the India issue to the highest political levels in their countries before the second and decisive meeting of the suppliers group. I decided to host a luncheon at my residence and invite ambassadors from only the six holdout countries. Internally, I called the event "The Recalcitrants' Lunch." I asked my staff to prepare a paper with six sections, one devoted to the development of each country's relationship with India over the previous five years. I knew that for each country during the course of my tenure that India was among the highest diplomatic and commercial priorities. The paper focused on their accomplishments, their improving trade balances with India, and their foreign direct investment progress. Many countries had sponsored multiple visits to India of various trade, education, development, and diplomatic delegations.

When the various ambassadors arrived at Roosevelt House and saw the seven place settings at the large round table set in the main reception room looking out into Roosevelt House's spacious, green garden, they knew this was to be a lunch for the select few. At the table I handed out the papers and asked them to read the three pages of country-specific information. Then I said that I had invited them to this gathering because the White House and the secretary of state were confused as to why their countries were prepared to sacrifice their impressive accomplishments with India over the past five years. To this comment there was a profound silence.

I continued that the United States was only confused about what appeared to be their common view not to join in the consensus that would permit India to return to the world of civil nuclear commerce and to become a positive participant in the global nuclear nonproliferation regime. The United States had important and intensive relations with each of their countries, which would not be disturbed by whatever decision they finally would make. India's reaction, however, to a decision to torpedo the U.S.–India Civil Nuclear Agreement, whether as a group or individually, would, I noted, be an entirely different story. I let them know that the United States did not understand why they would so lightly sacrifice five years of progress with India, because I had no doubt that India would impose a harsh and painful price on any country that sabotaged what for India was seen as their most important diplomatic breakthrough for the past fifty years.

The lunch went smoothly but quite quickly. As the ambassadors hastened out into the rising summer heat, I knew the lines to capitals would be singing that afternoon. I was also confident that the afternoon's messages would convey a sense of panic and be directed to the highest levels in their governments—well above their respective bureaucracies. No one left the working paper behind, and I sat with a cup of coffee, which all the "recalcitrants" had politely declined, and thought of the entertaining instructions printed on English fireworks back when I was at Oxford: "Light fuse and retire."

I did not attend the second plenary of the Nuclear Suppliers Group in early September. This meeting would simply record whether a perfect consensus could be achieved to support the proposed change in India's position in the world of civil nuclear commerce. Debate and lobbying in Vienna were over. We would soon know whether a small group of holdout countries, or even a single nation in the forty-five member group, would destroy the consensus for change. In the days leading up to the plenary meeting the "recalcitrant" group of small countries began to weaken. Opposing India, the United States, and the other large nuclear powers who supported the changed status for India would clearly carry a high price. At the meeting they all supported the consensus, together with China, which joined at the last minute after a call the previous night from President Bush to the prime minister of China.

There could be no doubt about the magnitude of this victory, and all of us involved in the effort shared an enormous sense of pride and achievement. In particular, we were very fortunate to have Geoff Pyatt, my former much-valued deputy chief of mission in India, serving as the deputy to our ambassador in Vienna. Geoff was knowledgeable, committed to the cause, and a skilled diplomat, who is now the U.S. ambassador to Ukraine. But our victory could only be short lived because we still faced what appeared to be the impossible task of working the final ratification through the U.S. Congress. When Congress reconvened on September 8 after its summer recess it was expected to remain in session only through mid-October before adjourning prior to the presidential election in early November. The original legislation passed in 2006 visualized a process for this final phase that would set aside at least thirty Congressional business days, which in the normal course of events could well cover up to sixty calendar days. Even assuming a "lame duck" session of Congress after the election, there simply would not be enough days before the administration ended on January 20, 2009. Only a decision by the Congressional leadership to change the rules could alter this prospect.

Pressure for this initiative came immediately from the administration. Recall, however, the political atmosphere that dominated Washington at that time. We were less than two months away from a strongly contested general election that stimulated highly partisan interests. In addition, the global financial crisis reached its peak in September 2008, when political leaders and finance officials found themselves staring into the abyss of a complete breakdown of the world's financial system. The meltdown of global financial markets was sowing panic in Wall Street, London, and Japan, and Congress was engaged in a frantic effort to enact economic stabilization measures.

On September 25 the president's economic stabilization legislation was defeated in Congress, and that evening he hosted Prime Minister Manmohan Singh of India for a small private dinner in the family dining room of the White House. The prime minister was accompanied by Foreign Secretary Menon, National Security Advisor Narayanan, and the Ambassador of India to the United States, Ronen Sen. Our side included the President's National Security

Advisor Stephen Hadley, Secretary of State Condoleezza Rice, and me. The dinner was memorable from the moment President Bush entered the room. Despite having had one of the worst days of his presidency, with collapsing markets and the defeat of his stabilization package in Congress, he entered with a calm and friendly bearing, conveying none of the frustration of his day. In fact, as we sat down to dinner he tipped back his chair and observed that after such a day there was no one in the world that he would rather be having dinner with that evening than Prime Minister Singh. The president referred to the example of calmness and peace always conveyed by the prime minister and expressed his gratitude for the prime minister being at the White House on this particular evening.

We exchanged views on a wide variety of subjects that evening, including prospects for congressional action on the U.S.–India Civil Nuclear Agreement. The president was confident that the measure would be passed by the Congress before the general election recess. This was the most heartening observation of the evening, and in less than two weeks it proved to be correct. The congressional leadership came together to agree to process the final very simple piece of legislation that would bless and activate the agreement. Once again, large bipartisan majorities were registered in both houses of Congress, just one month before a divisive U.S. general election. President Bush's legacy for India was secured. I believed then and still believe that this accomplishment with India by President Bush will be seen for decades to come as the cornerstone of modern U.S.–India relations, as well as vital to India's rise to world power status.

For me the vote was the culmination of nearly four years of effort on every aspect of the civil nuclear initiative, coupled with periods of patience and restraint as the process unfolded in our respective capitals and as all the countries in the global nuclear nonproliferation regime came together to express their support.

The signing by the president at the White House on October 8 of the U.S.–India Nuclear Cooperation Approval and Nonproliferation Enhancement Act was the event that crystallized the entire enterprise. The East Room was packed, with every seat and space for standing occupied. Across the back of the room were more TV cameras and still photographers than I had ever seen in one place, including most summit meetings around the world. Dozens of the cameras were directly linked to India, where I knew that in the heat of the late monsoon season the nation waited.

Jeannie and I entered the White House early to attend a private reception with the president and leaders of Congress. We noticed when entering through the East Wing portico that the Secret Service guards were permitting attendees to bring cameras and cell phones into the White House, despite signs clearly asking visitors to leave all such items at the gate. Perhaps the Secret Service had recognized that the large crowd of Indians and Indian Americans who had been critical to the lobbying success in Congress would resist leaving their cameras behind on this happy and historic occasion.

Inside we met the president and members of Congress to enjoy the moment and sense of accomplishment shared by all. Then we moved into the East Room, resplendent in brilliant lights and set up with a raised stage and a small table decorated with American and Indian flags, with the legislation laid out for signing. Vice President Cheney was present and a group of congressional leaders stood behind the President.

President Bush spoke from the rostrum before moving to the small table decorated with the Indian and American flags to sign the U.S.–India Nuclear Cooperation Approval and Nonproliferation Enhancement Act.

Jeannie and I were seated in the first row just before the signing desk. When the president spoke, we both saw him wink at us as he completed the opening passage. Then he moved to the table and in a few moments signed the ribboned legislative packages. Thousands of flash bulbs exploded with shutters making what seemed to be a wall of simultaneous clicks. Everyone stood with a great cheer, with the Indians immediately leaving their seats and surging forward. The president stepped off the stage and came straight to us to shake hands, to congratulate me and thank me for my efforts. He embraced Jeannie and kissed her on the cheek. Such was the consideration consistently shown by this president for the people who worked for him.

Jeannie and I at that moment and in the confusion that followed that the historic and boisterous occasion had been perfectly captured in time. We felt a swelling of pride and sense of true accomplishment. We knew that our decision in 2005 to stay the course in India, despite Jeannie's suffering and our long separation was truly an act of love and commitment that would carry forward for the rest of our lives.

On the evening of October 25, 2005, I was invited to visit the campus of the Pathways School, a relatively new boarding school about an hour's drive outside New Delhi. The school was founded by the Jain family in New Delhi and in less than ten years had established itself as a serious baccalaureate program educational institution. The occasion was a special evening for parents and guests in which the students put on a light show depicting the drama *Ramayana*, set around a small lake and stoneworks in the center of the campus. I was driven out on one of Delhi's first cool evenings after the long, hot summer, and the last ten miles down a narrow country lane at twilight under the rising of a full moon was lovely, cool, and picturesque in the fading light.

I spoke before the light show to the body of assembled parents, students, teachers, and visitors. When I finished, my security officer asked me to step away for a moment. He told me there had been a major terrorist bomb attack on Sarojini Market in New Delhi, with a large number of casualties. Within a few minutes I was on my way back into Delhi in a very different mood than on the outbound trip. Sarojini Market was not far from the diplomatic enclave; it was frequented by large crowds in the evenings, including many diplomatic personnel who were attracted by its convenience and huge selection of goods. I could not imagine the scenes of horror and hoped there were no American citizens among the dead and injured. Traffic going back to the city was heavy and I could understand why. Since the attack on India's parliament in early 2002 there had been virtually no significant terrorism attacks in India, apart from the almost daily incidents that swirled around Srinagar in Kashmir and periodic local violence in India's northeast. Sarojini was clearly an attack of a wholly different type.

No Americans were killed or injured in Sarojini Market that night, but the death toll numbered well over sixty and the destruction to shops and the market was widespread. In the the next few weeks, intelligence sources, both Indian and American, identified Lashkar-e-Taiba (LeT), a well-established terrorist organization that operates largely out of Pakistan, as the perpetrators of this outrage. The rationale behind the attack was that Lashkar-e-Taiba wanted to increase its visibility and the national impact of its terrorist activities in India. The violence it promoted in Kashmir was now so commonplace that the organization was gaining only minimal publicity benefits from them. A few hand grenades and some daily murders confined to Kashmir simply were not spectacular enough and had little impact on the nation of India. Their new strategy was to strike into the heartland of India with spectacularly destructive attacks, claiming dozens of human lives and sowing division, distrust, and communal tensions in India's dense population. These attacks were to be the weapon of choice for Pakistan's future terrorist operations in India.

India, it appeared, would now face the chilling prospect of a much-expanded terrorist campaign. Sarojini Market would prove to be a watershed event for India's internal security and a significant challenge for U.S.–India relations. The information pieced together by intelligence sources confirmed to the Indians that the attack was a new departure for Pakistan's terrorist campaign across India, which reached its peak three years later in the brutal terrorist attacks on hotels in Mumbai.

In the months that followed Sarojini Market, there were attacks in the markets of other Indian cities. These were virtually identical to the attack on Sarojini Market: crude pipe bombs, fire, panic, disorder, and bloody casualties. As soon as the attacks were over and police rushed in to hunt for suspects, crime scenes were cleaned, destroying any prospect for serious forensic work. Sketches of suspects were distributed, but there were few arrests and subsequently no significant prosecutions. The Indian intelligence community was sure that the terrorists were Pakistanis with no real local support from Indians, except perhaps for information or minor assistance paid for in cash by the perpetrators. For the Indian intelligence community, the new strategy proved a depressing and frightening challenge.

That the LeT could marshal a far more destructive campaign was graphically demonstrated in the coordinated bomb attacks that took place in Mumbai against the city's commuter trains on July 11, 2006. Over two hundred people were killed at the height of the evening rush hour as they made their way home. For months afterward the *Daily News and Analysis* in Mumbai published a personal sketch each day of one individual victim, his or her life story as a working person, a family member, wife, husband, son, or daughter, and how by sheer chance that person came to be where they met their death in a train ripped open by blasts in the midst of heavy monsoon rains. These accounts were graphic and conveyed the pain, injustice, and pure chance of death by the hand of crossborder terrorism.

These developments also raised serious problems for me as U.S. ambassador in India. In the years following 9/11 in the United States, when initially there was a notable sense of solidarity between the United States and India, questions arose in India concerning the apparent double standard of the U.S. government toward terrorism in India. The attack on India's parliament in early 2002, which had clearly been carried out by Pakistanis, was not followed by any punitive U.S. action against Pakistan. Instead, the United States appeared to be largely insensitive to Pakistani-led attacks across India following the Sarojini Market outrage in 2005. The U.S. continued to regard Pakistan as a critically important ally, vital to U.S. interests in Afghanistan. U.S. aid continued to flow to Pakistan without significant conditions. Providing new or modernized F-16s to Pakistan, for example, continued to be advanced as a policy objective of the U.S. administration, whereas in India the attitude was that F-16s are not used for crowd control in cases of domestic unrest; they can carry nuclear weapons, which in India were clearly seen as for deployment against India. Nevertheless, the State Department continued issuing statements expressing our outrage and unconvincingly citing our shared interests in fighting terrorism. In fact the State Department, the Department of Defense, and the intelligence agencies of the United States all continued to assume that India should fully cooperate with the United States in the field of counterterrorism, with no commensurate action by the United States against Pakistan.

As ambassador to India, I found this attitude toward Pakistan's involvement in terrorism damaging for our otherwise strengthening relationship. Despite initiatives proposed from time to time in counterterrorism intelligence activities by the United States, the Indians restricted their cooperation with us to the exchange of intelligence information, drawing the line at any operational cooperation. Their attitude, in my view, caused a quite unjustified disappointment in the U.S. intelligence community, followed by the typically superficial response that Indian attitudes just confirmed how difficult and unreasonable they could be to work with. Meanwhile, within the U.S. government I found as ambassador a surprising and irritating lack of cooperation from our own intelligence community. Obtaining information on Pakistani sponsorship or encouragement of terrorism in India was simply not forthcoming from Washington, in spite of numerous requests for a more-considered appraisal of the role being played by the government of Pakistan. Instead, I received the worn and utterly useless response that U.S. intelligence could not produce the "smoking gun" linkage required to convict the Pakistani government of actively planning and promoting terrorism in India.

By treating this life and death issue in India as if we had to meet the standard for guilt in a court of law before we could lift a constructive finger against the outrageous violence flowing into India from Pakistan, the United States struck a severe blow to its credibility in India. The slightest exercise of common sense would have justified some sort of punitive action against Pakistan. To broadcast our sympathy after each terrorist event and then to fail to follow up with any credible response on the ground in Pakistan was shameful for the United Sates and fully justified, in my view, the cynicism and suspicion our people found in both the government and society of India.

As my time in India began drawing to a close in 2008, and we had successfully revived the U.S.–India civil nuclear effort, there was every reason to renew our efforts to address counterterrorism. This was the one area of U.S.–India strategic cooperation that had remained at a standstill for four years. Several considerations came into play in trying to raise counterterrorism cooperation to a higher priority for both sides. Leadership in the U.S. intelligence community was improved by the appointment of better people. Congress began to show tentative signs of wanting stronger conditionality on U.S. aid to Pakistan. A new and highly classified technology that could be of key importance to India in its struggle to preempt terrorist activity on the ground in India was introduced for consideration between us. Finally, the continued pattern of more frequent attacks around India, coupled with the now quite impressive seven-year track record of the United States in preventing another 9/11 at home strongly suggested that India could benefit from a better understanding of U.S. domestic actions to improve internal security since 9/11.

High-level meetings began to take place. I approached members of the Indian government to encourage them to arrange to visit U.S. counterterrorism facilities in America to see for themselves how we had overcome the inherent conflicts in our federal, state, and municipal law enforcement structures to improve our ability to identify possible terrorist initiatives and in particular to disrupt attacks before they could take place. India's complex federal, state, and municipal structure of semiautonomous authorities raised many of the same questions we had faced when it was becoming increasingly obvious that India was losing the battle for ensuring internal security against terrorist attacks, whether from Pakistan or from the Naxalites within India. By October 2008 I felt sure I was getting their attention.

Then came Mumbai. On the evening of November 26, 2008, ten highly trained and heavily armed terrorists attacked Mumbai in what became India's 9/11. They came ashore in small rubber boats laden with explosives, heavy weapons, and ammunition. They set off for different targets: the railway station, a Jewish religious center, and three of Mumbai's most fashionable hotels. Everywhere they appeared over the next few hours they killed indiscriminately: innocent people in the streets and the main train station, police officers, a rabbi and his wife at Nariman House, and hotel guests and Mumbai families enjoying the restaurants and ambience of Mumbai's leading hotels. As the terrorists entered the Taj Palace and the Oberoi Hotel they shot the door staff and the check-in people behind the front desks, then proceeded to the busy restaurants, killing people at their tables. At the Taj they quickly proceeded to the manager's apartment and murdered his wife and small children. Fires were started in the hotels as the terrorists went room to room, killing and seizing hostages.

The initial shock of the attack was quickly replaced by the realization that Mumbai and especially the hotels were under siege for as long as the terrorists could hold out. In the end this proved to be seventy-six hours, during which nine of the ten terrorists were killed and one captured wounded but alive. During this attack, after the initial killings in the restaurant and lobby areas, the terrorists stalked terrified guests in the rooms and as they tried to escape from the hotels. Hostages were checked for nationality, and foreigners were not released. A group of hostages were assembled at the Oberoi, marched to an upper floor, and brutally slaughtered.

Outside the hotels vast crowds assembled to watch the flames coming out of the windows and on the roof of the historic Taj Palace Hotel. The police remained outside the hotels, seemingly immobilized, with any movement toward the hotels met with grenades tossed out by the terrorists, who seemed to know where the police were getting close to the buildings. Indian national television quickly staked out the hotels and reported nonstop on the unfolding horror.

Shortly after the attack began I was contacted in Phoenix, Arizona, where Jeannie and I had gone for a family Thanksgiving. It was Wednesday evening in Phoenix and Thanksgiving morning in New Delhi. We left immediately for India. Arriving in New Delhi Friday evening, the attack was still going on, with movement by the authorities to enter the hotels with commandos only just begun. The following day the terrorists were gradually overcome so that by late Saturday the attack was over and the authorities were left fighting the fires and searching hotels for bodies and survivors. Meanwhile, details of the street attacks, the railway station massacre, and the utterly depraved attack on Nariman House, the Jewish center, had emerged. Public outrage against the Indian authorities for what appeared to be a delayed and inadequate response swept the nation. Why couldn't the government of India protect its people against predictable terrorist outrages? The public seemed more intensely critical of their own authorities than against Pakistan, the suspected perpetrator of the attack. The view among Indians was that they expected this kind of outrageous behavior from Pakistan; it was India's inability to protect its own citizens that drew the ire of the Indians. Incompetence and inaction from top to bottom was the public's bitter judgment, which later, despite the personal bravery of many in the Mumbai police, proved to be for the most part true.

The most immediate political casualty was Home Minister Shivraj Patil, who resigned and was succeeded by P. Chidambaram, India's finance minister. Chidambaram, a lawyer by training and a leader from South India within the UPA coalition, had the reputation of being extremely able, articulate, and decisive. These qualities were quickly deployed at Home Affairs and in a fashion which immediately reorganized India's most urgent challenges following the attack. These were to identify and punish the perpetrators; to address India's obvious need for a coherent national security regime that could anticipate and disrupt future terrorist attacks; and to provide an immediately credible effort to identify Pakistan as the perpetrator of the attack.

We made the unusual offer to provide forensic assistance at the crime scene, and to our great surprise this was immediately accepted by the home minister. Indeed, a twelve-member FBI team was en route almost at once for India. Their agreed-on mission was to offer on-the-ground assistance to the Mumbai police. They were permitted to enter India at Mumbai instead of first going to New Delhi, and their sophisticated high-tech equipment was cleared for entry into India that same day at Mumbai airport. These were all remarkable developments by any historic standard that spoke of India's new attitude of urgency and the decisive nature of Mr. Chidambaram.

Within a few days it was clear that we had made a major breakthrough in counterterrorism cooperation with India. Much credit for this was to the FBI team members themselves, who were able to establish close and friendly working relations with the Mumbai police.

Eleven countries lost citizens in the Mumbai attack. India established the forensic effort as a serious process aimed at producing as quickly as possible a dossier of evidence that would indict Pakistan beyond question as the planner and perpetrator of the most professional and brutal terrorist attack ever on India. Progress was immediate and dramatic. The suspicion that the attack had been managed over some seventy-two hours by "handlers" in Pakistan was confirmed when the FBI was able to retrieve verbatim mobile telephone conversations between handlers in Pakistan and the ten terrorists on the ground in Mumbai. These exchanges, which were transformed into transcripts, were recovered from the damaged and in some cases melted mobile phones found on the bodies of the terrorists. They confirmed that handlers in Pakistan were following events in Mumbai on 24/7 news channels on Indian television, instructing the terrorists in the hotels on where the Indian police were deployed, whom to kill, and whom to free, among the many hostages taken in the hotels. In one case, the terrorists were instructed to seek out foreigners, take them to an upper floor of the hotel, and hold out their phones so they could hear the hostages being killed.

The reconstructed record of the attack made the most horrible reading. It confirmed that at the hotels the doormen and baggage handlers were killed outright, and the young and attractive front desk staffs were murdered as they stood. The terrorists went to the restaurants, killing people at their tables. An American man was killed before his thirteen-year-old daughter, who was wounded and escaped. She was later hunted down in the hotel and killed. At the Taj Palace, the terrorists went directly to the manager's apartment and killed his wife and young children. The final report also established that despite the loss of his family, the manager remained at his post for the duration of the attack. Fires were set in the hotels, and people were killed in their rooms or trying to escape. Some survived by locking their rooms and hiding. One could hardly imagine the horror of those seventy-six hours for all who were caught up in the slaughter and their anxious families on the outside.

Pakistan's immediate response was to deny that the attackers were from Pakistan, even though Azam Amir Kasav, who had been wounded and apprehended by the Mumbai police, admitted that he was from a village in Pakistan. Within a few weeks the claims of the Pakistani government that the attack had not been planned or carried out from Pakistani soil were proven beyond doubt to be blatant lies. A satellite cell phone found in one of the rubber dinghies used by the terrorists to come ashore in Mumbai provided inconvertible evidence. The joint team produced a map of northern India and Pakistan that showed bright yellow dots indicating where the phone had been each day for the previous four weeks. The phone had never left Pakistan. It had been in the border areas where terrorist training camps were known to be located until a few days before the attack. Then the phone had gone to a particular house on a named street in Karachi, and from there to the Karachi harbor and down the coast of India to Mumbai.

This and other revelations forced Pakistan out of its denial mode. It was forced to acknowledge that the attack was carried out by Pakistani nationals who had planned the attack on Pakistani soil. Yet it still denied government involvement, and the official position of the U.S. government remained that of no smoking gun having been found in Pakistan. Such was and apparently still is the capacity for denial in of the U.S. Department of State, the National Security Council, and the CIA.

Meanwhile, the FBI and Mumbai police completed their work in assembling the dossier of evidence implicating the government of Pakistan and distributed it to each of the eleven countries that lost citizens in the attack. The joint effort of the FBI and the Indian authorities marked a critical turning point in U.S.–India counterterrorism cooperation. Home Minister Chidambaram, reappointed minister of home affairs following the Indian general election of May 2009, has continued the effort with the FBI, and I have no doubt that from the tragedy in Mumbai yet another dimension of the U.S.–India strategic partnership will build greater trust and stronger counterterrorism cooperation for the future.

II

Epilogue

In the four years since I left India the financial and economic crisis that began in 2008 continues to dominate our world. There is little doubt that this crisis will stand over time as a major world-changing event comparable to the Great Depression or the world wars of the twentieth century. The vast, complex, multidimensional global economy and financial markets that evolved late in the twentieth century are being tested as never before. Will we move forward to an even more interconnected global economy with associated political transformations, or will we move backward to a divided, compartmentalized world of nationalism, protectionism, and conflict? The eventual outcome is by no means clear at this time.

There is a virtual industry of study and speculation as to why and how the crisis took place as it did. No doubt the roots reach well into the past as global markets evolved to support our rising world economy. More recent events also provoked and fed the crisis. More important perhaps is the simple fact that we are where we are today, and we must develop and implement policies to retain the world growth needed to move forward to recover a more prosperous and stable world. Much will depend on whether confidence can be sustained among the peoples and nations of the world in the type of open global economy that evolved over the decades leading up to the crisis. In a world of sovereign nations pursuing both common and competing interests, this is a challenge of prodigious complexity. In my experience, problems of great complexity require in the first instance clear, disciplined, and essentially rather simple thought.

In any global economic and market system that is to command the confidence of the great majority of participants there needs to be economic growth and coherent leadership. Today, five years after the crisis, we lack both these essential requirements. In the global economy that evolved in the second half of the twentieth century, leadership was provided primarily and consistently by the United States. Formation and development of international financial institutions and trade organizations, the management and functioning of the world's sole reserve currency, and the provision of a reasonable sense of global security were all led by the United States, which also had the world's largest, most innovative, and steadily growing economy.

These vital elements have now been weakened, not perhaps fatally but certainly perceptually. New realities have been brought about by events and by changes in attitudes and expectations in the United States and around the world. The will to lead is as important as leadership itself. The question is how well will the world economy perform and what its longer-term prospects will be without these elements as prominent as they have been these past fifty years.

Not particularly well, it would seem, and perhaps very poorly indeed. Consider the following. The U.S. economy, whose sustained growth has been the leading force in our global transformation, remains in a low-growth, heavily burdened mode. Europe, also in a low to negative growth mode, has fallen into what will surely be deep and long lasting economic and institutional challenges as it seeks to move toward some form of greater economic and sovereign unity. The rising world of newly emerged and emerging nations must be able to maintain post-crisis domestic growth levels, help preserve the benefits of an open trading and financial system, and participate more fully in efforts to provide stronger leadership in global economic financial governance. Our well-established and now mature global economic and financial institutions must reform far more quickly to reflect the changing power distribution in the world if they are to continue to command credibility and the constructive support of all nations. They must also be inspired and led by their most important members, especially the

United States. Finally, the suppressive influence of governments, and especially of unelected bureaucrats in governments and international organizations, must be overcome and made more practically rational by political and economic leaders responsible to the needs of their people.

These vital issues must be addressed as recovery continues.

The simplest reality about our world is that we must develop and implement policies to retain the world growth needed to recover a more prosperous and stable world. It is helpful to divide our present world into three broad component areas: the United States and Canada; Europe, including both European Union and Eurozone countries; and the large group of emerging market countries.

Since 2007 the United States has been embroiled in its own particularly virulent crisis. In its initial phase from 2008 to 2009, emergency actions were required by the U.S. and other governments to prevent a deeper catastrophe for the United States and Europe. By June 2009 the U.S. recession was declared by the government to be over, and some modest economic recovery was established in the United States. However, more robust growth of the type achieved following the U.S. recessions of both 1961 and 1981–82 has not been achieved in the United States. This failure is largely due to political considerations that have rendered the policies so successfully applied in the earlier recessions impossible to implement these past few years. As a result, the United States remains unable to provide its traditional leadership in global economic affairs, either by producing sustained growth that lifts the world or by fulfilling its role of the past sixty years to provide a sense of security and minimal orderly governance for world economic affairs.

These vital functions, though far from perfectly performed in the past and admittedly of U.S. self-interest, have been essential to the growth and development of the world as we know it today. In their absence, whether temporary or permanent, our world political economy cannot function as before.

The U.S. political establishment seems to have forgotten the tested policies that in past recessions restored growth within a short time frame. These policies have proved under both a Democratic president (1961) and a Republican president (1981) that growth can be restored in America quickly. The policies of President Kennedy and President Reagan, respectively, may not have been identical but they were more similar than different and they were not excessively complex. They involved in each case reducing taxes, exercising fiscal restraint, and removing regulatory, tax, and government disincentives to small business. People respond to opportunity and the chance to raise their standard of living. In a large, privatized democracy whose economy is based on the foundation of capitalist free enterprise, government must use its power to remove punitive barriers to productive economic activity and must cast policy in favor of incentives to which individuals can respond and from which they can benefit.

Looked at in this fashion one can see that this body of policy solutions is essentially nonpartisan in the sense that they have been deployed with success by both major U.S. political parties in times of significant economic distress. A government-sponsored and redistribution driven fiscal approach of the type seen since 2007 to create a new and radically different society in the United States is bound to fail to produce buoyant economic recovery. It might over time provide a different social and economic structure for America, but these economic and social policies will result in a poorer, more divided, more isolated society while generating no more than a feeble growth impulse. At the moment this is the direction in which America is moving. As long as these policies prevail we will not restore growth and recover our post-1945 role as leader in the global economic system. Indeed, if we fail to restore our leadership role it is doubtful the global economy we have seen emerge these past thirty years can be sustained.

Until the crisis of 2008 we had depended on a strong Europe and extensive transatlantic political, trade, and economic relations. The same was true of our relations with Japan. Now Japan, though still the world's second-largest economy, is only just emerging from a lengthy recession. Europe has moved into an even more threatened position with which the United States is intimately linked through our global financial system.

In the late 1980s and early 1990s events unfolded that have had a major impact on our world. Within the short space of a few years, the Soviet Empire collapsed, Eastern Europe was freed from decades of control and repression, East and West Germany were united , and Europe dramatically accelerated its own unification, particularly through the project of the single currency.

As the Soviet Union broke into its component republics, Russia had to act to restore its credit worthiness by turning to the Paris Club to negotiate an agreed debt restructuring. It also sought to liberalize its economy and to open its financial system. President George H. W. Bush made a priority of binding the smaller countries of the Soviet block and also the former Soviet republics to the West so that they could liberalize their state-run economies and not fall back into the Soviet orbit. This lay behind, for example, the rapid formation of the European Bank for Reconstruction and Development (EBRD) in which the United States took a leadership position. The EBRD's mission was to assist and help finance the development of market-based economies in the new countries of Eastern Europe. Perhaps the leading example of success is Poland, which after implementing a radical economic "shock" program and restructuring and reducing its official bilateral debt in April 1991, established and maintained steady growth for the past twenty years.

The most important development, however, was the vision for a United Europe. Both aging leaders in Europe and a new generation of European leaders worked together with renewed energy to advance European unity, believing that if greater economic and political unification and the creation of a single currency for Europe could be accomplished, Europe would never again be torn by tragic and destructive war. The United States has supported Europe's efforts, and our economies and financial markets have become increasingly intertwined throughout the 1990s and early years of the twenty-first century.

What did not materialize in this period was a deeper understanding of what these developments might mean for the global economic system. Europe became obsessed with its drive to unification and the challenges of launching the euro. The global policy cooperation dialogue that was housed in the G7 weakened significantly as Europe turned inward. Global imbalances reappeared, financial markets expanded across the world, and financial instruments became more diverse, more complex, and less closely regulated. In fact, markets grew so quickly in both scale and complexity that government-to-government efforts to coordinate policies were rendered less effective, even though the G7 dialogue continued in a desultory fashion.

The drive in Europe to create the euro involved a lengthy and positive process of "convergence" among the national economies of Europe. Countries such as Italy, Spain, Greece, Portugal, and others enjoyed strong growth, declining fiscal imbalances, and declining inflation and interest rates. Optimism about Europe's future was widespread. The newly united Germany gradually adjusted to the costs of unification and the euro was launched in 1998 to an optimistic world that appeared to enjoy benign financial and economic conditions. The optimism that prevailed in the euro's early phase now seems wildly excessive. In the beginning the financial world gave greater credence to the currency union than to the creditworthiness of Europe's individual national partners. Europe's new and "forever" currency union members could all borrow at euro rates close to the competitive rates enjoyed by Germany. The investment world, as well as the world of governments, cheered the success of Europe's currency union, disregarding the fact that there was no matching fiscal union and little effort to implement the national structural reforms necessary to improve the efficiency and competitiveness of Europe's peripheral members, and even France. Fundamental differences among the economies of still-sovereign nations in Europe were disregarded or perhaps overcome in the eyes of markets by the success of the euro as a currency in the years after its initial launch.

The financial crisis of 2008 changed everything, including the world's view of Europe. When Greece surfaced in 2009 as Europe's first case of insolvency, European leaders adopted a posture of denial. While acknowledging that Greece had a serious problem of indebtedness largely brought on by itself, the attitude of European leaders was that Greece simply faced a current liquidity problem that would have to be addressed by Greece tightening its belt and adjusting to the new reality. At no point in those early months of crisis did Europe's leaders see a deeply indebted Greece as a threat to the euro itself. As Greek spreads widened with no realistic support plan from Europe coming forward, international markets concluded that Greece was becoming a candidate for default and that other low-growth, heavily indebted peripheral states in the euro might face a similar situation. Valuable months went by with no concerted action plan coming forward from Europe's leading nations to address Greece as a unique problem that with concentrated action could be contained. Soon the notion of contagion emerged and markets panicked, with investors retreating to the sidelines.

Essentially, markets had come to the judgment that heavily indebted, low-growth, entitlement-dominated countries in Europe were no longer financeable at rates anything close to the narrowly favorable spreads over German bond rates that had characterized the early years of the euro. Early efforts in Europe to address Greece's problems were tentative and inadequate, encouraging contagion to spread and introducing, through a series of failed summit meetings, a new threat for the eurozone, namely, its own survival. At each phase over several years of worsening and more widespread deterioration Europe failed to understand and to act aggressively on the need for radical and well-financed action. By late 2011 the overriding question for global markets was: how much damage will Europe do to itself and to the world at large before it figures out how to resolve the fundamental issues posed by the eurozone problem?

Meanwhile, Europe's growth will remain low to flat with the significant risk of periods of negative growth and high structural unemployment as it seeks to address the euro's long-term challenges. Europe's negative demographics ensure that its political classes will continue to place benefits, environmental, and social issues above buoyant growth, with the result that Europe will not provide as in the past the same growth stimulus to the United States or to the emerging market countries. The EU's more favored members, such as Germany, Sweden, the UK, and Poland, may perform above average, and especially many of their leading global corporations, but overall the growth picture remains bleak for the foreseeable future.

The United States and Europe are both failing to provide the growth stimulus necessary for the emerging market countries to maintain their previously established momentum. At first after the crisis of 2008 these countries adjusted quickly to restore their growth levels, but as growth in North America and Europe failed to materialize in a positive and sustainable manner and the United States, the UK, and the eurozone introduced less helpful trade and monetary policies, the economic policy problems of emerging markets have become substantially more challenging.

The chief problem once again is these nations' inability to maintain the levels of growth they had formerly enjoyed, which over the past twenty years, helped emerging market countries to lift their people from poverty, strengthen their investment base and generally promote successful, aspirational societies. Reversing these dramatic developments will prove very painful indeed and in some cases may be linked with rising nationalism and aggressive political behavior. The shift in the distribution of power in the newly emerging world economy may take very unpredictable turns if the United States and Europe fail in the reasonably near term to reestablish growth and to reach out to resume at least some significant part of their leadership role.

Taking into account my experience in global economic affairs and international diplomacy, the key requirement to avoid continuing adverse global development is the restoration of solid 5 percent annual growth in the United States. This obviously is in the interest of the American people. The economic policies necessary to bring this about are well known and if implemented aggressively will work. That there are serious challenges in virtually every direction in the United States today to making this happen politically is also obvious. However, nothing among the diversity of popular political distractions will make this growth we and the world so sorely need a reality. The basics of creating growth remain simple in concept if difficult in execution, but moving to and achieving sustainable realities is a central part of America's history.

For many decades now the notion that America's economy is isolated essentially from the rest of the world is a complete myth. Our growth and prosperity have been influenced for decades by external developments, and our global leadership role has been a central reality for the United States certainly since 1945. The global alliance systems and international political, trade, and financial institutions that have played a key role in the development of our world were all created and led to a significant degree by the United States. The economic benefit to the United States of its global leadership efforts have been incalculably beneficial to the U.S. economy and its people. Playing a passive role in the radically changed world we face today is simply not an option if we wish to prosper as a nation. Recovering our leadership and influencing the future world we face—and should welcome—begins with the one overriding and essentially simple proposition: the restoration of robust growth in the United States.

Throughout my career in private finance and public policy I have always believed that if leaders can produce and encourage economic growth, all problems, including issues of fairness in democratic societies, become easier to resolve when growth is on the rise. This is as true on a global scale as it is as a national phenomenon. From 1980 through 2009 this simple proposition has been demonstrated to be valid. Such conditions do not provide a perfect world, or even a world free of dangerous challenges, but such conditions do provide a significantly more malleable world. That fact is easily confirmed by reflecting on the experience of countries in deep crisis, or periods of deep crisis and conflict in world affairs. North Korea and Iran come to mind today as examples, and the upheavals of the 1930s world economic crisis and Second World War provide the most striking examples of a world destroyed by economic decline and conflict.

A breakdown in leadership at virtually all levels of society is the common feature of these transformations, and our world today is no exception. Leaders I have most admired are of strong purpose, sound vision, pragmatic in the execution of their policies, and blessed with a knowledge of human history. If one attempts to give practical recognition to our failures since the year 2000, I would cite the following breakdowns as those that most threaten continued economic progress in a gradually uniting world.

The world taking shape in the fifty-year aftermath of the Second World War was a product of U.S. political, economic, and security leadership, strongly supported by a rising democratic Europe and later the emergence of a democratic and peaceful Japan. This world was not developed or kept in place by military power alone. Economic and cultural forces were far more consistently influential, in part because their benefits were perceived as desirable and achievable by a widening share of the world's population. The speed with which this reality was spreading, and its implications for future leadership in a far more diverse world in which power and influence are becoming far more diffused, are essential for Western leaders to understand and to act on in their policy objectives.

If one were to take as an example an area in which I have had experience in public and private life, I would point to the spread of global financial markets and how this phenomenon was managed or mismanaged over the years.

In the 1980s the United States embarked with new vigor on the world financial and economic stage. The success of Europe and Japan were recognized by the United States as important to a rising and improving world. The adjustment to the massive oil price increases of the 1970s had been largely absorbed, and the later years of the 1970s had demonstrated the cost of demoralizing the American people. The need for rigorous cooperation with rising economic and political allies was widely accepted, and the United States supported the world's cornerstone economic institutions, recognizing that while not always fully serving U.S. national interests, these institutions were essential to the management and better governance of the world economy. The process of economic policy cooperation between leading countries to reduce global imbalances and to address exchange rate misalignments, the globalization of private business and finance, and the recognition of the diversity of interests in the widening world promoted improving levels of world growth and relatively benign international economic conditions during the 1980s and 1990s.

I am very much aware and proud of the fact that during these two decades we lived in a world of rising growth and reasonable stability. Even the collapse of the Soviet Union, the drive toward unity in Europe, and the early rise of China were not destabilizing events to the world economy. Expectations continued to rise.

One must consider and recognize the success generated by world growth, chiefly the result of the spread of better national economic policies around the world and the willingness of leaders around the world to engage in a minimum of positive cooperation that recognized the reality of a shrinking more interrelated world.

The vision, however, could not last for a variety of reasons which, unfortunately, while in the control of world leaders, was not acted upon judiciously or with sufficient creativity. The collective leadership and cooperation of the G7 counties was permitted to decline and to atrophy without being transformed to provide broader, more credible leadership for the world. Europe turned inward to press ahead with its own greater unification. The United States accepted this withdrawal, failing to understand the need of transforming and yet maintaining a credible leadership group of countries for the rising global economy. The United States should have worked with Europe and other leading emerging countries to restructure the G7 to reflect the rise of China, India, and Brazil as well as the decline of Russia, with the goal of keeping the number of leading countries in the group at 7 or 8 in number. The United States made no effort to use its power to achieve a reasonably paced transformation of our world economic institutions (the IMF, the World Bank, or even the UN Security Council) to make them more reflective of the world to come and more credible in their representation of the newly emerging world economy.

This was a fundamental error of U.S. leadership. Such reforms would have been exceedingly difficult, but the United States held the greatest leverage to force change, including on itself, to maintain through reform the Bretton Woods Institution's global relevance. After all, irritating as the IMF and World Bank might be from time to time, they do enjoy broad world membership, huge bases of capital, and the credibility of successfully having had many of their reform policies accepted by countries all over the world. Revising the quotas or share ownerships of these institutions was vital to moving to the world we see today. Neither the IMF nor the World Bank are reflections of the world economy and geopolitical reality we face today. Instead, the G20 has been formed, a nonoperational body with no capital base, no track record of reforms or change, and populated by a grand diversity of countries that cannot effectively resolve world economic challenges. Even its membership today, which excludes Switzerland, for years a significant player in the G10 group of countries, but includes Argentina, a renegade country in economic and financial affairs presently defying the rest of the world economic community, is a sad commentary on the legitimacy and relevance of the G20.

Perhaps the greatest failure has been on the part of the United States, which from the late 1990s has lost its direction as economic leader of the world. It has effectively withdrawn as the leader of a now-defunct G7; it failed to recraft the G7 to make it relevant to the future of our rising world economy; it failed to understand and effectively engage China as it rose to new prominence in the global economy; it failed to grasp the importance and leadership role needed to bring reform to the IMF and World Bank; it utterly failed after military victory in Iraq to sensibly promote the building of a new nation and economy; and it failed to grasp victory early in Afghanistan from the jaws of eventual defeat in a country that simply cannot become a democratic country in the near term but instead remains an essentially tribal society.

More recently, the U.S. failed to prevent the IMF from being drawn into the Greek debt crisis, which in turn has brought the IMF into Europe at a level of participation and finance that does not serve its role as the monetary institution of the world. Greece, of course, as a member of the IMF, deserved to draw on its own quota at the IMF and to receive economic advice, but not to receive IMF funding of the size that has been accorded and under the strict conditionality of the IMF as opposed to the political conditionality of Europe. The Greek emergency financing was a transaction promoted by the IMF's managing director, who aspired to be the president of a France that had "saved Europe" and which in doing so used the over-represented European constituency in the IMF and the sleepy disengagement of the United States to push through a deal with other people's money that Europe should have and could have easily financed itself. This transaction and subsequent involvement in Europe of the IMF has further eroded its relevance and legitimacy as the "world's monetary institution."

The United States should and could have blocked this deal, which will now have a permanent and negative influence on the IMF's potential role in the world. One could have perhaps contemplated a "world decision" to assist Greece on a grand scale as a means of helping Europe to overcome its own eurozone crisis. Perhaps a fully reformed and properly representative IMF might have voted to bail out Greece as a major source of world financial risk. However, with Greece accounting for only some 2 percent of Europe's total GDP and without the largess of the United States Congress, I somehow doubt this would have been a starter.

At the moment, with the second Obama administration well advanced, the outlook for U.S. fiscal, regulatory, environmental, and job-creation policies that incentivize and stimulate the economy toward 5 percent growth is not favorable. However, the U.S. economy is recovering slowly, and the stock market remains positive and apparently reasonably confident about the future. A new recession is possible but not probable at this point. There is likely to be a period of bitter partisan conflict with a testing of our Constitution and the strength of the checks and balances that are such crucial points of U.S. democratic governance. Meanwhile, I believe the forces so threateningly apparent today will lose their dominance for the restored functioning of the U.S. economy. There is the critical issue of timing—how long do we have to make the adjustment to begin to awaken stronger U.S. growth?

An important part of this recovery process will be relatively free from Washington's depressive hand. This is the now-visible strengthening of the U.S. energy sector and the rise of U.S. energy independence. This prospect is already changing behavior and will help transform our economy, our competitive position in the world, and the perceptions of our geopolitical position in the world. There may be resistance from Washington, but the transformation taking place is not entirely under Washington's control. States want the growth, jobs, and the domestic and foreign investment that can flow from this change, which will enhance growth, create jobs, strengthen manufacturing, and raise U.S. spirits. One could say that our economy will improve in spite of ourselves and the federal government!

These optimistic thoughts will of course be derided by sophisticated experts, but it should be borne in mind that historically the U.S. economy has constantly surprised, consistently displayed the flexibility to restructure itself and once again emerge with new features during change and generating growth. I believe this is what markets are telling us as we face an uncertain future.

President Obama, however, has failed two of the most important tests for the president of the United States—restoring robust economic growth in the United States and providing global economic and financial leadership in our newly transformed world. Although many aspects of the economic crisis that President Obama faced when he took office lingered into his new administration, it has long since been possible to simply blame all economic problems on President George W. Bush. Policies that promote tax reform, reduce rates, widen the tax base, remove harmful and costly distortions, and incentivize small business will without doubt strengthen growth and make a significant positive impact on structural unemployment. If, on the other hand, we continue to follow today's policy prescriptions we may improve some measure of fairness in our society, but at the cost of a poorer, less-dynamic United States, and this is a cost that we and the world at large will bear.

The best hope is that we see a combination of gradually restored growth in the Unied States together with the gradual education of President Obama. Or perhaps President Obama will be transformed into a "lame duck" president by the successful blocking of his economic and social initiatives. Much of the early stages of refinancing and reinvigorating the U.S. economy can and will happen while President Obama is in office. He is likely to be more driven by adverse foreign policy developments, but this may lead to further withdrawal of the United States from global challenges. World realities will confront him with economic developments such as the continued rise of China and the continued subperformance of the United States and Europe, as well as global security developments such as growing chaos in Egypt, confrontation with Russia, the civil war in Syria, the probable loss of part or all of Ukraine, and rising tensions across the entire Middle East that threaten world peace and oil supplies. President Obama will face the full political manifestation of the threat posed to global stability as well as continued low growth at home and high structural unemployment, especially among the young generation.

When one considers the plethora of unsuccessful policies pursued by President Obama in the course of the global economic crisis, perhaps the unwinding of the Federal Reserve's second and third rounds of quantitative easing (QE2 and QE3) policies will prove the biggest threat to global economic recovery as his administration enters its final years. Provision of liquidity and support to the U.S. banking system was essential in the early going after the extreme crisis conditions of 2007 and 2008. However, the continued provision of huge liquidity by the Federal Reserve in the ensuing years has laid the basis for a long-term adjustment that the U.S and world markets will have to endure in coming years.

The Fed's continued provision of liquidity since 2009 has not produced a restoration of significant growth in the U.S. It has not created jobs and it has violated a principle of U.S. governance—namely, the conversion of the Federal Reserve into an unaccountable fiscal organ of the U.S. government, which in effect has sought to replace a presently divided and dysfunctional Congress in meeting its fiscal duties as prescribed by the Constitution.

The supreme confidence of Federal Reserve Chairman Ben Bernake and presumably his successor, Janet Yellen, that we can exit from the QE strategy of the Fed without damage to the United States and the world seems to be driven by a combination of academic confidence and intellectual hubris. Although markets have seen the risk of the adjustment that must come, they have been delighted by the largesse of the Fed's program and any sign that it gives that the ultimate adjustment of global liquidity can be pushed further into the future. This latter point offers the Fed one of its most market-disarming tools—namely, the management of micro information flows reported on a continuous basis that allows the Fed to manage market expectations at will.

Whether the United States ultimately experiences a significant rise in inflation is for the moment of lesser importance than the effect that tapering or unwinding of this gigantic program will have on world markets. The favorable credit spreads emerging markets countries have enjoyed over the past two years will prove to be illusory, just as those enjoyed by the peripheral counties in Europe from 2000 to 2007 proved unjustified and helped promote easy growth and inadequate structural reform in their respective economies.

If tapering, when it finally begins in earnest, as indeed it must, brings with it significant continuing market distortions that undermine growth and stability in the emerging market world, one could visualize a lengthy period of painful adjustment and rising political risk. The problem of future unwinding of monetary stimulus must also be faced from Europe and Japan.

The most depressing aspect of the historic challenge faced by the Federal Reserve is that President Obama, as in the case of so many of his international policy challenges, appears to have little knowledge and virtually no interest in the global implications of his domestic economic policies. If one believes that U.S. fiscal policies should be the responsibility of elected officials working within the checks and balances of the U.S. system of governance and ultimately acceptable to the public, we have clearly moved away from historic standards. If world growth and stability are seriously undermined by the adjustment world markets now face, or if inflation establishes itself in our recovering economy, the Federal Reserve will be discredited and face major efforts to transform its mandate.

However partisan President Obama's policies may be, he will feel the rising threat to the United States and hopefully begin to realize that the strength of the nation is being tested, that his legacy goal of a better life for Americans is also at risk. At the very least, President Obama will find that within the political and constitutional realities of the United States he will in effect be prevented from exercising his unrestrained will. What is accomplished by a massive dependence on regulatory fiat can and will be reversed or dismantled in the future. One imagines that President Obama is too practical a politician to simply see out a weakened, ineffective administration. Recent major policy failures, both domestic and international, suggest that we must be nearing some awakening of his personal and political concerns about his legacy as president.

Is it right to remain optimistic? Yes, because America and Americans are essentially optimistic. They will not stay defeated or demoralized. Even the so-called entitlement community will want something beyond a periodic check and minimal life support. It has ever been so and I do not see the basis for a permanent change in American attitudes.

Nevertheless, there can always be an exceptional, or perhaps historic, shift in public attitudes from which completely new features emerge—features that change everything and destroy the most peaceful and virtuous of societies. History is replete with examples, and it would be foolish to ignore these possibilities, especially in the United States today.

There are those who would argue that America is beyond the point of no return in becoming an entitlement society with policies that punish the wealthy, creative, entrepreneurial spirit. They would argue that we are rapidly becoming a low-growth, high-unemployment and eventually unfinanceable welfare state, that America is past its prime and is now in decline. They are obsessed with issues of fairness, political correctness, vigorous government regulation of our personal and business affairs, and the destruction of long-held American values, among them the functioning of the

Constitution of the United States and the foundation it establishes with the principles that sustain democratic government. Certainly, these features of modern U.S. society are there, but whether they are temporary or remain permanent fixtures and practices of American society and government, only time will tell.

America's relations with India have also changed since the end of the George W. Bush administration in 2009. The momentum in U.S.–India relations that gathered in the late years of the Clinton administration and which blossomed into five years of unprecedented growth and a transformed strategic relationship during the Bush years has declined significantly over the last five years. Part of the reason lies in Indian politics. The Congress-led coalition government elected in May 2009 did not live up to its promise of continued high growth and reform in a coalition that was free of the drag imposed earlier by its communist members. Growth in India has declined sharply in the past two years to below 5 percent per annum, partly due to continued low growth in the developed country economies and partly due to the 2009 Indian government's inadequate commitment to continued reform and sound economic policies.

U.S. relations with India have also weakened sharply, beginning from the very first days of the Obama Administration. The decision of the president to form a new Afghanistan-Pakistan (AFPAK) nucleus in U.S. South Asian foreign policy with Ambassador Richard Holbrooke appointed to lead the new initiative was unwelcome in India, rekindling new suspicions in India that U.S. relations with Pakistan and India would not be even-handed. India's significant aid effort and political influence in Afghanistan appeared to have been unappreciated by the new U.S. administration. Apparently, if Pakistan were to be the preferred U.S. partner for Afghanistan, it would be India that would be called upon to compromise its fundamental interests in Kashmir to induce stronger cooperation from Pakistan with the United States in the Afghanistan war.

Ambassador Holbrooke seemed immediately to confirm these suspicions in his first visit to India in early 2009. I was still serving as U.S. ambassador to India in the early weeks of the new administration. Holbrooke's visit proved to be a painful affair. He would visit India only after stopping first in both Afghanistan and Pakistan, contrary to India's request that he visit India after Afghanistan but before Pakistan. When he arrived in a U.S. military aircraft accompanied by three U.S. generals, India's Foreign Secretary Shivshankar Menon declined to receive the military members of the delegation, who were left waiting at the airport while Ambassador Holbrooke and I met with the foreign secretary. The military in India is firmly under civilian political leadership and control. Serving military personnel would not normally be included in a sensitive, high-level political meeting. No meeting was arranged with Prime Minister Singh.

In March 2009 I left India. I was not replaced by the Obama administration's new ambassador, Timothy J. Roemer, until July that year. Ambassador Roemer served in India for only two years and was followed, after another lengthy time lapse, by a senior U.S. Foreign Service officer appointed to act temporarily as chargé. He was in turn followed by another U.S. Foreign Service officer, Ambassador Nancy Powell, former U.S. ambassador to Pakistan. Without demeaning these particular officers in any way, the reality in India, and the historic record since independence in 1947, is that U.S. ambassadors to India have been prominent political appointees known personally to the president of the United States. U.S. Foreign Service officers, however skilled and well prepared, are not seen in the same light as senior political appointees with direct access to the president. The appointments since the departure of Ambassador Roemer in July 2011 have sent a clear message to India of its diminished status with the Obama administration. The same is true regarding the president's own reportedly lackluster visit to India and the visits made by both Secretary of State Clinton and Secretary of State Kerry. More recently, the insensitive manner in which the United States handled the case of India's deputy general counsel in New York, Devyani Khobragade, has seriously damaged relations and brought about the kind of disputive reciprocity atmosphere that can be particularly harmful to relations with India. By the time of India's general election of May 2014, which brought Narendra Modi and the BJP to power, the American ambassador to India had announced her departure from India and retirement from the foreign service, perhaps marking recognition by the Obama administration that a new beginning with India was needed.

India, with its declining growth, its diminished status with the United States, and its own less-friendly policies to foreign direct investment and trade from the United States and elsewhere, no longer appears to command the high U.S. interest reserved for China. This new reality is painful for India to accept after the warm sense of priority it experienced with President Bush.

Meanwhile, India has its own dynamic. Its sheer size, its favorable demographic structure that ensures a young, aspirational workforce for years to come, its functioning democracy, and the rural economic and social transformation now underway promise a lengthy period of growth, social change, and rising aspirations. In a few short years, India has created a national telecom system based almost entirely on mobile telephony that has allowed India to leapfrog an entire generation of investment in fixed landline infrastructure. Rising disposable income in rural India, still small but increasingly widespread, will bring major macroeconomic change: expanding local banking services, rising consumption of consumer products and vehicles of all kinds, changes in land use, influence on changing patterns of migration to secondary cities across India, and expansion of a wide range of services, from internal air travel to education and health care.

Within this improving economic picture, it is my hope and expectation that India will succeed in diversifying its domestic energy base away from imported oil and coal to other forms of energy, including in particular the expansion of civil nuclear energy for domestic electric power production. India's access to global civil nuclear technology as a result of the U.S–India Civil Nuclear Agreement of 2008 has been diminished by the mishandling in 2010 of India's own legislation to conform its civil nuclear liability laws to international standards. Until it does so, leading foreign companies in the field of civil nuclear development will be unwilling to assume the huge risks of India's inadequate nuclear liability regime.

Over the past twenty-five years India's progress in opening its vast economy to the world, maintaining sound fiscal and monetary policies, introducing critical structural reforms, liberalizing internal controls on foreign and domestic investment, and generally giving more freedom to its market economy has been uneven and too slow in implementation. Yet it would be wrong to say that little has been accomplished. Reform in India moves in waves over time, managed by complex coalition governments that seek to maintain levels of consensus among the coalition members that avoid bringing down its coalition governments in public, political crises.

Does this reality promote frustration and criticism inside and outside India? Yes, decidedly. Does this mean India is not moving forward? Emphatically, no. Like the United States, India has its own way of meeting challenges and addressing change. It may be inconsistent, take longer than seems necessary, and frustrate and discourage India's friends, but India is rising and will grow impressively well into the future.

The most dramatic evidence of this is India's remarkable general election of May 2014. Narendra Modi, the newly promoted head of the BJP, hugely successful chief minister of the state of Gujarat and a man of the Indian people, swept India in a landslide victory. With the first majority government elected in India since 1984, India has chosen the "muscular" CEO that the vast majority of voters wanted "to get India moving again" and to begin the attack on corruption that most Indians believe is out of control. India's problems may be both serious and complex to resolve, but I have no doubt that Mr. Modi's commitment to restoring growth and advancing reform will be realized in the next years.

Restoring relations with the United States will also begin, although so will new foreign policy initiatives by Mr. Modi with India's closer neighbors, especially China, Pakistan, and Japan. When one stands back at this early time, one has the clear sense that India has taken a giant step forward in its historic transformation and that this will lead to a whole new dimension in U.S.–India strategic and economic relations.

Significant opportunities clearly are taking shape as the United States advances its own transformation toward energy independence. Its dependence on Middle East oil is already declining. The new leading consumers of oil from the region will be China and India. The United States, however, will remain the country that provides security cover in the Indian Ocean, ensuring access for all to the Strait of Hormuz. India is anxious to develop its own naval power to offset China's naval ambitions in South Asia and the Indian Ocean. Here again is a major opportunity for U.S.–Indian strategic partnership between the two great democracies in coming years.

India's footprint in global affairs will expand as its economy grows and its strategic position strengthens. India's standing military, one of the largest in the world, provides the most promising defense market in the world for the United States and Europe. As in America, India's military is firmly under democratic civilian control. During the period of my ambassadorship, U.S. defense sales of sophisticated military and high-tech products expanded impressively, as have sales of U.S. commercial aircraft.

The growing and potential initiatives between us are virtually unlimited in both our private-sector civil societies and between our two governments—great democracies, halfway round the world from one another, in a shrinking and more interdependent global setting. We are now only at the beginning of a new era in global development and U.S.–Indian strategic partnership.

It has not, however, been the purpose of this book to foretell the future. Instead, its purpose has been to explain how we evolved these past fifty years to the more globalized world we face today, as seen through my personal experience. If this evolution can be continued as we exit successfully from our present global challenges, one can see a future of tremendous prospects for global mankind in virtually every field of human activity. Yet I have also been struck by how dangerous our world continues to be for those who believe, as I do, in American exceptionalism, both in our daily lives and in our unique history of freedom, democratic governance, and economic success. These are abiding but not necessarily dominant features of world history. Among my most poignant lessons from life is the simple and compelling fact that freedom and the values of America must constantly be espoused and defended against the counterforces that are ever present in our world.